Walford State of Mind

Also by the author:

Albert Square & Me: The Actors of EastEnders

Walford State of Mind

*EastEnders As Reported by
the Walford Gazette*

Edited by Larry Jaffee

East End Company
New York, New York

Walford State of Mind: EastEnders As Reported by the Walford Gazette

For more information:
www.wgazette.com

ISBN 978-0-615-42920-5

Cover design: Nicole Hock

This book is dedicated to my parents Skip and Ruth Jaffee, who have supported and encouraged my various endeavours, as well as to my children Jake and Annie, who have put up with my obsession with *EastEnders* since they were infants.

Acknowledgements

I would like to thank Dan Abramson for convincing me in 1991 that the world needed a newspaper dedicated to *EastEnders*. I would like to thank Michelle Collins and Mal Young, former BBC Controller of Continuing Drama Series, for their forewords and friendship.

I would also like to thank the many *EastEnders* actors and members of the creative team who granted us their time to provide insights into the programme, the craft of acting and their careers. I would like to thank the many agents and publicity staff at *EastEnders* who set up the interviews. I'd like to thank *EastEnders* company manager Carolyn Weinstein, BBC controller of drama production John Yorke, as well as former executive producers Matthew Robinson and Louise Berridge.

And thanks to Anne Trauben for her encouragement in creating this book. I would also like to thank the newspaper's Pamela Knight (copy editor) and Paul Field (webmaster). Their continued help allows me to keep the *Walford Gazette* on a regular production schedule.

I also would like to thank the ten public television stations that have stuck by *EastEnders* when so many have not, and especially those who have offered newspaper subscriptions and my two books as viewer thank-you gifts.

And finally, I'd like to thank the *Walford Gazette* subscribers and numerous contributors (it was so hard to pick articles for this book), who have come from all walks of life to share in the comings and goings of Albert Square.

Contents

III: Creative Team

IV: Advocacy

V: Fandom

VI: Reviews

VII: Epilogue

Foreword from the Cast

By Michelle Collins (Cindy Beale, 1988-1998)

Let's face it. Cindy Beale has been dead for a long time. But it never ceases to amaze me how fervent *EastEnders* fans can come up with all kinds of theories why she should come back from the grave to haunt Ian.

I don't take for granted even a second the fame that *EastEnders* brought me during those ten magical years. The series, and even Cindy—as much as she was so easy to despise—will always mean something very special to me. That is why I've always made time to sign autographs or take photographs when I'm recognised in public, or answer fan mail, which is actually how I first became aware of the *Walford Gazette* when I answered a questionnaire sent by an American fan who contributed to the paper, Mackenzie Jones Currey.

Around the same time, I was visiting New York—which I absolutely adore, especially for the shopping—settling in on some fish & chips at a takeaway on 14th Street, when I did a double-take. There were free copies of the *Walford Gazette*, including a photo of me! I thought, why don't we have this at home?

Soon thereafter I was contacted by the *Gazette's* co-founder and editor Dan Abramson, and we did a phone interview. I was impressed how professional it all went, compared to some of my dealings with the British tabloids.

A few years later, I met Dan's business partner, Larry Jaffee, when he and Deepak Verma were climbing up the stairs of London's Soho House, while I was going down. I hadn't seen Deepak in a while, and we shared many scenes on *EastEnders,* since Cindy was best mates with Sanjay's wife Gita. As it turned out, Larry was a good mate of Deepak's, and we decided to stay in touch and some time soon have a "proper meeting." Later that year we had a quick impromptu hello at Manhattan's Gramercy Hotel (a mutual friend tipped off Larry where I was staying), but unfortunately a limo was waiting to take me to JFK.

Larry thankfully came to London a few months later, and we finally spent a few hours over drinks at a hotel on The Strand, talking about show business and parenthood (his daughter is a year younger than mine). A few months later, he extended an invitation to help WLIW, the New York public TV station with fundraising live in the studio. Larry accompanied me and my New York friend Debbie Weiss in the limo ride to the Long Island studio, where I was treated like royalty. I was happy to keep that *EastEnders* flame burning (so what if Cindy died in prison?) because I'm always in favour of doing philanthropic work, even if it means crossing an ocean.

About six months later, Larry calls my mobile in something of a panic: WLIW has decided to cancel the show, and he wants to know if I can do a benefit meet-and-greet, that they need to raise $29,000 in a month or *EastEnders* will be history in the New York area. It just so happened that I needed to be in Manhattan that week for a screening at the Museum of Modern Art of *The Illustrated Mum*, an award-winning film that I starred in. Next thing I know, I am walking into a pub in Greenwich Village to the unmistakable sounds of Elton John's "The Bitch Is Back," which, of course, was what was playing on the Queen Vic's jukebox when Cindy returned to Albert Square after an absence. During a Q&A with Larry, I learned that it was *Gazette* contributor Tim Wilson's idea to play the song upon my entrance. Tim, who has met probably more *EastEnders* actors than I have, seems to know more about me than me, and endorses me to become a regular on *Desperate Housewives*. "Cindy was the original Desperate Housewife!" Tim quips. Obviously, I can't agree more.

Paparazzi working for tabloids back home picked up on the story of me helping to raise $1,700 that night, and I even got a mention in *The New York Times*.

I think it was then when I realised how committed Larry and his contributors are to *EastEnders*. The *Walford Gazette* is obviously far more than your typical fanzine, and I can't wait to read *Walford State of Mind*.

Michelle Collins first came to fame on EastEnders *as Cindy Beale from 1988-1998. Since then, she has gone on to star in other British television series including* Sunburn *and* Two Thousand Acres of Sky, *and is often starring in West End theatre productions and touring stage shows throughout the UK.*

Foreword from the Executive Suite
Walford State of Mine

By Mal Young

TV soap operas in the UK are a truly unique and wholly British institution. Long running, continuous drama serials such as *Coronation Street* and *EastEnders* revolving around the minutia of everyday life in urban working class communities, such as Manchester or London, broadcast all year round, in prime time and often with four or five half hour episodes across a week.

It's often said that if Charles Dickens was kicking around today, he'd be a staff writer. They're known as the juggernauts of British broadcasting, attracting huge, diverse audiences that can often give the reality shows like *Idol* and *Dancing With The Stars*—and anything with the word celebrity in the title—a run for their money.

And they've done this successfully for decades, non-stop. In the case of *Coronation Street*, the show that started this phenomenon, the viewers have grown up with it in their lives for 50 talkabout years. The BBC's flagship saga of everyday life in the East End of London, *EastEnders*, is now in its 25th year, and still keeping the nation gripped by its compelling reflection of contemporary working class Britain—and of course the occasional murder.

The States created the everlasting soap opera genre with their daytime shows, and other countries have hugely successful telenovelas, but those shows aren't often noted for their relevance to anything real or to which the audience can truly identify or relate.

During my TV career I've been involved with quite a few of these shows in the UK. I started out producing *Brookside*, set in Liverpool, for Channel 4, and quickly realized how such a show can have a positive impact on the audience. You see, us Brits, we've always been quite keen on seeing ourselves on TV—warts and all. The Brit soaps were born out of the very British tradition of playwrights striving to portray real life in all its earthy realism; they came out of theatre, novels, radio plays, and a new, gritty style of movie-making that emerged in the UK in the late 1950s producing socially realistic pieces such as *Saturday Night, Sunday Morning.*

Meanwhile American soaps always reflected a very different audience—an aspirational one who'd rather dream about the rich and famous than engage with ordinary blue-collar families struggling to cope with what life throws at them. Maybe it's as simple as everyone in America seems to think they could become the President, while no one in the UK would ever want to be Prime Minister. Although it seems okay to laugh at the underclass—there's a tradition in the States of some great comedies based around blue-collar families: like *Roseanne* and *All In the Family*– based on a Brit format incidentally.

So with that in mind, we producers of the big Brits soaps have always made our shows to appeal solely to the domestic audience. Sure, we occasionally heard stories about how our shows were subtitled and sold to small African countries for thirty pence an episode, but we never expected our gritty storylines and characters to have legs away from our home turf. The stories we chose to tell were and still are always most successful when they touch a nerve with the British viewing public and feel very much of the moment. A good Brit soap should feel like it was recorded just a few hours before transmission—then the morning after, as the nation discusses its impact, the episode is consigned to the archive, never to be seen again, until the special anniversary compilation episodes.

When I arrived at the BBC as Controller of Drama Series (the Beeb has always been fond of a fancy job title) I was given ultimate responsibility for the goings-on at Britain's most famous Square called Albert from 1997 through 2004. *EastEnders* had been hugely popular with its fans since its launch in 1984 and our fan base and accompanying daily sacks of fanmail was as great as ever—email hadn't quite caught on yet.

All the soaps have more than their fair share of committed, loyal, and sometimes frankly obsessive fans, but we started to be contacted by one especially dedicated super-fan.

We knew of fans from many differing backgrounds and nationalities, but they were usually resident in the UK—Larry Jaffee was different.

He appeared to know more about our show than some of our writers and producers and although thousands of miles away in the USA, he had followed the weekly installments of Eastend life rabidly for years on PBS stations in a galaxy far, far away. He represented a small but perfectly formed band of fans of our show watching from across the Atlantic. But what put Larry firmly into the super-fan league was that he actually conceived and published a regular fanzine, the *Walford Gazette*.

When I first came across a copy I thought it was something created by one of the crew or staff working at the BBC Elstree studios on our show. I was impressed. Even more so when Larry led a campaign to save the show from cancellation on BBC America. It was a valiant, but ultimately doomed effort. For all the reasons I've outlined, a British soap just doesn't travel well, even when held in such high regard back on home soil.

There were just not enough Larry Jaffees to keep the show on an emerging cable network who needed to get bums on seats and attract the advertisers.

But what an adventure Larry's been on. Without the enthusiasm and support of TV fans like him, we wouldn't get to make shows like *EastEnders*—and I'm pleased to say he even became an honorary Eastender when he got his wish of visiting Albert Square to live out his TV dream. As Del Shannon put it—Hats off to Larry.

Mal Young is a well known and respected producer who has been making TV drama for the past 26 years. He began his career producing the ground-breaking Brookside *for Channel 4 and went on to oversee and create many hundreds of hours of popular programmes when he became the BBC's Controller of Drama Series, his final BBC success being the relaunch of the iconic series* Dr. Who *to great acclaim. Most recently he has been working for Simon Fuller, creator of* American Idol, *developing and producing new shows for the US. He now divides his time between Los Angeles and London creating and producing new programming for a global audience.*

Preface

Once while on a Britain-bound transatlantic Virgin flight, among its in-flight entertainment I stumbled upon a movie called *Cruise of the Gods* about a fan club dedicated to a cult sci-fi British television show not unlike *Dr. Who* or *Star Trek*. The club's enterprising leader managed to round up some of the actors and creative team for a fan convention at sea.

As I watched, I thought to myself, "Oh no, I'm like that guy." I was on my way to London to interview actors of *EastEnders*, which enjoys something of cult status on the US side of the pond, thanks in part to my fanzine, the *Walford Gazette*, which I've published continuously since November 1992 as a quarterly tabloid. Periodically I kicked around the idea of mounting a convention similar to the one depicted in *Cruise of the Gods*, which starred Rob Brydon and Steve Coogan. In fact, Wendy Richard's husband in 2003 broached the idea with me, but we got sidetracked with figuring out the logistics, and it was unfortunately never discussed further.

Even though I'm not much of a sci-fi fan, I often likened the obsessive nature of *EastEnders* fans—you're either get it or do not—to the classic extra-terrestrial film *Close Encounters of The Third Kind*, in which people are drawn together, but they don't know why. Go to any *EastEnders* club meeting, and you will find similar disparate types from all walks of life. If it wasn't for this TV show, it's unlikely they would ever have otherwise met. Many of them ended up contributing to the *Gazette*, which, like every newspaper, needs multiple voices.

The would-be social networker in me often wonders how I could better serve this audience, and remarkably 18 years later I'm still plodding ahead with my little quarterly newspaper, firmly embedded in an old school media model, in this age of iPad delivery. I guess there's ink in my blood. Trained as a journalist, I never pictured myself doing anything else. The journalist A.J. Liebling once wrote, "Freedom of the press is guaranteed only to those who own one." It's an adage that I have long believed in, and that was long before thousands of journalism jobs have been lost, including my own.

But despite all I have achieved in the mainstream media (published articles early in my career in *The New York Times, Rolling Stone, Parade, Vibe*, among numerous others, as well as being the top editor of several business magazines and websites), I can honestly state that I am most proud of the *Walford Gazette* and last year's publication of my first book *Albert Square & Me: The Actors of EastEnders* among my professional achievements.

I'm not delusional to think that *Walford Gazette* makes me some sort of "Citizen Kane" character. But given my experience as a professional journalist and ability "to recognise a good story," I'm not surprised how many publications and media outlets gave coverage to my little fanzine right from the start. However, I was a bit taken aback when *The Times* of London ran a news article Aug. 18, 1995 on page 2 about the *Gazette's* co-founder Dan Abramson threatening to protest the BBC offices if *EastEnders* was cancelled in New York, next to an article about Iraq giving arms details to the United Nations.

Not that we always courted controversy, but sometimes it came from unexpected places. A year after Dan and I launched the *Gazette*, which was designed to provide American public TV stations with a thank you gift that *EastEnders* fans would really want instead of station-logo tote bags, I learned I had been banned from the BBC's Elstree studio. The reason? For publishing in the *Walford Gazette's* second issue a series of photographs of an American woman posing around the exterior sets. The cheeky headline read: "ALBERT SQUARE TRESPASSER!" Apparently, there was hell to pay within the security office. Eventually the ban was lifted, and a change in guard resulted in me being welcomed several times to the studio by a succession of executive producers. In 2003, I was rewarded by former BBC Controller of Continuing Drama Series Mal Young with a prop Walford street sign signed by the entire cast, as a token of appreciation for all I have done to keep *EastEnders* alive in the US. Later that year, BBC America pulled the plug on *EastEnders*, citing low ratings, when the real culprit was no promotion. I sprung into protest mode with a screaming *Gazette* headline: "COR BLIMEY! Fans Vow: We Will Not Go Quietly."

At the time, I was already planning a trip to London, and a friend who had just been made redundant by the BBC gladly fed me phone numbers of the internal BBC telephone directory, placing my calls at the offices to the highest executives. Eventually, one agreed to meet with me, and you can read here on page 117 the maddening, face-to-face conversation in all its glory. So despite my ability to get press, I wasn't always successful in getting the powers-that-be to realise that they were overlooking a programme that resonated across the Atlantic. But I did lead the effort to save the show in New York in January 2005 when the local public TV station made the decision to cancel *EastEnders*, but didn't have the guts to go let viewers know. The *Gazette* database of 1,200 fans in the vicinity came in handy, and within a month we had raised nearly $35,000 in response to two postcards I mailed, exceeding the demanded target of $29,000 to cover the BBC's license fee. And I'm happy to report the show is still on the air.

Two years later I came across a particularly disturbing interview with Garth Ancier, the new head of BBC America. He told an AP reporter that *EastEnders* was "peculiar to Britain," and that "it's not a particularly uplifting or inspirational show. It's a very dramatic serial but sort of depressing. The joke around the office is the lesson from that show is 'Life is miserable and then you die.'"

As the Cockneys say, "them's fightin' words," and I know of at least of a hundred teabags (get the symbolism?) that were mailed to Ancier to show him how severely he underestimates interest in *EastEnders*, and that it belongs back on BBC America. It's as if the BBC has learned nothing from fans being able to reverse cancellations in New York and Washington, D.C., by raising substantial sums of money for the their public TV stations in short periods of time. It's inexplicable why the BBC hasn't made more of an effort to make *EastEnders* a success in the US.

The *Walford Gazette* was created partly as a fundraising tool for the 50 PBS affiliates that broadcast *EastEnders* at the time of its launch in 1992; now there are nine left. Sometimes dealing with these non-profit stations has been frustrating, such as the time an executive at WNYC in New York insisted on taking only 50 copies of the paper as a thank-you gift for viewers' financial contributions, rather than the open-ended approach I suggested. Of course, the 50 copies sold out in two minutes, and somebody in the control room flashed on the live TV screen "NO MORE GAZETTES." I hate to think how much money the station and I lost that night.

You will sense my careful attempts to not bite the hand that feeds me, yet also be taken seriously when I corresponded with Rupert Murdoch on why he should pick up the US rights to *EastEnders*. When the *Gazette* tries to influence the powers-that-be, I suppose I'm practicing a form of participatory or advocacy journalism, albeit a much smaller scale, that Orson Welles portrayed in *Citizen Kane*. Still, I was chuffed for receiving an official citation for publishing the *Walford Gazette* as "an outstanding citizen" from the New York City Council on the occasion of *EastEnders'* 20th anniversary.

This book serves as something of a "Best of the *Walford Gazette*." Whereas my first book told the story of the series from the perspective of the actors (a volume 2 of *Albert Square & Me* still is in the works), *Walford State of Mind* provides a pot-pourri of what the paper delivers in every issue: interviews, inside information, analysis, humour, trivia, reviews, etc.

Besides Dan and myself, there are 19 contributors of articles that fall into distinct sections: **Analysis**, including examinations of favourite episodes, characters and moments; **Creative Team**, exclusive *WG* interviews with executive producers, directors, writers and a casting agent; **Advocate**, in which the newspaper finds itself leading campaigns to reverse cancellations and mix it up with the BBC and PBS station honchos over cancellation decisions; **Fandom**, in which various super-fans retell their encounters with *EastEnders* actors, including Wendy Richard (Pauline), Anita Dobson (Angie), Pam St. Clement (Pat), Barbara Windsor (Peggy), Michelle Collins (Cindy), and Shane Richie (Alfie); and **Reviews** of *EastEnders*-related episodes, videos, and books.

Perhaps my favourite piece in the book was written in 1994 by Lenny & Stephanie Kaye, "How *EastEnders* Saved Our Marriage," ending with Stephanie nabbing a anniversary autograph for Lenny of Steve McFadden (Phil Mitchell). Its sequel 11 years later, "How *EastEnders* Saved Our Marriage, Again," written by Stephanie alone is even better. In it, she explains how after a few-year-long separation, they both realised that neither her new boyfriend nor his new girlfriend could relate to *EastEnders*. Stephanie and Lenny's ritual of watching the show together ultimately served as the ties that bind.

That's where the title *Walford State of Mind* comes from. Non-fans of *EastEnders* just don't understand our fascination with the show. But those of us who do get it are hooked for life. Who else would understand the fictional London tube map depicted on the cover of the new book? Only a true fan would know that the fictional "Walford East" is situated between the real-life Upney and Dagenham East.

Putting out the *Walford Gazette* has not only given me the rare privilege to walk the cobblestones of Albert Square, but also meet and interview about 50 of the show's actors. I've discussed the finer points of *EastEnders* with personal heroes Ray Davies, John Cleese, Billy Bragg, Richard Thompson and Tracey Ullman, as well as had the opportunity to hand a copy of the *Gazette* to Paul McCartney and Elvis Costello.

I think the writing contained within *Walford State of Mind,* especially those articles written by others, speaks for itself, certainly worthy of being published in the finest publications. So *EastEnders* fans, please enjoy what follows; there's plenty more from where it came.

Ta,

Larry Jaffee, November 2010

I

Birth of A Fanzine

Where Did the Walford Gazette Come From?

By Larry Jaffee

Quite simply, if it wasn't for Dan Abramson, the *Walford Gazette* might have not existed.

It began with an offhand conversation with Dan at my then-new workplace back in late 1991, when I overheard Dan talking with another co-worker about *EastEnders*. I chimed in, "Oh yeah, I watch that too."

Dan turned around speechless—a wide grin on his face, most likely mulling to himself, "There's another one!!!" The next day I received in my office mailbox, an impeccably double-space typed, five-page memo about that week's most recent episode, intermittently punctuated by "IAN SHOULD BE SHOT!" Most of it contained Dan's brand of off-the-wall humour, unlike anything I ever previously encountered.

In our next conversation, Dan later claimed that I insisted, "We can make money with this." I don't recall saying exactly that, but it doesn't surprise me. I was looking for something entrepreneurial to do, and I genuinely loved *EastEnders* (although not nearly as obsessively as Dan).

It became apparent that our partnership would take advantage of our strengths. Dan was to be the in-house creative genius, churning out reams of copy about the intricacies of Albert Square. He also was friendly with Freddie Hancock, a BBC publicist who was married to the late British comedian Tony Hancock. She was instrumental in us eventually gaining permission to publish the *Gazette*.

Meanwhile, I knew how to put out a newspaper, came up with a marketing plan that would appeal to the public television stations, and would chip in stories here and there time permitting. We figured we'd lose a few hundred dollars on a first and only issue, and that would be the end of the *Walford Gazette*. We were wrong. Hordes of *EastEnders* fans came out of the woodwork, thirsting for as much information

3

about the series as we could muster. And major media outlets on both sides of the Atlantic the likes of BBC Radio, the *Times* of London, *The Guardian, The Independent, Time Out, Daily Mirror, USA Today, New York Post, Newsday,* et. al., were intrigued with our fledgling venture.

Dan was something of an odd duck, who had an unusual way about him. For example, when the *New York Post* ran a brief item about the *Gazette,* he lit up a cigar in the office we worked, as if we won the lottery or our IPO was the darling of Wall Street. Dan also had an undeniable talent for writing prose, a way with words that captured insight into *EastEnders* that I'm sure its creators never even considered. He also at times was very funny, best exemplified by his Top 10 lists.

We collaborated a few times on comical *EastEnders* fantasy scripts. The process would be he'd write the first draft, and I'd polish the lines, adding a joke here and there. It reminded me of Carl Bernstein polishing Bob Woodward's Watergate articles.

Dan also was incredibly well read, a self-taught historian bordering on savant-hood (reminiscent of *Cheers'* Cliff Claven), who could instantaneously cite the nuances of British Royalty going back centuries in one breath and the batting average of some hapless baseball player on the 1962 New York Mets in the next. (Admittedly, I possess a repository of useless rock 'n' roll trivia.)

When we'd put together an issue of the *Gazette,* I sometimes found myself playing the role of censor, letting Dan know from time to time that his references will go straight over the heads of most if not every reader. On the other hand, we were in agreement that the publication needed to be "an august intellectual journal," as our friend Jonathan once dubbed it, with the right balance of intelligence, humour and insight.

Occasionally, I had to point out to him some of his musings went a little too far, like when several years ago he wrote about the sexual attractiveness of the female castmembers of *EastEnders*, and wanted to use the byline of my then two-year-old son.

He also used numerous nom-de-plumes ("Sid Reilly," "F. Scott Fitz-Nigel," "Dora Kaplan," "Phyllis Domesticus," "Sir Walter Cockney," "Chris Orthodox" and "Alan Badelian Traherne") that occasionally would be attached to some of his *Gazette* articles. He'd use a pseudonym when he felt there were too many Dan Abramson bylines in an issue.

Another thing about Dan and his idiosyncrasies is that he had no interest in technology. By 1995, he was still writing on an electric typewriter. Dan finally agreed to use a computer when I and then-*Gazette* managing editor Aaron Berman (who was tired of retyping his articles) finally insisted that he get one, courtesy of the *Gazette*.

I never quite understood his reluctance to join the computer age, and told him if he ever learned how to use e-mail, he'd be dangerous. He was my only acquaintance who actually wrote letters to people. I figured that back in grade school he must have had a teacher who once gave a homework assignment that the class needed to write a letter to a relative. Dan never stopped writing those letters—to everyone he knew.

His allergy to computers reminded me of a lyric from an Al Stewart song about two friends who hadn't see each other in 15 years: "I have no use for modern tricks."

Dan often admitted that if wasn't for me his writing about *East-Enders* would have otherwise sat in some file unread by anyone.

At the beginning of our partnership, we split the duties. I'd handle the business deals and strategy; he'd deal with the subscribers and stations on a day-to-day basis. After six years of working together, we decided to call it a day, and I bought him out of the business. About a year later in April 1999, Dan died of colon cancer at the age of 45. His health was always suspect. In fact, the day I picked up from the printer the *Gazette's* preview issue in late 1992, Dan was recovering from a heart attack.

From the outpouring of condolences, I know that he was very well liked by our readers, who often would call him to find out what they missed in a given episode. Dan would provide total recall of every scene, including actual dialogue. (Thankfully, he didn't attempt the voices and accents.) Of course, some readers called him to complain that they hadn't received their *Gazette* after mailing in a check. Dan would stay on the phone with them for hours, winning them over with his charm and deep well of knowledge. He'd then inevitably forget to update the database, maybe subconsciously so that he'd get to talk to them all over again. In any case, I apologise for never being able to match the time and energy that he put in handling subscriber calls.

Here's another lament: the world's biggest Anglophile in his lifetime never got a chance to visit the UK. My guess is he would have been like a kid in a candy store. I once told Dan that when I had enough of the *Gazette*, I'd let him some day run wild, and let him put anything he wanted in the publication. That sadly never took place. I'm sure there would be plenty of outrageousness, but it would also have been damn funny.

• • •

Me & Arthur Watching Young Martin Grow

By Dan Abramson

(Editor's note: Dan was so prolific in his writing about EastEnders *that often there wasn't enough room to print all that he wrote. As a result, there was always a backlog of material. This was one that I was saving, waiting for Young Martin to grow up a bit so stateside viewers could better relate to Dan's analysis. It ended up getting published after his 1999 death, making the headline—written by him—all the more poignant. In 2006, when James Alexandrou visited New York, I presented him with a copy of the issue containing Dan's article; he was pleased and proudly showed it to his then-girlfriend Kara Tointon,* EastEnders' *Dawn Swann.)*

Watching those Walford Kids grow up has been one of the distinct intellectual pleasures of *EastEnders*. It provides a sense of community—folk memories of the Young 'Uns—just like in the real world, except that, in Albert Square, the conversations are better-scripted. I shall refrain from singing "Sunrise, Sunset" in this context. But that can't stop me recalling... Young Martin, aged five, climbing a long staircase on his first day of school as his unemployed Dad watches with joy and fascination... Kofi Tavernier starting a serious friendship with Vicky Fowler, in emulation of their parents' Romeo & Juliet routine... Twelve-year-old "Junior," the son of a con artist, bravely defending his Aunt from an abusive husband... Junior's little girlfriend Melody resisting a potential child abuser by biting the hand that pets her... An entire roomful of children at an Albert Square birthday party, reacting in amazement to an ex-rock star doing an awesomely grotesque Elvis impersonation... Clare, Janine and Sonia playing "Nancy Drew" with the life of an elderly Holocaust survivor and scaring half the neighbourhood...

These are golden memories for me—part of the experience of living in Walford which I can convince myself I am sharing. Let's face it, kids were one of the key reasons for having communities in the first place. Their growing pains and happiness are the hallmarks of life going on. And *EastEnders* deals with children in a beautiful manner. Not as diminutive geniuses, not as exceptionally cute and constantly lovable. The Walford kids are sometimes quite pleasant and sometimes massive annoyances. Usually, their behavior lies between those two polarities.

Trysting Martin

Just how much that Walford Y-Generation is beginning to mean to me was brought home recently, when a friend from England sent me tapes of an episode that has not yet been broadcast here in America. The complicated set of plotlines included the first time that Young

Teenaged Martin is invited by a girl to engage in what used to be called "heavy necking."

This, of course, means that Martin is now getting into adolescence, but he and the girl were both so sweet and skinny that it amounted to childhood romance. There was no heavy trauma involved, just a nice little Tom Sawyer & Becky Thatcher In The Hayloft kind of thing. Martin was a guest in the home of the young lady's parents. She invited him to sneak out to her favourite trysting place after the rest of the family had gone to sleep. And, presumably, the two wholesome Byronics had a very pleasant time together. In any case—by the next sunrise—Young Martin's face was defined by one of the most delightfully silly grins I personally have ever seen.

Those of us privileged to witness this occasion did not get to see the actual necking. (Among other things it was left in the minds of the beholders as to whether Martin & Friend went beyond mere kissing and fondling.) But this is one of the better aspects of the Walford Canon—the fact that sex almost never takes place in full view of the audience. You maybe see the first kiss. The rest is silence, with a fade-to-black on the video monitor. After all, there are very few sluts or exhibitionists in Walford. If Cindy Beale is sufficiently ladylike to have all her sexual encounters take place off-camera, then we can only assume that Young Martin is enough of a gentleman to do the same.

Which made the whole matter of Martin's Tryst delightfully poetic in an extremely tasteful sort of way. Especially since this is a boy whose existence we first became aware of on-camera six months before his birth.

Louisian Anger

You see, Arthur had been out of work for two years and he and Pauline were overjoyed to have a new infant on the way—sixteen years after Michelle. (Two years of unemployment would have left most men impotent. Arthur, however, had a very strong sense of family.)

But his mother-in-law, Lou, did not want another smelly child on the premises, which precipitated a decade's worth of psychodramas as Arthur graphically told off Lou. Pauline sided with Arthur for once and Michelle overheard and sided with Lou and a traumatic time was had by all.

We visited in Young Martin's childhood as he was born.... years later when he had appendicitis.... his role as Joseph in the Christmas pageant....the trauma he experienced as Pauline threw Arthur out of the extra-marital house....and then there was Martin-aged-five having trouble with doorknobs. All these could have been incidents from anyone's childhood—especially the doorknobs.

And I have a particularly fond memory of Martin and Vicky—both holding hands with Arthur—walking around a corner on Bridge Street just as Pat Butcher punches out Santa Claus. (Saint Nick was sexually harassing her, but it's kind of a long story.) Martin's facial expression was memorable.

With any luck, we will still be watching *EastEnders* a dozen years from now, as Martin brings up his own children in Albert Square. Maybe we'll even see Martin's son or daughter at First Kiss. Ah, the delicious continuity of it all! In my old age I'm hoping to get acquainted with Martin's kids. They'll probably be quite nice.

• • •

Ethel & Dot's Two-Hander Down Memory Lane

By Dan Abramson

The episode where Ethel and Dot commune on a wet winter's day is probably the best-half hour of *EastEnders* that I have ever seen. This is one of the famous "two-handers," in which only two characters appear onscreen. Of course, between them, Ethel and Dot have enough character quirks to equal a cast of dozens on any other series. Even by Wal-ford standards, Ethel Mae Skinner and Dorothy Cotton are marvel-ously multi-faceted in their good and bad qualities.

The memories they voice in this episode institute a wonderful bit of time travel among the ghosts of Walford Past. Mrs. Skinner has lived in Albert Square since her birth circa 1910. The comparatively Young Ms. Cotton was pushing fifty when this was taped in 1987 and she had spent part of her childhood in Wales. So we can think of her as "The Newcomer." In any case, Dot & Ethel qualify as what in Africa are called "griots," the oral historians who know all there is to know about the life of their home village.

During this 30-minute mini-drama, The Dynamic Duo provide viewers with fascinating insights as regards what was happening in sleepy Walford Town before the BBC-TV cameras first showed up in 1985. And those insights provide all sorts of psychological information that help us to more fully understand the likes of Dennis Watts and Kathy Beale and everyone else who grew up under the watchful eyes of Dot & Ethel.

Ethel's Larder

Our Cold Day in Walford episode begins with Ethel checking the food supply in her bedsit. She has enough money to go out and buy a nutri-tious dinner (or, anyway, something filling.) But it is so cold and wet outdoors that Ethel does an inventory of her in-house reserves. She ascertains that she has the fixin's for many pots of tea, along with half a tin of tea biscuits. And Ethel would rather get by on that for the next sixteen or eighteen hours than run out and buy food.

Enter Dear Dot, the neurotic Good Samaritan, who asks if Ethel needs anything from the Cash 'n' Carry. The episode then consists of: a short conversation between the two ladies; followed by a few minutes in which Ethel falls asleep while alone in the apartment; after which Dot returns and mistakenly concludes that Ethel has died.

The heaviest physical action involves Ethel lying down. They speak to each other in polite, almost genteel tones. Neither woman has any dramatic news to report. There are no fancy camera angles. It all takes place on the one dingy stage set. And the result is 30 riveting minutes of the artform known as television.

One of its true golden moments has Ethel reflecting on the fact that—while she may presently be just the old woman who helps clean up the pub—The Queen Vic is sacred ground to her. That's because, Ethel explains, one night in 1942, an American sailor and a British soldier got into a fist fight over her at The Vic.

"Why ever did they do that?" asks Dot.

"Because I led them both on, silly!" replies Ethel.

"Why ever did you do that?"

"Dot, weren't you ever young?"

That final question is phrased by Ethel with such existential despair that it helps if you seen every previous episode of *EastEnders*. Because then you would have picked up the fact that Dot's troubles in life began when she was a three year old whose home got blown up during The Blitz. And Ethel and Lou Beale (Pauline's mother) went over to comfort the crying child and found themselves enlisted as surrogate-Mums-for-1ife.

This led to a beautiful friendship between Ethel and Lou, who probably would not have become close for any other reason. (Pre-Blitz, Lou was a respectable, almost puritanical, married woman, while Ethel was the sort who caused fist fights in pubs.) Let's face it. programmes with this kind of depth are hard to find. They don't have psychological character development like that on say *Home Improvement*.

Nor would most programmes even attempt the level of comedy/ drama that is achieved by Ethel in remembering a rather forceful woman who lived around The Square 40 years earlier. Ethel gleefully recalls how the woman's teenage son had been allowed to place repeated bets at the local horse parlour. Then, when the boy actually won a sizable wager, the bookmaker had hypocritically told him that he was too young to be betting and that the winnings would not be paid. So the boy had gone straight to his forceful Mum and she had beaten the stuffings out of the bookmaker.

For Ethel, that bookie-beating Mum is a happy memory. Dot recalls her as "a vicious old woman." Which provides very heavy ongoing insights into the nature of Ethel & Dot.

The main appeal of this two-hander lies in the performances of Gretchen Franklin (Ethel) and June Brown (Dot)—each of whom displays an astonishing ability to find truth in their characters. Each brings subtlety and power (which is a very rare combination) to her portrayal. There is genius present in the language of Ethel's elderly body and the timbre of Dot's neurotic voice. Together, they herein weave a very special panel in the ongoing tapestry of *EastEnders*.

Welsh Lullabies

The threads from this Ethel/Dot dialogue also worked nicely into a later episode from the tapestry, when a teenage runaway named Disa O'Brien has given birth and is occupying the apartment downstairs from Dot. In her two-hander with Ethel a few years earlier, Dot told a fascinating story about how, after her home was Blitzed, she was evacuated to Wales, where she lived with a family who treated her extremely well. Dot tells Ethel of the wonderful memory she has of falling to sleep to a lullaby sung in Welsh. As Ethel knows, the rest of Dot's childhood was a continuing story of emotional abuse by her mother and stepfather in Albert Square. So Ethel just smiles in a surrogate-motherly way, as Dot recalls this one delightful childhood memory.

Two years later, Dot is left alone with Disa's infant and Dot suddenly—hauntingly—begins singing a lullaby in Welsh. You either remember this from the Dot & Ethel episode or you don't. One of the great things about *EastEnders* is that they never go to flashbacks and almost never include speeches about how this happened to her three episodes back and now she's doing this to him. The creative team at Elstree takes it for granted that nobody gets hooked on *EastEnders* in the first place unless they have impressive powers of concentration. This occasionally pays off in spades, as in Dot's lullaby to Disa's baby. Anyone in the audience who recalled the two-handed programme received a powerful emotional jolt when Dot began singing what was—in effect—an ode of love to her own unhappy childhood self.

Shortly after the lullaby and with the best of intentions, Dot hands over Disa's baby to a villain—simply because he claims to be the infant's father. Devastated at the effects of her own childish naivete, Dot then moves heaven and earth to recover the infant. In so doing, she displays an intelligence and skill at communications which would normally seem beyond Mrs. Cotton's ability. Even the police are impressed with Dot's efforts (and Dot is the sort of person usually referred to, in police lingo, as "a massive pain in the a%*"). It is, of course, a case of Dot seeking to preserve and protect her own inner child. And Dot's high-level of efficiency in recovering Disa's kid provides further fascinating insight into the sort of adult that Dot might have been, if childhood circumstance had given her half a chance.

But to fully understand Dot's melody of love, you sort of had to spend a winter's day hearing her converse with Ethel in the confines of a bedsit. And to watch what happens when two superb thespians turn a pair of seemingly mundane old women into works of the finest art.

. . .

The Life & Career of Gretchen Franklin

June Brown & Larry Jaffee Interviewed by BBC Radio5

BBC Radio 5's weekly obituary programme Brief Lives *interviewed June Brown and Larry Jaffee regarding the passing of Gretchen Franklin in July 2005. Here is a transcript of the broadcast.*

Hello, I'm Dotun Adebayo and this is *Brief Lives*. The celebrations marking the 60th anniversary of the ending of the Second World War were a reminder how the people of the East End of London refused to be defeated by the Luftwaffe bombings from the skies in the 1940s. That East End spirit was embodied on television by one of the most famous *EastEnders*, Ethel Skinner. Sixteen-and-a-half million of us mourned the passing of Ethel on the series five years ago. Actress Gretchen Franklin, who played Ethel, was part of an *EastEnders* double act with her friend and colleague June Brown, best known as Dot Cotton.

June Brown: She was acerbic. She could be very sharp, but she had a very kind heart and was one of those people who didn't suffer fools gladly. She didn't suffer them at all, and also was hot at all sentimental. But underneath she was caring. She had loads of friends of different ages from different walks of life. She was a very complicated kind, being from the theatre for years and years and years. She was quite a girl, very pretty, very sparkling eyes, blonde curls and a wide mouth. And she could sing and dance. We once did a scene for Pat and Frank's wedding. We were outside in the street, and Gretchen decided to do a dance. She got a tea tray. She's 78 or 79. And there she is on top of the tea tray kicking high kicks. It was marvelous. She did it once; and did it again and again and again. I thought it was going to give her a stroke or heart attack, and she gamely went on.

Dotun plays an audio clip with Ethel and Dot arguing over an umbrella, which Dot claimed was "from a big store in London, prob-

ably Harrods, while Ethel insisted it was "from a sale at the community centre."

June Brown: They (Ethel and Dot) were constantly at loggerheads, scoring points off each other, and yet you were aware of this deep friendship: As I said, Gretchen was the most unsentimental person.

There was a line when she had to say, "I love you, Dot" or "You're my best friend, Dot." She said, "I'm not going to say it." When it came to it, it was right at the end—her last words—she did. And it was really quite moving. It was really quite sad to do because [Gretchen] had become so frail.

More from the clip of them arguing over the umbrella.

June Brown: She always liked the last word, and if the last word was yours, she would always answer it. Finish it off—you get the last shot then. She was very generous in some ways too, Gretchen. Although she liked being number one. 1 told my PA Jim, Gretchen had died that evening, and he said "I won't say anything." I said, "What do you mean, Jim?" And he said, "Well you know, you wouldn't want it to get around." I said, "What are you talking about? Gretchen was a star. She wanted a big audience. She would want everybody to know. She was number one. Tell everybody you think of."

Dotun Adebayo: *Larry Jaffee is the publisher of the* Walford Gazette, *the* EastEnders *fanzine from America. He met Gretchen Franklin many times, and I asked him did the real Gretchen Franklin have a little bit of Ethel Skinner in her.*

Larry Jaffee: Every once in a while it would come through, little sayings or little quirky things that she would come out with. 1 always looked at her as sort of the British gran I never had. I'm an American journalist and once had a conversation with the English musician Billy Bragg. I had known him for about four or five years and never mentioned the *Gazette* because I thought it might ruin any kind of cool status I had with him. But he laughed for about 30 seconds and said, "I once watched an episode at my mum's. It was one of those two-handers between Ethel and Dot reminiscing about the war. And I was glued to the set. Those conversations took place in my house with my mother, my aunts." It shows what a great programme *EastEnders* really is. I think everyone bas an Ethel in their family.

Dotun Adebayo: Larry Jaffee and June Brown talking about *East-Enders* actress Gretchen Franklin, who has died at the age of 94.

• • •

20 Best Moments In EastEnders History
A Completely Subjective, Unabashed Opinion

By Larry Jaffee

(Editor's note: Apologies for those stunners that have come since No. 20 on the list. Blame it on BBC America canceling EE in September 2003, and stateside fans having to put up with watching episodes more than six years behind the BBC1 broadcasts in Britain.)

Once viewers are hooked by a television serial, they pick up on character/plot-development nuances that make more and more sense as time goes on. At least once a year, *EastEnders* delivers a gripping storyline that sets the stage for a pivotal event, thus forever changing life in Albert Square. This can take the form of someone dying, leaving the Square, or personal relationships veering off into a new understanding about who they are. These pivotal events in some cases can take an entire half-hour episode (see Nos.5, 6). But in others, it can merely be a split-second, tunnelvision-like look (#10, 13, 14).

The passages in bold explain the overall significance of the moment. They're listed roughly in chronological order. I think it would be an exercise in futility to list them in terms of importance. They're all precious in their own way, and could stand up on their own as minidramas whether or not the viewer has any prior *EastEnders* knowledge.

1) **Den Watts kicks down the door to find the dead body of Reg Cox; later chucks Nick Cotton out of pub.** What a way to kick off a series. Episode director Matthew Robinson pointed out to me in 1998 when he was executive producer that it was no accident that the first episode ends with a fist (Nick Cotton's) coming through the door.

2) **Ali and Sue find/deal with their baby's crib death.** Imagine how painful this type of thing is, even to act.

3) **Den and Michelle discuss Michelle's pregnancy.** I still find it hard to believe that this could happen, or when 'Chel slept with Grant.

4) **Den and Angie fight in the pub.** This happened fairly often, so I'm not sure if any row stands out in particular, but they certainly were sort of a latter-day Richard Burton-Liz Taylor a la *Who's Afraid of Virginia Woolf.*

5) **Dot and Ethel reminisce about the old days.** One of the most requested "two-handers." You find so much about what made them tick.

6) **Kathy confronts her rapist Wilmott-Brown with ex-husband Pete present.** I had a house-guest while this was airing, so I didn't catch it all, but the little I did see appeared to be gripping.

7) **Gill dies of AIDS.** This was ensemble acting at its best.

8) **Michelle and Sharon's night out; Clyde and Grant look for them at the college.** The best shot was the very last with an aerial night-time

view of the campus showing 'Chel and Sharon going in one direction, and Grant and Clyde walking in the other.

9) **Arthur tells Pauline about his affair with Christine; Pauline bashes Arthur on the head with a frying pan.** Arfur acted so guilty about his affair that he probably felt he deserved it.

10) **Grant beats up Eddie, returns to his flat looking manic while blasting opera on the stereo; Frank mobilizes Arthur and Pete to teach Grant a lesson a la *High Noon*.** Grant's manic look is priceless. Frank, Arthur & Pete probably saw too many John Ford westerns on telly.

11) **Grant finds out about Sharon's affair with Phil, plays tape in front of everyone at the Queen Vic; beats up Phil at the Arches**. Probably one of the most effective shots of a car tape deck. The party was getting kind of boring.

12) **Ricky's bachelor party ends three hours before the wedding with the groom waking up in a country field with Grant, Phil and Nigel thinking that they're in France.** The best bit is Nigel trying to speak French.

13) **David realises how mentally ill Joe really is.** The camera does a quick scan of Joe's tin-foil-wrapped bedroom; David's silently aghast.

14) **Phil, Grant, Ricky and Bianca go to Spain in search of the Mitchells' sister Samantha, who ends up in bed with David—Ricky's half brother.** Sam is Ricky's ex-wife. They're all utterly shocked, amazed, embarrassed, confused. Probably the second funniest scene, after #12.

15) **Phil and Grant's car takes a dip into the Thames.** They don't do

them often, but usually an *EastEnders* car chase is gripping viewing (see #16), and this location shoot in Greenwich was no exception. Made great use of the Millennium Dome as a background prop.

16) **Steve gets blown up after the car chase**. *EastEnders* usually doesn't spend this much money on an expiring actor contract, and we were sorry to Martin Kemp and his suits go.

17) **Zoe finds out that Kat is her mum.** Sure, the situation owes plenty to the Hollywood film *Chinatown*, but so what?

18) **Alfie in search of a condom for his big night with Kat.** Yeah, it was implausible, but you could really feel for him.

19) **The Ferreira wedding party.** I know most critics consider this attempt at an Asian family to be ill-conceived, but this celebration gone awry stands out.

20) **Dot Cotton thinking she's seen a ghost.** Den Watts as a latter-day Lazarus in the eyes of this Believer.

• • •

In Search of Walford

By Larry Jaffee

(Editor's note: The following was first published in 1993.)
Taking my first trip to London this past May since launching the *Walford Gazette* in April 1993, I was anxious to get first-hand British reactions to our Yank-created publication, which lovingly pays homage to *EastEnders*. If we tapped the pulse of a loyal viewing cult in the colo-

nies, wouldn't the Limeys go absolutely barmy over a newspaper that chronicles their favourite BBC television series week-in-and-week-out?

What follows are excerpts from trip diary:

May 13-May 14: Waiting for my red-eye Virgin Atlantic flight at JFK to be called, I proudly wore my *EastEnders* t-shirt in hopes of sparking conversation with other faithful viewers from both sides of the ocean. Unfortunately, no one even noticed the latest issue of the *Gazette* that I happened to be casually/obviously perusing. I attributed the lack of attention to the reserved nature of Brits, or the flight's abundance of businessmen who couldn't be bothered. Too bad their wives weren't along. By the time I finally made it to my London hotel in Kensington, I found out that my room wouldn't be ready for several hours. So I took a bunch of *Gazettes* and made the rounds with the local newsagents to see if they had any interest in selling the only newspaper in the world dedicated to *EastEnders*. I was greeted with suspicion, which is partly understandable since they had never seen the *Walford Gazette* before. Excuses ranged from "you have to talk to the owner" to "I have no room."

May 15: On Sunday, I decided to take an "Eastenders (sic) tour" of the "Jewish East End," as promoted in *Time Out* magazine. As it turned out, the real East End is a far cry from the show's cockney neighborliness. The streets we walked along seemed to have more of an Indian feel than the ethnic mosaic we see on *EastEnders*. The Petticoat Lane market is much more crowded than the stalls we see in Albert Square. Once again, I tested local merchant interest in selling the *Gazette*. These guys can sell anything, I figured. As I moved from stall to stall, the general consensus was that they were licensed only to sell specific merchandise, not contraband like the *Walford Gazette*. I mused, "I suppose Tricky Dicky, the market manager, will issue you a citation if you accept these complimentary copies from your friends in the States." Where were Pete Beale, Frank Butcher, even Nigel Bates, when I needed them most?

May 16: Kicking off the work week, I had scheduled a business meeting with Vicky Mayer, editor of *Inside Soap* magazine, which was pictured on our last issue and whose publishing company just co-published a book on the history of *EastEnders*. Vicky and I compare notes on the differences between our stateside and the British appreciation of *East-Enders*: they classify the programme as a soap, not the high-art drama that we Yanks at the *Gazette* make it out be. Seeking some publicity for the *Gazette* and my visit to London, I contact the *Daily Mirror's* television critic, Simon London, who has the great idea of me squaring off with Vicky for an *EastEnders* quiz. I explain to Simon that I never pretended to be a trivia buff, and that my contributions to the *Gazette* have been more on the business side. But I played the good sport. Of course, there's no excuse for not knowing the first names of Dot Cotton's husband and Phil and Grant's mother. Vicky and Simon are happy to talk to me about *EastEnders*, but they're absolutely mad over *Melrose Place*.

May 17: No UK trip would be complete without a sensationalist tabloid headline about an *EastEnders* character. The People came through with: "TRICKY DICKY QUITS EASTENDERS; BBC shocked as sex rat says I've had enough." It was also a pleasure to hear the morning radio team raggin' on the preceding night's *EastEnders* episode, imitating Grant and Phil's voices, how they were being "stitched up" by a local hood named Jimmy. (I later found out that the slang meant being to be set up.) The DJ also commented, "I can't believe that Michelle kissed to him," referring to the new, older man in 'Chelle's life, Geoff. With some of the local newspaper critics, there seems to be an *East-Enders* backlash, in which the general consensus is that the quality of the shows has gone down noticeably.

May 18: Gretchen Franklin, who *EastEnders* fans know as Ethel, invited me to interview her at her home! On the telephone, Miss

Franklin sounded exactly like Ethel. In person, she appeared decades younger than her real age (on 8 July 1994 this wonderful lady and talented actress celebrated her 83rd birthday). We had much to talk about, as she over the next three hours told me all about her fascinating career before and on *EastEnders*. When she caught a glimpse of the *Gazette*, she said, "It's quite charming, isn't it?" If interviewing Gretchen Franklin wasn't enough, I also manage to catch Todd Carty (Mark Fowler) in his dressing room between scenes, calling from *Inside Soap's* offices.

May 19: Today was a shopping day. On my list was of course anything related to *EastEnders*, but in particular the record by Michelle Gayle (Hattie Tavernier), who scored a big UK dance hit last fall. After searching virtually every record store in Soho and Camden Town, I finally found it at HMV probably what was the last copy for sale in all of London. I also purchased audiocassettes of Mike Reid's (Frank Butcher) comedy act, as well as one called *Mike Reid Sings*, a thoroughly enjoyable collection of standards in the Tony Bennett/Frank Sinatra vein. In between shopping expeditions, I managed to hold meetings with several executives at the BBC Television Centre and BBC Enterprises (White City tube station) about the unavailability of official *EastEnders* merchandise, which the *Walford Gazette* would like to sell to eager subscribers.

May 20: My only disappointment during the week-long trip was not being able to visit the *EastEnders* studio in Elstree, Borehamwood. Despite giving three weeks' advance notice and having various BBC staff and executives request my entrance, the *EastEnders* publicity and producer's offices stuck to their guns of me being "banned," apparently to resulting embarrassment in the *Gazette* running a series photographs of an "Albert Square Trespasser." Gretchen Franklin was flabbergasted at the way I was being treated, and said it was too bad that she wasn't working that week because I could have tagged along with her as her dog minder. "Nobody would have any say in that but me!" Another creative team member, who I met for lunch at a nearby hotel and shall remain nameless, also thought it ridiculous the way I was denied entry. Even though I explained to the powers-that-be all I wanted to do was walk around the set, take a few pictures and leave, my request was refused. Reasons cited included: the hectic production schedule to meet *EastEnders'* three times-a-week telecasts to a planned strike against the BBC the following Tuesday. Also, I was told simply, "no one can visit the I set," especially if they're from "a fan newspaper." My protest that the *Walford Gazette* is a publication sanctioned by BBC Lionheart Television (the BBC in America) and largely responsible for keeping *EastEnders* alive in the US fell on deaf ears with the Elstree honchos. I was told that BBC Lionheart has no say in arranging *East-Enders* set visits. I was in *Catch-22* hell.

I left Friday open to go to Elstree via British Rail and see for myself what the big deal was about, and met up with *Gazette* correspondent Darren Nelson for the trip. Borehamwood turned out to be a sleepy little hamlet that just happens to be home to several movie and television studios. The *Gazette* made a small sensation on Elstree's High Street, especially with the staff of a bookstore where I picked up a few of *EastEnders* paperback tie-in novellas.

I proceeded to the set's security gate, where a guard bellowed, "We know all about the *Walford Gazette*. You printed a story about how some body trespassed!" I was surprised that this alleged breach in security, as documented in issue #2, would be taken so seriously. At my urging, the guard called the producer's office to see if someone would see me, and of course, the response came back negative. It didn't stop Darren and me from peering over the residential fences to see some of the exterior sets, viewable from the sidewalk. After hanging around the front gate for a half hour in the late afternoon in hopes of catching an *EastEnders* actor coming or going, we called it a day.

Epilogue

On May 23, the day after I returned, the *Daily Mirror* published a full-page article asking rhetorically: "Can you out-score the No.1 *EastEnders* fan in the West?" Way too kind, Simon London wrote: "The biggest *EastEnders* fan, isn't a chirpy cockney, a Londoner or even a Brit—he's a Yank called Larry Jaffee and he lives in Manhattan." A few weeks later, *Time Out* magazine published: "My eyes were opened when New Yorker Larry Jaffee turned up in our office the other week bearing a copy of what looked like a tabloid freebie, proclaiming it to be 'an intellectual journal about *EastEnders*.' He seemed like a nutter," wrote Elaine Paterson, the assistant TV editor. "After security had escorted him from the building, I took a closer look at the 12-page paper and realised I had done Jaffee an injustice." Paterson called me a few days later when I was back in New York to apologise for making up the story that I was shown the door by security. Apology accepted, and I didn't even mind being referred to as a nutter; after all, any publicity is good publicity.

• • •

Walford Found

By Larry Jaffee

(Editor's note: The following was published in 1996.)

Two years ago on these pages (Vol. 2, Issue 2), I lamented on how I came so close—but yet remained so far—from encountering Albert Square for real, only to be rejected by the then-*EastEnders*-powers-that-be and their so-serious security force. However, in my quest to visit the BBC's Elstree studios this past June I turned out to be triumphant.

The new production regime, led by series producer Jane Harris, expressed gratitude—and amazement at the *Walford Gazette's* efforts to keep *EastEnders* alive in America these past four years. So dear readers, I'm happy to report that I actually walked the cobblestones of Albert Square, and didn't even have to jump over a fence or pay off some sympathetic series staffer, as some fervent US fans have been known to do.

I'm sure the turning point for the *Gazette* in terms of being taken seriously by the BBC, with whom we admittedly share a sometimes-tenuous relationship, was the interview editor Dan Abramson conducted with former series producer Corinne Hollingworth, as chronicled in Vol. 3, Issue 4.

When I found out a month or two after we published the article that Ms. Hollingworth was planning to leave *EastEnders* for a new job elsewhere, the pessimist in me figured that Corinne's successor may very well look at our publication the same way as her two immediate predecessors did (both viewed the *Gazette* as a nuisance from a couple of obsessed Yanks who should have something better to do, living in America and all).

However, much to my delight, after informing the *EastEnders* office of my impending holiday to England, I was told by staff assistant Rachael Lund that a quick tour of the set, and even a short meeting with Ms. Harris could be arranged.

So one Friday morning in early June, I embarked on the 30-minute BritRail/ThamesLink trip from St. Pancras station in London to Borehamwood with a slight, uneasy case of deja vu, circa May 1994. I keep telling myself, "It's been arranged." I make my way up to the all-too-familiar Elstree security office ("We know all about the *Walford Gazette*" will forever ring in my ears), which was just like I remembered/left it, only this time I'm greeted by a smiling, bearded officer who quickly finds my name on his clipboard. Relief. He then directs me to walk down a couple hundred yards and make a left to a four-story office building off the famous lot, where I'm to rendezvous with Ms. Lund.

Tempted to take a detour and search for where they hid Den Watts' body, I wisely reconsider so I don't miss my appointment. We accidentally stumble across the parked *Walford Gazette* van, but I'm denied permission to give it a spin around The Square.

Once I set foot in Walford City Limits (every *EastEnders* fan's dream), my first impression is that everything seems a lot smaller than it does on the telly. "It's all done with camera angles; they've got it down to a science," Rachael confides. She adds that The Queen Vic and the outsides of the houses are really facades, and only a few of the locations, such as Kathy's cafe, are functional. Rachael is graciously showing me around the studio, as I peek into interior sets like the Jacksons' house.

Recently, the prop masters had been instructed to put more garbage on the streets to give it a more authentic East End feel, Rachael explains. We stopped at the Walford World War II Memorial, and notes that most of the surnames on the monument included the family names of practically everyone who has worked on *EastEnders* in any capacity, as well as the familiar "Beale" and "Fowler." Walking down these empty, albeit familiar, streets gives me an eerie feeling. I almost expect to see a startled Nigel burst out of the swinging doors of The Vic, or Mark arranging the fruit at his market stall. Rachael asks where we are in the storyline in The States, and I respond that we just finished up with the love triangle between Ricky, Bianca and Natalie. Rachael reveals that Sid Owen (Ricky) recently took a sabbatical from the series for a holiday in Thailand. She then ushers me into the producers' office, where I meet Jo Ward, one of the three *EastEnders* producers under Ms. Harris. Ms. Ward says the current regime is grateful that American cares that much about the show.

A brief comment about the few current episodes (the UK at the time was about 14 months ahead of the US; that's inflated, as of 2010, to more than six years' gap due to the increase) I watched on telly those two weeks. I won't play the spoiler and divulge plots, but you almost need a road map to figure who's who with all of the new castmembers aboard. And these are not minor characters. It was almost as if your favourite sport team traded its starting lineup overnight. I watched literally for 15 minutes before I found a familiar face (Kathy).

The British media still has a love affair with *EastEnders*, as evidenced by the entertaining conversation I stumbled upon between a radio deejay and a tabloid television critic. "Is there anyone Ian Beale is not related to on The Square?" the DJ asks. The critic can't think of anyone.

Speaking of Ian, I was slightly disappointed being on the set and failing to run into Adam Woodyatt (Ian) or Ross Kemp (Grant), with whom we've been trying to land interviews. Still, this was a trip of few letdowns, the biggest being the discovery that the miniature replica "Matchbox Cars" from my childhood are now Chinese-manufactured imposters and no longer "Made In England," in the East End no less, as was the case in the early 1960s. This may very well be the root cause of why I am an Anglophile.

• • •

Happy 25th Birthday, EastEnders!

By Larry Jaffee

February 19, 2010, New York—It was 25 years ago today Julia Smith and Tony Holland taught the Albert Square band to play. Almost two years later, I became riveted to the screen as I watched that very first episode on WETA Den Watts bar Nick Cotton for fighting with Ali in the Queen Vic. "Is that blood on my shirt?" the dapper yet ultra cool Den asked, looking down on his white Oxford button-down.

The silver anniversary is quite a milestone for the BBC and the series, considering that few other TV programmes have had that kind of longevity. Over here, *The Simpsons* just recently set a non-soap record with 21 years. *Gunsmoke* only made it to 20 seasons and *Bonanza*, 14 seasons, trailed by *M*A*S*H* at nearly 12 seasons. In the British soap world, *EE* rival *Coronation Street* debuted in Britain in December 1960. In the US, *As the World Turns* celebrates its 54th anniversary on April 2, and *The Guiding Light* lasted for 57 years until last August.

Last spring astronauts from America, Russia, Japan, Canada and Europe aboard the International Space Station orbiting the Earth demanded that episodes of *EastEnders* would be broadcast live to their living quarters on Mondays, Tuesdays, Thursdays and Sundays for the omnibus edition. It's the only TV programme ever been beamed live to a spaceship.

We who watch via public TV in the US are actually in *EastEnders'* 19th year. That time-warp means that the UK is about to welcome back Alfie & Kat to Walford when we never saw them become a couple. And meanwhile the UK has been gripped in recent weeks by the cliffhanger, "Who killed Archie?" Please pardon my unfamiliarity, but who's Archie and 80 percent of the rest of the current cast?

This issue goes to press on the anniversary. We in America watching via PBS affiliates won't see today's live (not prerecorded) UK episode for another six or seven more years, but you can imagine how crazy things must be at the Elstree studio for the cast and crew. Here's to another 25 years of *EastEnders*. You can be certain we'll still be watching.

II

ANALYSIS

Our transplanted UK correspondent suggests: How to Reinvigorate EastEnders in Four Easy Steps

By Sherry Chiger

Editor's note: The following was published in 2007 when the EastEnders *episodes that US residents were watching via local PBS stations didn't need reinvigoration. But in the opinion of our transplanted correspondent the episodes she was watching in England lacked oomph. The author, a Yank, has since moved back the States after a three-year sojourn in Ole Blighty.*

It was interesting to read in a previous issue of the *Gazette* how many Brits have stopped watching *EastEnders*. In fact, the newspapers here in the UK, where I moved from New York in June, tend to be quite disparaging of the programme, comparing it unfavourably with *Coronation Street*.

Having watched both shows regularly throughout the summer, I can see why. I don't necessarily agree that *Corrie* is better than *EE*, but I can understand why so many other people do. But *EE* can rise again. Here is my four-point plan for reinvigorating the show:

1) Base the storylines on real life, not life on other TV programmes.
Corrie has a psycho teen—and what do you know, now Walford does too. *Corrie* recently had a will-they-or-won't-they wedding—as did *EE*, at the same time. The best—stories have always been grounded in real life: Den fathering Michelle's baby, Kat admitting that she was Zoe's mum, the Grant-Sharon-Phil triangle. I'm not saying that psycho teens should be verboten—the Joe Wicks storyline was one of my favourites. But that's because it was handled with great attention to authenticity, evolved over time, and featured some wonderful actors. (Though Aaron Sidwell, who's playing Steven Beale, this year's psycho teen, is doing a credible job as well.)

EE's current psycho teen plotline was sprung upon us, featuring a character we haven't had the chance to get to know before he goes ballistic. It seems that this character was written in purely as a plot device, nothing more. Of course, most characters are plot devices in one way or another, but here it's particularly blatant and artless. And the aftermath of his breakdown is ridiculous. Despite having inflicted bodily harm, he's not sectioned (committed for mental health reasons in UK parlance) to a hospital, he's provided with no aftercare, and perhaps most unbelievable, hardly anyone in the Square knows exactly what he did during his breakdown except the parties involved. When was the last time anyone in the Square could keep something secret?

2) Enough with the gangsters.

This ties in with my first suggestion about basing storylines on real life. There was a spate of violence in the UK this past summer (a spate by UK standards—just another summer by New York or L.A. standards). Most of the violence involved teens shooting teens.

Headlines moaned that adults were afraid to venture into city centres at night for fear of meeting up with 'hoodies'—delinquents who favour hooded sweatshirts because the hoods obscure their faces on CCTV footage. There was much talk about the effectiveness of ASBOs, Anti-Social Behaviour Orders, most commonly associated with out-of-control teens who, after vandalizing shops, drunkenly urinating in public, harassing passers-by, and brawling in the streets, are banned from certain areas.

So who recently ripped up the Vic and terrorised its patrons? No, not some drunken teens. A Firm—all because the leader of this particular bunch of saddos wanted a recent addition to Walford, who had moved to the Square to start afresh, to rejoin the gang. Making matters worse, during their rampage the Firm inadvertently injured a heavily pregnant character, who subsequently went into premature labour. And of course the baby wasn't breathing properly upon delivery, and we were meant to believe that he had died, but apparently that was a bit depressing even for *EE*, so he was miraculously revived.

Yes, yes, premature labour and senseless violence and retribution are all cornerstones of serial dramas, but I think *EE* could opt for more realistic, relatable angles that are "ripped from the headlines," to quote another long-running series, *Law & Order*. Where are the ASBO-flouting hoodies wreaking havoc? Where are the Polish and Bulgarian immigrants and the tensions between them and the Anglo residents, who fear that the newcomers are taking "British jobs from British workers" and straining the health and education systems here? Where are the young Muslims who are becoming too westernised for their parents' liking, which in the most extreme incidences have resulted in so-called honour killings?

While we're at it, where's the cultural diversity? I live in a town in North Devon, one of the more remote and rural counties of the country, and my street is nearly as diverse as the Square. Granted, my family—Jewish-American, with a Chinese-American daughter—is responsible for much of that diversity, but still, you get the point.

3) Use the characters or lose them.

There are some Walford hangers-on who haven't been part of a decent storyline in ages. Which is well and good, except that they aren't given much to do as supporting characters either. Is it because the characters aren't well defined? In that case, define them, or ship them out. Is it because the actors are limited in their dramatic ability? Then ship them out as well.

Pat, Dot, Peggy, Frank, Bianca and Ricky grew richer and more faceted over the years because they were fairly complex and well-rounded characters to begin with and/or because they've been portrayed by fabulous actors. When they left the show, even temporarily, the Square felt a bit unbalanced, at least for a while. I don't know how many of the characters that have been introduced to *EE* during the past year would have a similar effect.

A number of the younger cast members deserve a chance to test their chops, though. For instance, Melissa Suffield, who plays preteen Lucy (the daughter of Ian and Cindy) did a cracking job with an intriguing storyline this summer and could well be another Susan Tully or Letitia Dean, someone we'd like to watch come of age.

Similarly, Madeline Duggan, who plays another preteen, Lauren Branning, seems talented enough to be tested with a meaty storyline—how about having her develop obsessive-compulsive disorder (a common condition that I've yet to see portrayed well on TV) or begin to question her sexuality?

4) Avoid the cheap laughs.

A relatively new character, Heather, is clearly meant to be nothing more than comic relief. She's overweight, socially inept, in love with a character who is in love with someone else, and saddled with a horrible perm. Despite the writers, and because of Cheryl Fergison, the actress playing her, Heather has turned out to be one of my new favourites. If the writers would stop treating her as a sight gag, she could well end up being a worthy long-term addition to the Square.

There you have it: My suggestions for shoring up *EE* so that it becomes the critics' and the public's darling once again. And to the powers-that-be at BBC: If you want to do lunch, give me a call. The publisher of the *Walford Gazette* will give you my number.

• • •

Walford's Jewish Community: Beyond Stereotypes

By Dan Abramson

The portrayal of Walford Jewry has been one of the few weaknesses in *EastEnders'* first 800 episodes. The producers started out trying to be too nice—one might say, condescending—in their depiction of Jewish characters.

For more of the show's first half-decade, the only Hebrew-in-residence was Dr. Harold Legg, who is something close to a saint. There was then a period of trial-and-error featuring several moderately interesting Walfordians of Jewish ancestry. These were followed by the arrival of the show's one truly fascinating Jewish character: delightful, hardworking, generous, neurotic, and unlucky-in-love Rachel Kominski.

That is not to say that a character such as Dr. Legg has no basis in reality. There certainly are physicians as noble and honourable as Legg and some of them are Jewish. The problem here is similar to the one which caused African-Americans 30 years ago to protest Sidney Poitier movies. When only one member of a minority group shows up onscreen and he possess superhuman moral character, it amounts to an act of lefthanded bigotry.

This is most unfortunate since Legg is portrayed by Leonard Fenton, an actor of marvelous range and subtlety. When *EastEnders* premiered in 1985, Fenton was already appearing in *Shine On, Harvey Moon*, a miniseries set in England of the late 1940s. His role in … *Moon* was that of a Jewish butcher who escaped Hitler but still furious with the rest of the human race for having permitted The Holocaust to take place. That character was an intriguing mixture of good and bad impulses. Too bad Fenton was not permitted such creativity with Dr. Legg.

Because SuperLegg is so perfect, he has never really fit into the community of deeply flawed individuals who live in Albert Square. Arthur Fowler, for example, bemoaned the dearth of respect paid to modern-day Father Figures while lacking the courage to go out and look for a job. James Wilmot-Brown maintained the pretense of being a perfect gentleman right up to the minute he committed rape. Lou Beale showed impressive affection for her grandchildren before it was revealed she in younger days had been an abusive parent.

But the One Jewish Guy in Walford had to be, like Caesar's wife, above suspicion. Attempting to rectify this, the East End creative minds went to the sociology books and discovered that there were once many Jews in Whitechapel and that a fair number of them were pawnbrokers. So they created "Uncle," the world's most decent and lovable pawn-broker. It didn't work. While there are tens of thousands of decent and lovable Jews in England, those are not the ones who tend to become pawnbrokers. Even if they do, the job tends to make decent folk rather mean. In any case, a pawnbroker who tries to do business in a decent and lovable manner will invariably go bankrupt. "Uncle" was a creature of fantasy.

The next significant Jewish character was Legg's nephew, Dr. David Samuels. This young Israeli marked a step in the right direction, since—like Walford's Christians and Muslims—he was a combination of posi-tive and negative qualities. David also offered an interesting twist on Zionism. Born in Israel, he resented what that nation had become and so concluded that his true ethnic roots were in the East End of London.

Unfortunately, David was a two-dimensional character. This, admit-tedly, put him one-dimension-up on his uncle and Uncle, but still was not as interesting as, say Pete Beale or Dennis Watts. David had sex problems (this happens to Jews as well as gentiles) and he was obsessed with modernizing Legg's medical practice. The fact that said problem may have contributed to his obsession was never explored.

When it became obvious that David was not working out, the producers got rid of him by having his exquisitely beautiful Israeli girlfriend arrive in Albert Square to propose marriage. They then left hand-in-hand for supposed Happy Ever Afters in Israel. This was in direct contradiction to everything we already had been told about David, who supposedly hated Israel and feared women.

And so Uncle begat David and David gave way to "Benny Bloom," who almost married Ethel. This marked a great leap backwards. As if trying to compensate for their past mistakes in creating too-wonderful

Jews, the producers made Benny cheap and politically loud-mouthed. This came very close to racial stereotype. Benny's marriage proposal to Ethel did, however, resulted in *EastEnders* best line about Judaism. Dot Cotton tries to argue Ethel out of marriage to a Jew. Ethel heroically stands up in all her four-foot-eleven-inch magnificence and bellows: "Do you know what you are, Dot Cotton? You're ANTE-SEMAN-TIC."

Benny's death was followed by a long stretch in which Albert Square, with the notable exception of the Good Doctor, was a virtual Jew-Free Zone. Enter Rachel. What is wonderful about Rachel is her three-dimensionality and mixture of strengths and weaknesses. At first, Rachel seemed a believable and fascinating person who just happened to be Jewish. But along the way, hints were dropped that Rachel's difficulties in dealing with life lay in her roots within a traditional Jewish family. Then we were treated to a visit from her Crazy Jewish Mother. Rachel became, if not an object of pity, at least the sort of person with whom most people can sympathize.

The episodes with her mother revealed that Rachel had suffered a nervous breakdown at 14 after being forced to have an abortion. We learned this after two years of watching Rachel interact with and form a delightful Alternative Family with Michelle and Vicky, key figures in a later teenaged pregnancy. Life with these two young gentiles was a healing process for Rachel, who became noticeably less neurotic during those two years.

A memorable scene showed Rachel meeting Vicky at the school bus one afternoon. No dialogue was needed to show the love and affection that had developed between these two. This is the sort of deeply felt moment that sets *EastEnders* apart from mere television. We can only hope that future Walford Jews will be as fascinating and complex as Rachel. The Square could use a few more like her!

• • •

My Favourite Scene:
Donde Esta Samantha en Espana?

By Dan Abramson

The episodes where a half-dozen residents of Albert Square went on a Spanish holiday se qualifado as "video magnifico." Iberia has not seen such an entertaining flow of hormones since Hannibal's army left for Italy in 218 B.C. These three half-hours had everything—sex, love, romance, filial devotion and—best of all, truly magnificent drunk scenes, ranking among the finest in the history of television.

And marvelous was the fact that there was not so much as one single on-camera bullfight, or other "touristy-travelogue" type event that might have been used as padding on such American equivalents as *The Facts Of Life Goes To Australia* or *A Very Brady Pearl Harbor.* So let's get to the *Gazette's* version of what happened in the telenovela *Hola EastEnders!*

Itinerary

To begin with, the scripts for these Spanish episodes were brilliantly conceived. It took considerable artistic courage to construct a series of romantically deep, dramatic moments around a plotline that would have been perfectly suited to bedroom farce (with everyone winding up in the same boudoir at the same time). This is especially true when you consider the importance to *EastEnders'* ongoing storyline of David being father to Bianca and Ricky's devotion to Samantha. Putting Sam in flagrante with David – just as Ricky & Bianca charged into the room—established what might be described as a romantic quadrangle among the aforementioned foursome. (It may actually qualify as a romantic sex-stangle if you take into account the platonic love that Phil & Grant have for Samantha, plus the platonic hate that Grant has for David.) Too bad there are no sexual sparks flying between Ricky & David because that would then qualify Walford's sextet as the most complicated set of interpersonal relationships since The Beatles.

Meals & Snacks

Nobody from Walford ate an authentic Spanish meal despite the delicious paella of subplots that was tossed together. Neither did these Walford pilgrims seek any other form of cultural enrichment while in the historically blessed and artistically impressive Land Of Espana. This was realistic writing because, let's face it, blokes like Grant Mitchell do not go on holiday in order to their chances of someday winning big on the British equivalent of *Jeopardy*.

They travel, instead, to get drunk and chase women. Phil, in fact, asked directions to the raunchiest sort of nightclub during his first meal in Torremolinos. That was called a "Bellybuster Breakfast Special," served at a Bridge Street-style cafe. That breakfast probably contained enough cholesterol to sink a battleship, but the waiter understood Phil perfectly and provided excellent travel tips about how to get to the nearest sleazy dive.

This was the first of a series of polite conversations between the Walfordmeisters and such Spanish natives as: the bartender in the nightclub; the bartender in the hotel; and the bartender in Sevilla (where Phil & Grant met up with the two available blondes).

However, we in the audience were blissfully spared the American TV approach to these matters. For example, not one of Our Travellers ever took time out from their ongoing hedonism to have a philosophical encounter with a hardworking Spanish peasant. Bianca did not leave Ricky for a few hours in order to have a deeply meaningful conversation with a priest. Phil did not step in, like a good Samaritan, to fix the broken-down limo of a woman who turned out to be The Crown Princess. In fact, nobody in the entire three episodes went out of their way to be nice to anybody else. This is always your best immediate clue that you are watching British Television rather than American.

Beverages

One other key difference between The Idiot Box and Telly lies in the drinking of wines and spirits. These days, one rarely sees alcohol consumed on America's cathode rays.

By contrast, the characters on Britain's television seem to frequently imbibe. And, on *EastEnders*, boozing is raised to the level of an art form. Let us take, for example, the scene of Phil & Grant on their last night together in Spain. They had just returned to their home base in Torremolinos after going hundreds of miles by car in a Wild Sister Chase after Samantha.

Settling down in the bar adjacent to their hostelry, The Mitchells agreed to a request from David Wicks that they stay out of the shared hotel suite where David was about to entertain an amorous young woman. Since The Mitchells did not realise that David's room guest was, in fact, their own sister, they decided that the only logical manner in which to spend the next few hours was to continue drinking. Being London macho-men with an instinct for "Alcoholic Chic," they sat down on the floor of that public house, with their backs against the wall.

What followed was something close to perfection in its portrayal of how machismo types behave when they get close to the cerebral-saturation point with whiskey. Steve McFadden (Phil) and Ross Kemp (Grant) are both extremely good at conjuring up the image of those Inner Children who reside within their personalities. In this case, they surpassed themselves by illustrating the Inner Adolescents who are Peggy Mitchell's Boys. These fictional scoundrels probably first got drunk at age twelve or thirteen. In Torremolinos, once the booze kicked in, Kemp-as-Grant began doing a marvelous impression of a twelve-year-old getting zany with his elder brother and some liquor. Kemp's laughter, facial expressions and especially his speaking voice were all fascinating images of what this character could have been like at twelve.

McFadden did him one better, though, by sliding downwards out of the scene while Kemp was in closeup. This led to a fascinating sequence where Grant dominated the right half of the screen, with the left half empty of all human activity except for Phil's disembodied voice rising up from below camera range. Talk about a commanding screen presence! McFadden's presence is even more effective in his absence. This is what superior acting—and drinking—is all about.

Of course, The Mitchells soon raced upstairs for their Date with Destiny in the same bedroom as Sam and the rest of Walford Armada. This was truly a great comic moment, which included something else you don't often see these days—a gifted actress offering a truly insightful portrayal of a nymphomaniac. Walford's Spanish Holiday ended rather abruptly on that note. So does this essay.

• • •

My Favourite Scene:
Angie Finally Leaves Den

By Linda Gessel

My favourite scene from *EastEnders* was the one in which Angie, once and for all, left Den and ran off to Spain with her new love, Sonny. This followed an episode in which a drunken Mr. Sparrow, the area manager for the Brewery, asked an equally drunken Den to explain the secret of his success with women. Den's reply: "Never let them know what you're thinking, Mate!"

The episode, which ends with Angie & Sonny going off together, could have been called either "The Secret of Den's Success With

Women" or "Never Let Them Know What You're Thinking, Mate!" Either way, and whatever the episode actually was called, it was a gem. The scenes which led up to my favourite portrayed a certain tenseness in the air at The Vic, as several of Angie's closest friends speculated as to what she could possibly be up to this time. Because she was definitely up to something!

Only Den seemed not to be the least bit concerned. When Pete Beale inform him that Angie was packing, Den's only response was to sing "Every Time You Go." Later, when Frank Butcher told Den that Angie wanted help carrying her suitcases, Den left for the relative safety of his daughter Sharon's party. He clearly hoped that, in this manner, he would avoid the potentially loaded emotional confrontation.

(Den had allowed his facade of indifference to Angie to slip on only one previous occasion. That was when he came home after a fight with his girlfriend and found Angie unconscious from an overdose of pills. At that time, Den begged Angie not to leave him. But there was no risk involved, since she could not hear what he was saying. When Angie recovered, he did not give her a clue as to how distraught he'd been at the thought of losing her.)

So, true to form on this particular evening, Den intended for Angie to leave Walford once again without a clue. But Angie was determined to have her ego-reinforcing moment of showing Den that—even if he didn't "Give a monkey's"—another man did. So she followed Den to the kitchen and quickly closed the door so that, with Sharon present, she could make her dramatic departure without Den bolting. Den (through the superb dramatic acting of Leslie Grantham) conveyed to us a multitude of emotion without saying a word.

Den looked like a trapped animal. He glanced at the ceiling, and it appeared he might lose control. But Den could not let that happen; and when they were interrupted on two occasions he used that brief private time to carefully compose himself. Den just had to keep a straight face and give a good performance! Sadly, where Angie was concerned, it was to be his last. He did not disappoint himself.

What he came up with was Den at his best! He walked Angie to the cab where Sonny was waiting, wished them both a nice flight, tossed them a bag of barley sugar as a farewell present and then dramatically knocked on the cab top as he ordered the driver to go "Double speed to the airport."

Den's final act of defiance was to tear up the letter explaining why she was leaving him for Sonny. Den stood in the early spring evening in Walford, deeply affected by his sense of loss. Then he suddenly remembered that Sharon was there and he willed himself out of his trance. The sad thing about Den & Angie is "what might have been" if Den had been willing to expose that part of himself that he chose to keep so well hidden. The positive effect on his own life, and that of Angie and Sharon, might have been immense.

• • •

My Favourite Episode: Arthur's Funeral

By Phil Hansen

I'm sure I won't be the only fan who picks Arthur Fowler's funeral as my favourite *EastEnders* episode. That half hour of television contained many unforgettable moments: Mark's soliloquy; the entire cast standing in the Square as the funeral procession drove by; Willie Roper getting a well-deserved punch in the snout; and the lovely final shot of Pauline at Arthur's grave (accompanied by a touchingly rare use of incidental music). The last rites for Arthur were handled in an appropriately moving and respectful manner. However, the best things about this episode, the things that reminded me just how much I love *EastEnders*, had nothing to do with Arthur.

It is remarkable that in the episode as devastating as this one, *East-Enders* still finds time to entertain. The subplots of Nellie's feud with Aunt Betty and Kathy's growing awareness that Cindy is back to her old wicked ways represent *EastEnders* at its funniest and most dramatic. These subplots act as counterpoints to the main plot of Arthur's funeral, suggesting that while everybody has gathered to celebrate Arthur's history, their own personal histories will not be forgotten. It is this rich vein of character that *EastEnders* continually taps into that ensures my constant viewership. Aunt Betty has been referred to now and then throughout *EastEnders'* history, but this is the first time we've ever seen her. It was a stroke of genius to have her accompanied by her incredibly tactless boyfriend who has to be taken away from the wake before he puts his foot in his mouth again.

This would have been enough comic relief, but Tony Jordan's script hilariously takes things one step further, by including a long-standing feud between Aunt Nellie and Aunt Betty that stretches all the way back to World War II! The feud culminates in a scene in the Queen Vic where Nellie and Betty row about the man Betty stole from Nellie all those many years ago, with some of the best dialogue I've heard in *EastEnders*. (Defending her wartime sexual promiscuity, Betty says: "It was the only thing that wasn't rationed!") What is notable about this comedy is that it is all character-based and that Betty and her boyfriend are only in Albert Square for one episode, yet are incredibly well delineated. Only in *EastEnders* would such minor characters be so well written and acted.

This attention to minor characters does not in the least mean that the major players will be shafted. Two of *EastEnders'* most integral characters, Kathy and Cindy, have a scene in this episode that seems so out of nowhere—Kathy is all moody and quiet, so Cindy asks if she's done something to bother her. Kathy lays into Cindy like a sledgehammer, letting her know exactly what she thinks of her (not much) and promising that if Cindy hurts Ian in any way she'll have Kathy to answer to.

This scene is explosive and thrilling. It does not feel imposed upon the characters just for the sake of drama, but instead grew naturally out of the interaction between Kathy and Cindy and their history. When Cindy returned to Albert Square, there was a confrontation in the Queen Vic between her and Kathy. Cindy was smug in her power over Ian, promising Kathy that if Ian had to choose between his mother and his wife, Kathy would be the loser. Kathy was so stunned, she was speechless. Five years down the line, she finally responds. This works on a purely visceral level for the casual viewer, yet for the long-time viewer, this scene is nothing less than a vindication for the audience who have been patiently waiting for a long time for Kathy to call Cindy a selfish cow.

With these two excellently developed subplots added onto the main storyline of Arthur's funeral, you have a pretty potent episode of *EastEnders*. With the funeral of such a major character, a fan such as myself would be bound to appreciate this episode, but the attention to character and history is what really makes this particular segment so special to me. Not only did I love this half hour, but my partner (who can be termed a casual *EastEnders* viewer, at best) actually sat down, watched the show and loved it as well.

This episode is a perfect example of how entertaining, upsetting, funny and damn good *EastEnders* can be. I only hope that *EastEnders* will continue to reach such artistic heights time and time again.

• • •

Playing Happy Families in Walford Faces Change, But Names Stay The Same

By Sherry Chiger

If, as an American *EastEnders* fan, you were to catch an episode of *EastEnders* in the UK today, you'd probably find yourself wondering, Who the heck are all these people? They have the same surnames as the lead characters in the episodes airing in the States—Mitchell, Slater, Beale, Banning—but they definitely aren't the same characters.

During the past few years *EE* has introduced new members of several core families. In some of the instances, the appearance of the characters made sense. But in others, there was a clear sense of desperation. (Okay, here come the spoilers!) For instance, when Peggy and Phil had to leave London and the Queen Vic in a hurry following Phil's near-miss of another disastrous marriage, lo and behold! Two long-lost Mitchell cousins arrive, ostensibly for the averted nuptials—although neither Peggy nor Phil recognise them, let alone seemed to recall inviting them.

Luckily the two Mitchells—sisters Ronnie and Roxy, who'd been running a pub in Ibiza but were apparently just as happy to take temporary charge of the Vic in Peggy and Phil's absence—keep up the fine Mitchell tradition of boozing, sleeping with inappropriate partners, feuding with Ian Beale, and generally wreaking havoc. Roxy in particular is a hoot, the Grant to Ronnie's (slightly) more sensible Phil. All pushed-up boobs, heavy eyeliner, and swinging gold hoops, incapable of walking without sashaying, Roxy is pure id. It's almost inevitable that she is now married to, and carrying the spawn of, the reigning resident psycho, Sean Slater.

Sean is another new branch on an existing family tree. His grandmother was Charlie Slater's sister, making him a cousin of the Slaters Kat, Little Mo, Lynne, and Zoe. He came to the Square about two years ago, having bumped into his teenage sister Stacey, who had moved in with Charlie and Mo a few years earlier, after her (and Sean's) bipolar mother, Jean, had been sectioned—that's institutionalised to us Yanks. Jean, like Sean, now lives in Walford as well.

Appearance wise, Stacey in particular fits the Slater bill: brunette, curvy, partial to short skirts with no stockings (then again, that describes a sizeable subculture of England). She also has the Slater sass and the healthy Slater libido (more of which in a minute). She's surlier than the other Slaters, though, which must have come from her mother's side of the family. As for Sean, he's so surly he makes Phil and Grant look like Little Miss Sunshine and Mister Happy.

Sean was in the armed forces and, like Grant, suffers from mental problems as a result. But there's also strong evidence that the forces alone aren't to blame for his hair-trigger temper, fondness of inflicting bodily harm, and periods of catatonic staring. (The last, in fact, may be the fault of the actor playing him, Robert Kazinsky, whose range is closer to that of your local molehill than to the Rockies or even the Poconos). In fact, Sean is so fearful of having inherited his mum's mental illness that he all but refuses to have anything to do with her.

I can't blame him for that—not because we should avoid people with mental illness, of course, but because Jean is an amazingly annoying character. Jean's dippiness and fluttery overbearingness are not symptoms of her illness but of her personality, and it's a shame that many *EE* viewers may now think of people with bipolar disorders of being vaguely inappropriate and fully irksome.

Stacey, on the other hand, is only partially irksome. With her smart mouth and ballsiness, I think we're meant to find her as charismatic as Kat. But Kat at least smiled on occasion. I can't recall seeing Stacey's teeth except when they were bared in a grimace or a growl. Even her romances don't seem to bring her joy. Maybe it's because they're ridiculous.

One of the long-running current storylines involves her on-again, off-again relationship with yet another young sprig from an old family tree, Bradley Branning. He's a grandson of Jim Branning, which would make him a nephew of Carol Jackson; his father, Max, another relatively recent addition to the Square, is Carol's brother, though I don't recall being aware of his existence back at the wedding of their sister Suzy, at which Alan proposed to Carol. Then again, back then Jim Branning was a flaming racist, a figure of hate; he was long since transformed into a lovable coot, more sinned against than sinning. (See also: Mitchell, Billy.)

Bradley and Max do bear a physical resemblance to each other. Both are redheads, in a country where "gingers" are one of the few minorities it's still okay to malign, and where they are indeed maligned to a degree that's difficult for an American to understand. Max is a slick salesman who is surprisingly effective with the ladies, despite being a) ginger, b) balding, and c) married. Bradley wants to be slick, but he's a true geek: He goes to *Star Trek* conventions and wears plaid short-sleeve shirts. Yet somehow we're supposed to believe that he and Stacey fell passionately in love, to the point where they married. Only they broke up for a while between first falling passionately in love and getting married, at which time Stacey took up with Max.

The reason I'm giving away so many plot points (I warned you!) is to demonstrate how artificial some of the goings-on have been. It's deus ex machina gone wild. And too often, IMHO, the introduction of long-lost or never-before-mentioned relatives of major characters is an awkward way of shoehorning in an already awkward plot contrivance. (Wait till you get to the buried-alive plotline—talk about awkward shoehorning...)

Where *EE* has done well with extending the family trees is with the offspring of several long-standing characters. Sadly, Ben Mitchell, son of Phil and Kathy is not an example. His loathing of sport and his love of dance draw the ire of his father, which would make Ben sympathetic if he weren't played by such a wooden little actor. (I don't like running down child performers, so let's see this as my running down the casting director of *EE* instead: Was this the best boy thespian you could find?)

But the now-adolescent children of Ian and Cindy are brilliant, in terms of characterisation and casting. The kids who play Peter and Lucy physically resemble their fictional parents: blond, pale, pleasant looking rather than striking. And Peter resembles Ian in his desire to toe the line and please his dad. (Ian haters, don't forget that he started out as a fairly sweet, good-natured kid, anxious to make dad Pete proud.) Lucy, on the other hand, has Cindy's scheming gene and Ian's Machiavellian instincts, and Melissa Suffield, who plays her, makes watching Lucy as much fun as spitting out some of her lines must be. The success of these additions to a stalwart Walford family almost make me wish for the appearance of a teenage Courtney Mitchell.

• • •

Women Working in Albert Square: Yes, They Do, Sometimes

By Priscilla Mayfield

As lovable as *EastEnders* is and has been, there have been occasionally over the years subtextual themes that gave pause. One that has been repeated enough now to look like more than just a plot contrivance seems to be the inability of any capable young woman with a decent job to keep it.

Most of the women in Albert Square have paying jobs. Pauline and Dot have always run the service washes at the laundrette, and there is usually a barmaid at the Queen Vic.

Whoever is currently landlady is seen behind the bar—Angie, Peggy, Sharon, Pat when she's not driving a minicab or doing the books at the car lot, and sometimes whilst — but with the hired help of Melanie, or the occasional Tracy. (Good old Tracy, seems she's always amenable to filling in when needed.)

However, not one of the ladies has been able to hang onto the business. Inevitably it reverts to one of the rotating roster of men who have owned it in the past, will own it in future, will win it in a do-or-die card game. And in addition, woe betide she who would be Queen Vic landlady, as far as her personal life is concerned. But woe, of course, betide every Albert Square denizen to some degree, usually the greater rather than the lesser. The few young women who have good jobs hold them happily, even easily, for a while. But it cannot last, and after not long they inevitably become unemployed whinging harridans, or unemployed mopey self-sabotagers.

The character of Natalie, for instance, after running her own business, and creating the Night Café, at every turn presented as the de facto family breadwinner, eventually was left with only unhappy marriage and unfulfilling motherhood to fill her time, and seemingly no desire or ability to take enough action to make herself happier or more productive. (Career-wise, anyways.)

Lisa's experience of motherhood, in contrast, is joyous, if complicated, in the way things are complicated on *EE*, especially if one's baby's father is Phil Mitchell, who not only kicked one out in a most humiliating manner but who went and survived one's shooting him. After a strong start upon her introduction, Lisa's work life, however, is adamantly not successful. From a very good job overseeing the market, sharp-dressing, clipboard-carrying, decision-making all day long, she unfortunately plummeted amazingly quickly into turgid self-pity. Lucy Benjamin, the actress playing Lisa, is extremely good-looking, and it took some major costumery to make her look downtrodden. Ian Beale's vengeful tattling went a ways towards her actually losing her job, but it was the character's sudden, immense poor judgment that gave him the opportunity.

And for Lisa as well, there seems to be no recovery of job-related self-esteem, or any other sort of self-esteem, in sight. The character was reduced to alternate modes of carping, blubbing, and lying to those close to her. Not to mention the aforementioned attempted murder; however at least in that showing a bit of self-determination.

Laura appeared on the Square as nanny to the children of Ian Beale, a job to which she committed well above the call of duty, resulting eventually in her marriage to Ian, but not before single-handedly propping up the shreds of his businesses as well as running every other facet of his and his children's life, including cannily organizing and financing the purchase of the fish and chips shop, remodeling the flat above so as to have a place to live, as well as covering school tuition and clothes for the children. Defying her father's opposition to her marrying Ian, she settles in as a full equal, or more than equal, partner in the growing Beale empire.

However, as with Natalie and Lisa, it could not be sustained. The character inexorably made a sharp wrong turn into money mismanagement, nearly burnt down the fish and chip shop (sending one of the children to hospital with smoke inhalation in the process), and allowed herself to become vulnerable to a predatory landlord. All achievement and independence were cut out from under her.

It is true that the men of Albert Square have hardly better job security. But many are self-employed, with troubles stemming more from Albert Square's stunningly high rate of graft, bankruptcy, business feuds, or angry wives torching the place, rather than the vicissitudes inherent in working for The Man. But that is another story.

• • •

The Importance of Being Pauline

By Mackenzie Lambert Wood

(Editor's note: The following was published in 2007.)
Wendy Richard's Pauline Fowler has been a cornerstone of *EastEnders* from the very beginning. While Lou Beale may have been the matriarch of the Beale/Fowler clan during the series' first few years, Pauline was the true backbone of the family. As the first episodes aired and the storylines unfolded, Pauline was there to bolster the family unit, and it was clear that she would be an important part of Albert Square, as well as the Fowler home.

From the first episode, Pauline has always been my favourite character on the show, though for a while there, Punk Mary the Punk was a close second. Wendy Richard's portrayal of an East End working-class mother of three was a far cry from the role that she had been famous for until then, Shirley Brahms, in the comedy farce, *Are You Being Served?* For the first several episodes of *EastEnders*, she does tend to keep the higher-ranged ranged voice of Miss Brahms but she soon settles into the role of Pauline. Images of that other character are erased from your mind as you watch the daily struggles of Pauline and the Fowler family in the Square.

Through the years, we have seen Pauline and her family deal with many of life's joys and tragedies. Among them, the birth of her third child at the age of 41; the deaths of her mother and her twin brother, Pete; her daughter's teenage pregnancy; her eldest son's rebellious teenage years, as well as his diagnosis of HIV and subsequent death. Not to mention her marriage to the hapless Arthur, who never seemed to pick his battles well. His death was another blow to Pauline, though she stayed true to form, keeping up appearances and grieving in private. The Fowler family was a real family, and Pauline was the one to try and hold things together, even when she was laid up in hospital with exhaustion or working all hours at the local launderette. Wendy Richard played the role perfectly, making viewers to really care about her and the family.

In spite of Wendy's many protests, and visual proof of what the character wore during the series, Pauline Fowler did not live in a tatty cardigan. Where this idea came from is anyone's guess, but for the most part, Pauline tried in her own way to be fashionable. She also managed to have some fun. Remember the ladies' darts team outing to Greenwich? And who can forget the "Glamorous Granny" competition at the Vic? No cardigans that night! But tatty sweaters aside, Pauline's wardrobe in the beginning was very much in line with what someone would wear in her living situation. No flashy skirts and tops like

Angie Watts, and no latest styles like her sister-in-law Kathy. Pauline was a hard-working woman with an out-of-work husband, raising three children. She didn't have the money or the time to dress any way but functionally. Up until the last several years, her hairstyle and make-up also reflected this. I must say it is a bit off-putting now to see the year-round tan and ever shortening hairstyles of Wendy Richard that have crept into her portrayal of Pauline.

In the course of writing this, I have gone back and watched some of my old tapes of *EastEnders*, as I have the first 10 years or so on VHS, and it is so interesting to see Pauline in the early years of the show. Her character really is true to life, and she shows her inner strength and backbone from our first introduction to her. It is clear that her family is her life, and though her relationships with her children have never been as close and trouble free as she would have liked, it is also clear that she would move heaven and earth for each of them. Over the years, she has had more than her share of crises and drama... Arthur's Christmas Club fraud and subsequent nervous breakdown, the search for Mark and his fight with the HIV virus, Arthur's jail term and his affair with Mrs. Hewitt, Pauline's own flirtations with Danny Taurus, her brother Pete's connections to the mob, Martin's antics, as well as his one-night stand with Sonia that resulted in the birth of Pauline's third grandchild. These things, and much more, added to Pauline's burdens in life, but with all the deaths, births and dramas, she held her head high and put on a brave face for the people in Albert Square. It is hard to imagine life in Walford without Pauline Fowler.

Many people thought that Barbara Windsor's arrival in the Square, as the Mitchell trio's mother, Peggy, would over take Pauline as the unofficial matriarch of Albert Square. This fan, however, never saw it that way. To me, Peggy will always be a bit of an outsider. She has moved away from Walford several times and had too many long absences to be considered in such a role. Pauline has been there her whole life, and until the announcement of her departure recently, I would have thought she would be there until Dr. Legg arrived to sign the death certificate.

As I watch the current episodes, I am starting to feel that maybe perhaps it is time for both Pauline and Wendy to move on. Her character has changed in the past several years, and though yes, people do change a bit over time, it seems that Pauline has undergone both a physical and emotional change that definitely isn't for the better. With no offence at all meant to Wendy Richard (I am a big fan of hers), Pauline is becoming a bit too much like Wendy, and the writers have made some choices that have affected the very soul of the character. The same thing happened with Barbara Windsor after a few years on the show... she stopped wearing her Peggy Mitchell wigs and wardrobe, and simply looks like Babs Windsor serving drinks behind the Queen Vic bar.

Over the last few years, Pauline has taken more than a few trips to America to visit Michelle... am I forgetting that Pauline has won the lotto to be able to pay for these spur-of-the-moment trips? Returning with a darker tans, shorter hair and heavier make-up each time, it is clear that this was the choice of Wendy Richard and it distracts from the character of Pauline. The writers, too have written dialogue that has taken Pauline from a solid, loving, caring mother to a selfish, domineering, unreasonable shrew who has alienated her youngest son, and nearly driven off her more-than-patient second husband, Joe. She has spent more time literally looking down her nose with squinted eyes at nearly everyone in the Square than she has folding smalls at the launderette these days. I am surprised that anyone would want to spend any amount of time with this woman, when she used to be the one that so many people came to for a cup of tea and a chat in her lounge. I just watched an episode from about the second year of the series, with Angie and Pauline sitting at the table sharing a concern over their teen-age daughters' interest in boys, over a bottle of stout. It is hard to imagine that same woman today, sitting at that table, sharing more than the sharp side of her tongue with whomever is in her sights at the moment.

This being said, the Square does need someone like Pauline, or at least the Pauline Fowler that we have loved over the years. Who could step into the space she will leave? Going over the women currently residing in the Square, the only name that jumps out at me is that of Jane Collins. She may be in a dodgy story line now with Ian trying to pull the wool over her eyes yet again, but she is definitely the strong character with a big heart and decent morals that the Square needs. She can grow into this new role, once Pauline has moved on. It is easy to see her as the one that the teenage girls come to for advice, that the teenage boys secretly have a crush on, and the regulars of Albert Square can depend on. With her fling with Grant Mitchell behind her, she can still learn from her mistakes and find her own footing, though I think we all believe she can do better than her current version of Arthur Fowler.

Pauline Fowler and Wendy Richard will both be dearly missed. The Fowler house will seem empty without Pauline's strong presence and begs one of the biggest questions of all....Will she be taking her cut-glass fruit bowl with her?

• • •

Queer As Walford:
How Gays Are Portrayed on EastEnders

By Phil Hansen

Watching two strands of *EastEnders* on PBS and BBC America, what really sticks out to me are 1999 *EastEnders* and 2003 *EastEnders'* depiction of gay characters. On the episodes showing on my local PBS station, Tony and Simon have just left, and Dr. Fred Fonseca has not come out as yet. In the BBC America 2003 *EastEnders*, Derek now seems firmly established as part of the Fowler family.

Over the years, *EastEnders* has always strived to present gay and lesbian characters as part of the diversity of modern life, with prominent storylines devoted to Colin and Barry and, later on, Binnie and Della. How do the current episodes of *EastEnders* measure up?

At best, Tony and Simon can only be written off as ambitious failures. Tony and Simon burst onto Albert Square as the most high-profile, interesting gay characters *EastEnders* had ever shown. Unlike previous gays in Walford, Tony and Simon were related to major families in *EastEnders*, thus ensuring front-burner status in storylines. The initial plot of Tony going out with Tiffany only to fall for her brother Simon led up to a highly controversial kiss on Blackpool pier. (Reportedly, this gay kiss was snipped from 45 seconds to about three seconds when shown on the BBC's Sunday Omnibus replay of the week's episodes after viewer complaints!)

The Tony/Simon/Tiffany story was fantastic and unlike anything *EastEnders* had shown before. Unfortunately, all this promise evaporated. Once Tony and Simon became a couple, Tony seemed to wake up in the morning and fancy girls again. Polly (that hair!), Frankie (bitch!) and Teresa (slag!) all hooked up with Tony to no noticeable dramatic effect. It seemed like the writers of EE had no idea what to do to keep Tony and Simon interesting so they made Tony bisexual. It's a pity that nothing noteworthy occurred because of that.

What happened to Simon was even worse. It's hard to tell how much of it had to do with the actor who plays Simon, Andrew Lynford, or the *EE* writers, but Simon grew more and more irritating. He forever seemed to be whining and obnoxious, not having a kind word or glance for anyone but his Mum and Tiffany. I even started to like the homophobic Terry and Irene more! When Simon got a new boyfriend who wanted an open relationship, I couldn't help thinking that anyone with Simon as a boyfriend would naturally want to see other men! My dislike of Simon grew to mammoth proportions after the death of Tiffany. His speech at her funeral, where he blamed Grant for Tiffany's death, struck me as grotesquely inappropriate and in fact spoiled a moving, dramatic episode. Simon's kidnapping of Courtney, climaxing in a ridiculous (literal) cliffhanger with a deranged Simon on a cliff with Courtney, felt borderline homophobic in its implications. I don't think the makers of *EE* intended it to have that effect but, as shown, it felt like the evil homosexual was being portrayed as a destroyer of the family and family values.

Simon's redemption as a result of his almost burning to death would have been welcome at this point. What we got instead was an EVEN MORE obnoxious Simon, who rejected Tony after Tony steadfastly stood by Simon's side through his trauma. Tony got Simon's flat ready for him and even cooked him dinner the day Simon got out of the hospital and Simon still threw Tony out! It is unbelievable that Tony continued to have such strong feelings for Simon that they were able to ride off into the sunset together, to travel around the world presumably forever. Good riddance!

EE's next gay character, Dr. Fred Fonseca, barely made a blip on the radar. I must confess I have not seen as yet the episodes where the good doctor comes out, or the fallout from that. When I started watching the BBCA episodes, he was gone. In the episodes I've been watching from 1999, Dr. Fonseca is bland as tofu. He hardly does anything or speaks to anyone. Occasionally he doles out medical advice.

Dr. Fonseca is the epitome of a sexless gay character, whose only purpose is to prop up the more colorful straight characters. He doesn't exist as a character in his own right. This is a waste of talent, as Jimi Mistry went on to show considerable charisma in films such as *East is East* and *The Guru*. Dr. Fonseca was a huge missed opportunity for the writers of *EE*.

Happily, the same can't be said of the production team of current *EE*. Their sole gay character, Derek, has unconventionally settled into the show as a replacement father figure for Mark and Martin, and as Pauline's best (only?) friend, making him and Pauline a sort of geriatric *Will & Grace.*

It is also notable that Derek is *EE's* first older gay character. Derek's introduction was excellent. Pauline ran into her old school friend as part of the cast of the community pantomime and she started to fall in love with him, only to discover Derek was gay when she was introduced to his boyfriend! After Derek broke up with his lover, he started to appear more and more in Albert Square until he was firmly established.

What I love about Derek is how likeable he is. The story in which Martin rejected Derek because of harassment by his friends about Derek's sexuality to his gradual acceptance of Derek worked so well because of the sympathy I felt for Derek. It's great to see Derek be there for Martin when it looks like Martin might go to jail.

When Derek fought with Pauline over her recent disowning of Mark, it was heartbreaking to watch Pauline lash out at Derek Equally moving was Derek's recollection of Pauline protecting him from bullies when they were at school and their eventual reconciliation. It is also refreshing that a gay man can be shown to be part of a family without having lust for any of the male members of that family. A nasty anonymous letter and Martin's so-called friends accused Derek of hanging around the Fowlers because of lust for Martin but that is not the case. Derek has nothing but unconditional love for Pauline and her family. While Derek is not defined by his sexuality, I would like him to gain some kind of romantic interest, if only to see Pauline's reaction! (I can hear her now. "You're not good enough for my Derek! He doesn't need you—he has me!")

While *EE* has had mixed results with its depiction of gay characters, the show has scored with one fantastic gay storyline that doesn't have any gay characters in it.

I'm talking about Steve and Matthew's hilariously homoerotic relationship! They are forever acting as if they are sleeping together and don't want anyone to know! Notice how Steve is always touching Matthew—putting his arm around him or grabbing his head. His gifts of money to Matthew and Matthew promising "not to tell" can totally be interpreted the wrong way. I thought I was the only one seeing this until Annie Palmer accused Steve of having a relationship with Matthew! I have such a laugh when the camera focuses on Annie's bewildered expression every time she sees Matthew and Steve together.

Seriously, it is the chemistry between Martin Kemp and Joe Absolom, who played Steve and Matthew, that makes for such riveting viewing. That is one thing *EastEnders* has never got right: a compelling gay couple, like Keith and David on *Six Feet Under*. What are you waiting for, *EastEnders*? Give Derek a boyfriend. Let him be subjected to a typically tortured Walford relationship!

. . .

EastEnders Embraces Britain's Rich Musical Heritage

By Pamela Vera

Refusing to use off-camera music between the opening and closing credits of *EastEnders* contributes heavily to the overall sense of realism. This ploy also underlines what a superb work of piano-and-strings Leslie Osborne and Simon May created for those credit sequences. The combination of music and one man's whistling is a gorgeous mosaic of East London audio. It mixes Caribbean flavour with just a soupcon of Indian curry to accentuate the idea of Albert Square as a multinational Our Town. Where else would you find a steel drum in counterpoint to a sitar?

The whistling itself is a bow towards Cockney good-old-bad-old days, when Music Hall provided employment for hardworking whistlers. (During World War Two; the British Broadcasting Company actually had a weekly programme called *Community Whistling*.) For what it is, worth, superstitious Anglo-Saxons used to believe that any boy who could whistle would grow up heterosexual. There is, of course, no truth in that Old Wives' Tale and *EastEnders* is far more interesting when it focuses on young wives' tails.

The creators of this show also make excellent use of the on-camera music that originates from such sources as home entertainment systems and the Queen Vic jukebox. "Dirty Den," for example, was often at stage center when said jukebox played a classic Sixties guitar lick known as "Apache." This was possibly the ideal work of melodic anarchy with which to illustrate Den's anti-social but charming character, especially since "Apache" is also French term for lowlife hoodlum.

That technique of a recurring tune for one character has not been repeated, which is probably a good idea. The show's soundtrack doesn't contain a special theme for Kathy Beale or Clyde Tavernier, for example. But clever use has been made of such one-shot aural puns as playing The Beatles' "Michelle" at the hen party that preceded Young Ms. Fowler's wedding to Lofty Holloway.

This suggested the delightful idea of Arthur and Pauline having named their daughter after the song they were listening to when they conceived her. An even better use of rock music to chronologically define certain characters was the ballad "You Belong To Me," which Pat and Frank sang tearfully on meeting again after many years. Thematically, this placed that couple in the 1950s, from whence so much else about them derives. This musical footnote was repeated just once, on their second anniversary together. Significantly, Frank's teenage son Ricky found that fifties reprise a crashing bore.

Homage has also been paid to other musical eras in this manner. For example, at Frank & Pat's wedding. For example, Ethel Mae Skinner sang a Music Hall ditty called "Who Was You With Last Night" that beautifully conjured the wholesome-but-sexy era of Ethel's youth. In that same episode, Frank was asked to sing at his own wedding, but only did so as backup for Sharon Watts' rendition of "When I Fall In Love, It Will Be Forever." This served to identify Frank's role as a nurturing gentleman and Sharon's as the sort of girl who knows the Old Standards as well as Heavy Metal.

Even more fascinating was the use of opera on the night when Grant Mitchell returned home after beating Eddie Royle senseless: Grant's high-decibel playing of a Verdi aria implied that he and Brother Phil are the sort of thugs who were brought up in a culturally enriched home. Incidentally, to get back to the matter of whistling: those opening credits are accompanied by an actual human whistler, while the finale recreates that lip sound via synthesizer. This gives the closing credits an ethereal quality, suggesting some sort of "Ghost Of Walford Past."

My personal theory is that the synthesizer is impersonating the spirit of Dennis Watts, stalking the streets of Walford in search of good, dirty fun. But, like so much else about *EastEnders,* this is strictly in the mind of the beholder.

• • •

God Save the Kinks and EastEnders

By Larry Jaffee

In 1975, the quintessential English group The Kinks, part of the mid-1960s "British Invasion," released an album called *Soap Opera.* Coincidentally, almost 10 years to the day, the BBC broadcast the first episode of *EastEnders.*

Kinks leader Ray Davies, author of such hits as "You Really Got Me," "'Til the End of the Day," "A Dedicated, Follower of Fashion" and "Lola," committed blasphemy, in my opinion, when he was quoted in a 1994 *Q* magazine interview promoting his recently published autobiography that he "hates" *EastEnders.* But when I met Davies at a New

WALFORD STATE OF MIND

York book signing, he denied that he felt that way (not the first time a British publication printed an inaccuracy), which made me feel better, especially since he's always been one of my musical heroes.

Had Davies really hated *EastEnders*, one wonders whether hidden behind this hatred are the numerous Kink song lyrics that uncannily might have served as inspiration for many an Albert Square character and plotline. To wit:

- Frank Butcher: "The taxman's taken all my dough / I've got a big fat mama (Pat?) trying to break me..." (from "Sunny Afternoon")
- Mandy & Aidan who are living on Dead End Street: "Out of work and got no money! What are we living for?" (from "Dead End Street")
- Nigel, a Dedicated Follower of Fashion: "One week he's in polka dots / the next week he's in stripes..." (from "Dedicated Follower of Fashion")
- Arthur [Fowler?] was "born just a plain simple man/In a plain simple working-class position..." (from "Arthur"; The Kinks 1969 concept album *Arthur: The Rise and the Fall of the British Empire*, in this critic's opinion, their finest LP.).
- Pauline Fowler, who dreams of moving to New Zealand where her brother Kenny lives: "Opportunities are available in all walks of life in Australia." (from *Arthur's* "Australia"). Well, it's still Down Under!)
- Christine Hewitt, who's so tired waiting for [Arthur]: "I was a lonely soul/ I had nobody 'til I met you/ But you keep me waiting all the time..." (from "Tired Waiting for You")
- Den Watts, A Well Respected Man: "He adores the girl (Michelle?) next door /'Cause he's dying to get at her..." (from "A Well Respected Man")

Further Kinks *EastEnders* connections abound. "'Til Death Do Us Part," the gem on 1973's *The Great Lost Kinks Album*, was the theme song for the UK television series of the same name (which served as the precursor to America's *All in the Family*). The pilot episode starred none other than Gretchen Franklin (Ethel), who was in Davies' 1985 film directorial debut *Return to Waterloo.*

And Nick Berry ("Wicksy") recorded his 1992 album at Davies' Konk recording studio, not to mention the aforementioned *Soap Opera* album, which was engineered by one Roger 'Beale,' who also handled the controls for many other mid-1970s Kinks records. Hell, the pub pictured on the cover of the Kinks' 1971 album *Muswell Hillbillies* could very well be the Queen Vic! God Save the Kinks & *EastEnders.*

• • •

Deadringers: Why Do They Look Like Rock Stars?

By Larry Jaffee

At first I thought it was just a coincidence that *EastEnders'* younger characters remind me of British rock stars. After coming up with more than dozen examples, I'm convinced that the casting directors are also keeping an eye on the UK pop charts.

Some of my friends think I'm nuts with these comparisons, which I admit is not that far removed from the American TV show *Cheers'* Cliff Clavin's insistence he grew a potato with the face of Richard Nixon.

So we at the *Walford Gazette* are going to let you make up your minds. Granted, you may not have heard of some of the musicians who make up these twosomes. Most are not hit makers, but they're prominent cornerstones of my record collection.

Ricky Butcher, played by actor Sid Owens, is a dead-ringer for U2's lead singer Bono (both in the early 1990s were prone to ponytails).

Put Grant Mitchell (Ross Kemp) side by side with Matt Johnson of The The and they appear to be twin sons of different mothers. The most common characteristic is their receding hairline. Johnson grew up in London's East End, a family-owned pub no less. "It was always a rough area; but it was lively. There were street markets and stuff. But they've ripped-the heart out of it," Johnson told *Details* magazine. When Matt and his three brothers were young, the pub was packed every night, frequented by the likes of Rod Stewart and the notorious Kray brothers. I wouldn't be surprised if Barbara Windsor was there too. And speaking of receding hairlines of rock stars and *EastEnders* characters, what about Grant's brother Phil and his likeness to Phil Collins?

Besides having the same first name, the actor behind the character (Steve McFadden) lists on his CV the 1988 Collins movie *Buster*. *Q* magazine describes Collins' 1993 CD as a "downbeat album from what sounds like a very puzzled and unhappy man." (Sort of sounds like Phil and his once-unrequited love for Sharon, but since then you could fill in the blanks. "Things happen in love and life," Collins told the *Q* interviewer. Asked if the singer/drummer ever gets violent, Collins replies: "I'm a Jack Russell [terrier]. I can bite. I've never been that physical, although I suppose I've been driven close to it many times. I put my fist through a wall when my first marriage broke up." As we *EastEnders* fans know, Phil, unlike Grant, usually keeps his temper in check. My favourite Phil Collins music video is "Take Me Home" in which his wife calls out: "I know where you've been, down at the pub!" Better you it was the Queen Vic.

Often-dour Mark Fowler (Todd Carty) easily matches up with the always-sullen Morrissey, former lead singer of The Smiths. Yes, it's no surprise both their first names start with "M." Often misunderstood, moody and morose, both these gents have (or only appear to have) lived through the world's miseries. Mark's huge HIV secret of course would be fodder for a perfect Morrissey song. Both have the tendency to wear button-down shirts. Both have sideburns. When Mark fled Walford the first time he ended up in Manchester, Morrissey's home town.

Not surprisingly Morrissey was once photographed on the set of

*EastEnders.*When *Q* interviewed Morrissey in 1993 no wonder the first question was whether he could sympathise with Gillian Taylforth (Kathy Beale, Mark's aunt) over the media circus that surrounded her in relation to libel suit she filed against a tabloid. Morrissey replied that he had "Nothing but sympathy for her," adding that "it's common knowledge *The Sun* is a vile publication."

Mark was interested in his sister's roommate Rachel Kominski (Jacquetta May) who resembles closely Kate Bush. Besides their striking looks, both women were born in Kent, in their mid-30s and fiercely independent and provide a certain arty sophistication usually lacking on *EastEnders*. Remember how Rachel used to write erotica in her spare time? Bush has an album called *The Sensual World.*

Top Ten Plays
By Eugene O'Neill
Set in Albert Square

1. Long Day's Journey to the Vic
2. The Aidan Cometh
3. Desire Under the Fowlers
4. Mourning Becomes Tricky Dicky
5. The Emperor Celestine
6. More Stately Taverniers
7. Bound East For Clacton
8. The Hairy Beale
9. Beyond the Allotments
10. The Great God Vicky

– Dan Abramson

III

CREATIVE TEAM

EastEnders and Me

By Andrew Collins

(*Editor's note: This article first appeared in March 2003 in the debut issue of* The Word, *www.wordmagazine.co.uk, and was reprinted in the* Walford Gazette *in 2008 and again here with kind permission from the author and the editor of the magazine.*)

I cannot tell a lie—I killed Nick Cotton's son. I murdered Ashley Cotton in cold blood. It was me who drained the brake fluid out of Mark Fowler's motorbike the night before. Ashley, in a fit of pique after an argument with Mark that I instigated in the Queen Vic, hopped on the bike and revved it up. It was me who arranged for the keys to be conveniently left in the ignition. Then off he roared, narrowly missing Dot Cotton, his own grandmother, outside the Vic, and smashed into the laundrette, coming off the bike and landing in a heap on the road.

Even Dr Trueman couldn't save him.

Throw on the bracelets, guv, it's a fair cop.

This all happened on Thursday 14 June, 2001, when episode 1149 of *EastEnders* was first transmitted. It was one of mine. I wrote it. All of it. It was I who penned the fatal stage direction, "DR TRUEMAN EXAMINES ASHLEY'S HEAD—WE SEE FROM HIS EXPRESSION THAT IT'S NOT GOOD."

Oh but it was good. In total, I wrote 11 episodes of Britain's premier soap opera over a two-year period: that's six-and-a-half hours of primetime television drama, watched by around 16 million people, give or take the odd 0.2 million. *EastEnders* was the best and the hardest job I've ever had. More fulfilling than running *Q* magazine, and more arduous than collecting trolleys for Sainsbury's in Northampton town centre week in, week out, when I was doing my A-levels. (Come to think of it, harder than doing my A-levels as well.)

Of all the potentially glamorous and exotic gigs I've had within the media since arriving in Big Town from the provinces in the mid-1980s, becoming an *EastEnders* writer has generated by far the most interest and inquisition, from people in and outside the biz. A friend of my sister's in Northampton actually accused her of lying when she told them what I did. Acquaintances who half-know me say they saw my name on the credits at the end of an *EastEnders* and assumed it must be another Andrew Collins. They can easily conceive of me interviewing Paul McCartney or pontificating on Radio 4, but writing *EastEnders*? No way! That's "other people," isn't it?

Well, it was me for a while there, a small but significant cog in the giant perpetual motion machine that is *EastEnders*. And being asked to write the episode in which Ashley Cotton—an established character and spawn of Walford's long-time arch villain Nick—drew his final breath on the back of a motorbike was my proudest moment. (I also introduced a brand new character, but it was only a pet goldfish called Posh so as you can imagine the folks back home in Northampton dine out on it a lot less.)

How did I come to be writing *EastEnders*? That's always the first question. (Can you bring Dirty Den back?—that's always the second.) How did a music journalist with no qualifications even to be a music journalist end up moving Phil Mitchell, Steve Owen and Kat Slater around Albert Square like pawns in a giant game of soapy chess? And what's it like?

To get to Albert Square, we first have to pass through Brookside Close and a place you may never have heard of called Charnham. Whilst working at *Q* in 1994 I despatched myself to the suburbs of Liverpool to write a short piece for the magazine on the inexorable rise of *Brookside* (this was body-under-the-patio time). I watched the Channel 4 soap religiously, and genial series producer Mal Young, having given me a thrilling tour of the set, suggested I might think of writing for the programme. Me? But I'm a humble music scribe, I protested. I review

Sleeper albums. Mal explained that many an untrained scriptwriter had found employment at *Brookside* (it was that kind of community-minded, rather 80s set-up)—indeed they encouraged new people to try out. Watching the programme religiously, he said, was sufficient qualification.

I thought nothing more of it. But when Mal was poached by the fledgling Channel 5 in early 1997 and brought down to London to launch their five-nights-a-week soap, he called me up again. With a limited budget and an unforgiving turnover (the other Britsoaps were still only on a leisurely two or three times a week back then), they needed as many keen writers as they could get their hands on, and wanted to start one or two out from scratch.

I was still sceptical. My only experience of script-writing had been a few radio comedy sketches, plus I was by now the Editor of *Q*, a full-time job, with car and everything. But Mal is a very persuasive man. I went to some early meetings, where the characters and stories were being thrashed out, and was given a commission, my own episode (#19) of what was now called *Family Affairs* and set in fictional Charnham—which may or may not have been just outside Maidenhead and later miraculously grew its own tube station to make it seem more metropolitan. (It's still running every weekday on C5, by the way, which is more than can be said for poor old *Brookside*.)

They gave me a couple of sample scripts by professionals from which to ape the page format, and a "story document" providing the bare narrative bones for my "ep." (Let's call them eps, it's what people in telly say—they also shorten cliffhanger to "cliff" and break stories down into "beats," i.e., individual events. Now we're talking.)

All of a sudden, I was a soap writer.

It's important to note here that soap writers don't, as a rule, come up with the plots. This would not be practical. For an "ongoing drama" (the BBC are still quaintly shy of the term "soap") to work, storylines must be plotted way in advance, the major ones—a murder, a pregnancy, a new family, anything above a new goldfish—across months, sometimes a whole year. There are teams of people working full-time on this called storyliners. In conjunction with producers and script editors, they form the engine room of any soap. Writers are generally freelance, but a big soap like *EastEnders* will have 50 or more on their books, and the work can be regular enough to constitute "a living" (unless of course you fall out of favour, as I eventually did at *Family Affairs* after two-and-half years and over 30 eps).

A commission will mean a meeting round a conference table with stewed coffee and Danish pastries. Here, all writers and script editors working on a given week of programmes will converge to discuss their eps with the storyliners—ask questions, suggest changes, sometimes swap "beats" with other writers (hey! jazz!). The 70-page story document, from which everyone works, lays out an entire month's storylines— these snake through the eps like lettering in a stick of seaside rock. I always think of an individual episode as a slice of salami cut from a huge ongoing sausage—the writer's task is to move the action along for 26 minutes and leave everything in the right place for the next writer. Eps must of course join up, seamlessly, and continuity is paramount, so even though writers go off and write in tortured isolation in their garrets, constant recourse to the bigger picture is required, and at least four drafts of each script are built in to what can be a ten-week writing and editing period. At *EastEnders*, six months pass between Danish pastries and transmission. (This is why fireworks night and other public holidays are always celebrated in soaps—it's the only way to make them seem current and topical.)

The planning or story document contains important information like "TX" (transmission) dates, all key deadlines inbetween (commission, first draft, second draft, final draft and "rehearsal script"—which is the one the actors actually get to see, about a month ahead of filming), plus sunrise and sunset times for the week the ep will go out, and "other info," such as characters' birthdays and school terms.

In your idealised writer's world, you imagine Bridge Street market swarming with the entire cast like a scene out of *Oliver!*, but actors have rights, and holidays, and you can't expect June Brown to be on standby just so that her character Dot can deliver one withering aside at the Fowlers' fruit stall. *EastEnders* weeks are shot in overlapping fortnights—week one: outside on "the Lot" and permanent sets only (the important ones: pub, laundrette, café); week two: permanent sets and studio only (all other sets are erected and dismantled as required, but for practical reasons have to stay up for no less than two weeks). Of the ep's 26 minutes, 19.5 minutes should be shot in studio and 6.5 minutes on the lot. Keep up.

One surreal feature of the commissioning meeting is haggling over sets: each week's writers must "inherit" three existing sets, and add three of their own choosing ("I can live without the B&B, but I must have Pat and Roy's kitchen"). Then, just when you think you're getting somewhere, under all the sunsets and birthdays on the cover sheet you reach the dreaded "CAST RESTRICTIONS."

Eek! It reads, "Pat—Week 2 Only." That means Pam St. Clement, who plays matriarch Pat Evans, is unavailable for the first week of filming and can thus only be seen inside. No chats in the market, no quiet words outside the Vic, and bang goes that dynamite exchange you'd envisaged when she comes out to pick up the milk from the step in her dressing gown.

Before you can sit down at your PC and open a new document entitled "EastEnders/ep#1149" and type in: "SCENE 1. COTTONS' LIVING ROOM. INT. DAY LIGHT. 07.30" there are so many factors to, well, factor in. You require Peggy to be in the Laundrette in Scene 5, and behind the bar of the Vic in Scene 7—would she actually have time to get from one to the other while Scene 6 is playing out? It's a logistical minefield, and requires military planning to get right and keep real.

One of *EastEnders'* most revered veterans is Tony Jordan, a master-writer (untrained, used to be a barrow boy) who began in 1989 and now occupies a consultancy position. He offers invaluable workshops to new writers where he'll run an old *EastEnders* from the Arthur Fowler years and break down exactly why it works, drilling into you the idea that structure is everything, dialogue is just window dressing.

Back at five-nights-a-week, corner-cutting *Family Affairs*, few of *EastEnders'* planning luxuries were afforded. I don't recall ever having to do even a second draft until I went off the rails towards the end. No time for such fripperies. Three months between pastries and TX, none of your six. As a result of the tight schedule, very little leeway was given to writers when I was there—individual scenes were plotted out for you. It was basically a dialogue-writing job, window dressing, although a priceless apprenticeship in the craft and the pressures of the process.

I loved *Family Affairs*, there was a real have-a-go spirit there. Plus, it allowed me to fulfil the old cliché and actually give up my day job. (Interestingly, you are always getting told off for using clichés in soap, apart from the ones that soap invented, like nobody in East London having a washing machine.)

The other great thing about *Family Affairs* is that nobody watched Channel 5 then, so it was like paid training without the embarrassment. (Actually, an unprecedented amount of people watched it when most of the cast were spectacularly killed in a barge explosion, as per the ratings-grabbing plan of the new producers. Pity they didn't tune in again the next day. Or the next.)

I got my *EastEnders* call in July 1999: an invitation to "try out" for the show, engineered, it must be said, by a Mr. Mal Young, who had by now been poached by the BBC as head of drama series. After 30 eps of *Family Affairs*, I felt I had paid my dues, but the journey from C5 to BBC1, from a million viewers to 16 million, was far greater than the unlikely tube ride from Charnham Common to Walford East.

To use another transport analogy, being able to drive a car does not automatically qualify you to fly a 747. However I passed my audition—it's a bit like applying for a university: there are a certain number of "places" available, and hopefuls must pass an entry exam, which involves writing a full scene breakdown and half a dozen actual scenes of dialogue based on a real *EastEnders* story document.

My first actual, commissioned ep was #931, transmitted on 24 January 2000. You're sure to remember it—Jeff got a mobile phone ("Very posh!"), Barry and Natalie came home from their honeymoon and Terry bought a car. I know. Not a ground-breaking or ratings-grabbing episode (it was a Monday; Mondays rarely are), but ideal for the Square virgin. I even got to work in my own self-contained sub-story, in which then-landlord Dan Sullivan kept asking punters to help him with a crossword. It was Pinteresque I tell you.

While creating my first ever ep I absorbed the ancient wisdom of Walford, all contained in the oracle-like Writers' Guide. There are a number of hard and fast rules. Never write phonetic "Cockneyisms" in your script (ain't, 'ere, dunno, darlin', innit)—leave that to the actors. Equally, try to avoid "Can I have a quick/quiet word?"—it's a phrase that has been overused and is thus banned until further notice. Don't use exclamation marks too often, it only encourages the actors to over-act. Never start a line of dialogue with "Listen" or "Look," as actors tend to put these tics in anyway and need no encouragement. Characters can't say "God knows" or "Jesus Christ!" because of the Sunday afternoon omnibus. Come into scenes late and get out early: in others words, don't waste time with hellos and goodbyes. End each scene on a reaction shot eg. OUT ON JIM, FUMING.

Certain among the cast are well known for polishing their own dialogue, but this is a privilege well-earned. Mike Reid, once star of the show as Frank Butcher, would famously add his own choice phrases, like "What do you take me for? Some kind of pilchard?" (How I wish I'd written that.)

Each new scriptwriter is also equipped with a handy map of the Square and what's known in most TV dramas as "the Bible," a fat document giving all the characters lengthy and detailed biographies (their "backstory" if you will). Herein, you will discover that Pauline Fowler had childhood dreams about marrying Stewart Granger, and that Ian Beale took up boxing as a boy to please his Dad, touches that have never been seen or mentioned but add to the reality of the show. What's telling about the Bible I was given in the summer of '99 is how many of the characters are now gone (Conor Flaherty, anyone? Lenny Wallace? Lilly Mattock?). There is also a full-time 'Enders archivist and two researchers, whom you may consult at any reasonable hour to find out if Terry and Irene have an ansaphone and other such vital stuff.

Another potential niggle you learn is that you can't use real names. When, in my first ep, Barry and Natalie came back from what was obviously Eurodisney, we had to call it Theme Park Continental. I invented the name of Dot's favourite hair salon for one episode—Mario's—and this had to be checked out against every existing hairdressers in the country to avoid a clash. Inevitably, there already is a Mario's, so I had to come up with a new one. Bernardo's (named in honour of the great Italian film-maker Bertolucci) was fine.

The truth is, you have to live and breathe *EastEnders* to successfully work for it. You must find the Mario's/Bernardo's conundrum vital, even thrilling (luckily, I did). You must watch the programme religiously—at the expense, I would suggest, of any other soap, indeed any other programme that might interfere with your total absorption in the task ahead.

A single draft of *EastEnders* takes two weeks (there is no deadline-surfing here). Now I'm the type of indecisive multi-tasker who likes to have a number of plates spinning at one time, but I soon found out that writing *EastEnders* is not something you can "tap away at" between other jobs when the muse strikes. You must wake in the morning thinking of your episode, and go to bed at night similarly focussed: eat, drink, breathe, dream, shave *EastEnders* (like you've got to time to shave!). It's the only way to fully immerse yourself in what is, lest we forget, a tough job—creating a workable 26-minute drama that will not only stand up to the scrutiny of crack script editors but also some of telly's most hardcore viewers, who (Ital)will(unital) notice if Terry and Irene suddenly acquire an ansaphone.

The first draft is the hardest: structuring the story so that up to seven storylines interweave logically and dramatically and every single scene "moves the action along." The average script is 8,000 words long—that's approximately 70 pages, comprising around 30 scenes. Usually, you'll find you're still on Scene 20 when the word-count moves into the final 500; cramming it all in is the big problem. Using the Jordan Method, you will have drawn a grid with all the scenes on and used different coloured pens to mark the "arc" of each story. By the end of the first draft, this will look like one of Russell Crowe's crazy maths calculations from *A Beautiful Mind*.

It's difficult to think about anything else when you've gone native in Walford. Getting Sonia home from college in order to accidentally bump into Zoe and Jamie on the market without making it look like she just came home to do this is the sort of stuff that haunts you. What if there was a burst pipe at college? In August? Perhaps she forgot a folder? She forgot a folder last week! Like any good drama, the audience must never glimpse the gears going round. You, the writer, sometimes feel as if you are caught up in the mechanism like Charlie Chaplin in *Modern Times*.

When you've finished a draft you then have to endure the mental torture of waiting for your first set of "notes" from the script editor—usually some bright young thing many years your junior. (SCRIPT EDITOR SITS DOWN FOR MEETING WITH WRITER—WE SEE FROM HIS EXPRESSION THAT IT'S NOT GOOD.)

These notes can go on for pages, even if your draft works. It's like being back at school, with teacher applying ticks and crosses to your work. Draft two is like draft one, except with twice as much information to process ("Can we change Janine's reason for coming in the Minute Mart"). Draft three should be a "dialogue polish" but unless you're Tony Jordan it never is. That'll be draft four—if things have gone phenomenally well—by which time they'll be baying for a rehearsal script for the director (who comes in quite late in the game). I wrote six drafts of the episode where Garry proposed (for the second time) to Lynne. There was blood on the walls in that one. Mine. I have seen writers replaced at a very late stage if the draft isn't working out. This is not a drill, this is *EastEnders*.

It's all something of a mindfuck, to use some non-TV jargon. As is keeping schtum. Beans must remain resolutely unspilled at all times (after all, tabloids would pay good money for *EastEnders* storylines six months in advance). Confidentiality was a high enough priority when I started; it was stepped up to war footing during "Who Shot Phil?"

The attempted assassination of Square hardman Phil Mitchell in 2001 was shrouded in maximum secrecy. The identity of his assailant was strictly need-to-know—writers and script editors were kept well out of the loop. Story documents were censored. Around this time an *EastEnders* writer was burgled and their PC was taken; thereafter we were all advised by bomber command to save our episodes on disc and not the hard drive. I was always vigilant not to put old script documents into the Lambeth recycling bin until the episodes covered had been broadcast, and as an extra security measure I renamed the *EastEnders* folder on my desktop "Time Team"—that would keep snoopers out!

It really is like working for the secret service. Even when drunk you must guard what you know, and I am proud to say I never blabbed. Although it was easy when people asked me who shot Phil: I had no idea.

The warm glow of satisfaction when your episode is finally shown on telly is hard to beat. Most writers do it for the magic of this moment, although the money is very nice too (mainly thanks to sales—you get an instant repeat fee for the omnibus, and further royalties when *EastEnders* is sold abroad or shown on BBC Choice, and if you're lucky enough to have a clip used on This Morning, there's £50 right there).

Once the rehearsal script is signed off (it's called "going to white" as that particular draft is printed on white foolscap), your work as a writer is done. No falling back exhausted onto a bed made of script editor's notes though. If you're in heavy rotation you will be deep into your next ep when your previous one is shown. Once you reach a certain level of competence and reliability, they'll commission you to write a double: two consecutive eps, a Thursday and a Friday, which is a bit like being king of the world. If you imagine that a double is twice as much work as writing a single, you are wrong—it's harder than that (for a start, you don't get twice as much time to do it in). I never found the time to go up to Borehamwood and watch one of my eps being filmed, a perk that was always on offer.

I trod the hallowed tarmac around Albert Square—it's much smaller than it looks on TV, that's what everyone says—but apart from that my relationship with *EastEnders* was a distant one, conducted mostly on the phone or by email. That's the way it should be. I did meet a couple of the stars: Barbara Windsor at a posh BBC reception (she kissed me!), and Todd Carty at the BAFTAs (I wasn't on the *EastEnders* table, by the way, I wangled my ticket through the Radio Times—soap writers don't get invited to award ceremonies unless they're Tony Jordan).

It was weird chatting amiably to Todd Carty. I confess I almost called him "Mark" when we were introduced (the name of his *EastEnders* character), proving what an easy trap that is to tumble into, soap fans. We agreed that writer and actor should probably keep a professional distance. You're never going to become firm friends. What sort of conversations would you have?

"Loved the way you delivered 'I'll get my helmet' in ep 1149! You really got the subtext."

"Thanks. Could you do me a bed scene?"

At the end of the day, you're just a writer, an interchangeable name on the front of the latest script to land on Todd Carty's doormat in a jiffy bag. He's the star, he's the one autograph hunters hang around for (or did—Mark Fowler has since been retired from the Square). If you're doing a good writing job on a soap, no-one will notice. Your agonised-over episode is just a slice of sausage.

I was eventually forced to give up writing *EastEnders* when I landed a job on the radio which meant my days were no longer my own. We parted on good terms, so it's not inconceivable that one day I might return to the Square, like Ethel—albeit hopefully not to die like she did.

It remains the best job I ever had—whether my sister's friend believes I ever had it or not—but it's a blessed relief not to have to watch the programme religiously any more. Four nights a week? Who's got the time? Apart from the actor who used to play Ashley Cotton, obviously.

• • •

Yorke's Aim: Continuing The Tradition

By Larry Jaffee

(Editor's note: As of December 2010, John Yorke is Controller of BBC Drama Production; EastEnders still reports to him.)

"A lot of the things changed; a lot stayed the same," reflects John Yorke, *EastEnders'* new executive producer since January 2000. He's comparing what working on the programme is like in contrast to what it was like five years ago when he left as the series' script editor. When the opportunity came up to return to *EastEnders,* he thought "long and hard for about 24 hours" before deciding to take the job. Yorke was selected by Mal Young, BBC Head of Drama, for whom he produced two other shows.

On this January 2002 day that I visit the set, Yorke is covering for a producer who's very pregnant and has a doctor's appointment. Consequently, our conversation is punctuated with him half-looking—for which he apologises—at the monitor, checking the taping going on in the internal set next door. I realise that I'm being granted a rare opportunity to see how *EastEnders* is created.

The particular demanding scene that's being worked on involves Frank (yes, he's coming back, sorry for the spoiler) working behind the bar, doing his best Tom Cruise-in-*Cocktail* impersonation. He flips the shaker up, and attempts to catch it without looking in hopes of impressing Peggy with a W.C. Fields-like "my chickadee..." delivery.

Frank's alter-ego, Mike Reid, apparently was taking a few liberties, adding an ad-lib here and there because Yorke presses the intercom button to tell the director to relay to Mike that he should "stick to the script." Five or six takes later, Yorke seems satisfied, which I'm sure made Reid very happy.

Getting back to the differences between Yorke's first and second stints in Elstree, he points out that a few of the creative team remain, some in new jobs. "*EastEnders* hasn't changed that much. The traditions of the show are very strong [and continue] what founding co-producers Julia Smith and Tony Holland created in the first place," Yorke explains.

In his first tenure at the show, Yorke worked under three producers: Leonard Lewis, Barbara Emile and Corrine Hollingworth. I ask what he learned from them. "You have to be fair; you sometimes have to be hard." I point out that Hollingworth was the *EastEnders* executive who showed the *Walford Gazette* any respect and appreciation, and in fact was interviewed by Dan Abramson over a transatlantic call. I have no doubt that it was Corrine who helped pave the way for her successor, Jane Harris, to lift the ban on me to visit the studio the next year (1996), as chronicled in Issue No. 14. Yorke tells me that he has every intention to continue the great relationship we had with Matthew Robinson, and that he too appreciates all the hard work that the *Gazette* does in keeping *EastEnders* alive in America. This, of course, puts me at ease.

I noticed that in the room on the wall is a front page of one of the tabloids with the banner headline "Well Done *EastEnders*." I ask about the series' relationship with the newspapers, and Yorke responds that it's fairly good and sometimes the criticism is warranted. I tell him that the *Gazette* veers clear of tabloid-style coverage of the actors' personal lives. Yorke says that he's sure the approach is appreciated.

"It's a good time in *EastEnders* history," the executive producer tells me, adding that it's no small feat to produce 157 quality shows a year—but they do it. Yorke then sets the record straight on two rumours that have popped up in the press: no, Anita Dobson (Angie) isn't coming back; contrary to continuing speculation, no *EastEnders* isn't moving to four times a week from three to better compete with *Coronation Street*. *(Editor's note: a year later, they did start producing four a week.)*

Following my interview with Yorke, I caught glimpses of newcomers Martin Kemp (Steve Owen) and Tamzin Outwaithe (Melanie), who recently won British Soap Awards for Best Villain and Most Sexiest Actress, respectively. Both have been in the cast for nearly two years, and presumably are months away from showing up on our stateside PBS screens. They seemed to be busy preparing for a scene so there wasn't any time for introductions, and I myself was late to be interviewed by *EastEnders Revealed*, a behind-the-scenes series on the BBC Choice channel that is available to UK households that subscribe to digital cable or satellite service.

As my [bad] luck would have it, there wasn't time to snare any quick interviews with castmembers, despite being in their midst. An *EastEnders* publicist insisted that I would be welcome back in the future, and she'd do her best to arrange transatlantic phone interviews in the meantime if I'd like.

I then rendezvoused with the producer of *EastEnders Revealed*, Mary Templeman, who was keen to interview me (how's that for a reversal?) about the *Gazette* and how Americans view *EastEnders*. After crossing the Square, video camera in tow, we settled down on Arthur's bench.

Mary then gave me a quiz on Cockney expressions, which I failed miserably. She wasn't all that impressed by my Grant impersonation, "OI!!!!" The segment is scheduled to run next September.

At lunchtime, I made my way over to the studio canteen, where I saw Marc Bannerman (Gianni di Marco) having lunch with his on-screen brother Michael Greco (Beppe di Marco). I met Marc last year during my visit to the studio, and he remembered this and then invited me to have lunch with them. I had to do a double-take since Beppe (sorry for the spoiler) appeared to be killed off in the episode I watched with Gretchen the night before.

I tell Marc and Michael that the di Marcos are about to arrive in America, which they're pleased to hear. I also mention to Marc that I'm headed to Manchester on Friday for an appearance on *Soap Fever*, which coincidentally is hosted by his real-life girlfriend Nadia Sawalha, who *EastEnders* fans know as Annie Palmer, the daughter of Peggy's boyfriend George. Also joining us at lunch was John Bardon, who plays Jim Branning, who US viewers might remember as Carol Jackson's father. He's returned for a permanent role signed up through September 2002, and in fact, in the previous night's episode there was a memorable scene between Jim and Dot, in which she accuses him of trying to get her drunk and take advantage of her.

John also is riding high from his appearance in *East is East*, which recently opened in the US and is currently a big hit on video in the UK He tells me that he heard that ticket lines are around the block in the States. I tell him that I don't know about that, but the night that I saw it the audience applauded afterwards. He complained how he only earned £150 a week for about six weeks' work. I pointed out to him that it was the director's first film. "It wasn't mine! Put that in your *Gazette*!" Bardon bellowed, getting laughs from Bannerman, Greco and me. It was all very casual.

Marc and John had to go back to the set, and I chatted with John for another 10 minutes. He seems especially fond and proud of Natalie

Cassidy, who plays his on-screen granddaughter Sonia Jackson, and who just celebrated her real-life 17th birthday. As I was talking with John, I noticed Adam Woodyatt (Ian Beale) ducking in for a quick word with a woman I didn't recognise. Adam is one of the few cast-members with whom we've been unable to snare an interview. But before I knew it, he was gone in a flash.

• • •

A Chat With Executive Producer Louise Berridge

By Larry Jaffee

British TV veteran Louise Berridge, who in 2009 became a novelist, twice worked on *EastEnders*. She returned a second time in January 2002, and then the following May was promoted to executive producer, succeeding John Yorke, her old *EastEnders* production team colleague who actually reported to her in the mid-1990s when she was series story editor.

The *Walford Gazette* caught up with her via a transatlantic telephone call, providing observations regarding her first two months on the job, covering such topics as the workflow process, what makes *EastEnders* special, where it needs to be careful and what she thinks of American television.

In a pre-interview e-mail, Louise congratulated me on the *Walford Gazette's* 10th anniversary. "We'll have to do something special," she wrote. When we finally spoke, I recounted for her the early days of the *Gazette*, which her predecessors had viewed only with suspicion and at best as a nuisance. Louise pledged continued support and appreciation for the way the *Gazette* is helping to keep *EastEnders* alive in the colonies. This, of course, was music to my ears.

She also expressed interest and empathy in the trials and tribulations that stateside fans are currently going through regarding the continued threats of cancellation, both from public TV stations and BBC America. When I told her of BBC America's June plans to air *EastEnders* only on Fridays at 3 p.m., Louise responded, "Oh no," concurring that the time slot was not exactly conducive to working fans who would rather not have to program their VCRs to catch it. "They missed a chunk [of the potential audience]," she said, appreciative of finding out to what extent her show is exposed across the Atlantic.

I also took the liberty of bending her ear on the *Gazette's* long quest to get the BBC to make available official *EastEnders* videos and t-shirts.

WG: You've been on the job a little more than two months. Has it turned out the way you envisioned?

LB: Not at all. It's been great, but on my very first day we went into a major crisis with an actor being ill, which meant we had to rewrite 53 scripts, including the one we were shooting that day. That's part of the buzz of *EastEnders*. They're real people [who work here]. They get sick. They have real problems. They have real lives. You just have to react to it constantly. It's not like you make a carefully laid five-year plan for the show and that's what you follow. The cast behaved superbly. They all pulled together. You know, the show must go on. The cameras never stopped filming. Everybody had to work overtime—the writers, the script editors. Actors had to cancel their holidays. They had to pull in people who weren't scheduled and change their stories on the spot. It worked out fantastically, but it did make for a very exciting start. And the audience never noticed the difference. I'm really proud of that.

WG: You worked on *EastEnders* in 1994 and 1995. How have things changed?

LB: It had just gone to three episodes a week. I started as script editor and became story editor. The first big story that I did was "Sharongate." Now we have four episodes a week. It's almost just too much for one script editor to cope with comfortably. It's too much for one writer to write all four episodes. It's pushed everything just beyond the breaking point, so we've had to add far more personnel than we've ever had to before. When we were doing three episodes we could do it, only shooting five days a week with only one team shooting. That made life really easy in terms of scheduling. But four episodes means that sometimes we need to use Saturdays, and people must work six-day weeks, which makes them very tired. It also means that four days a week we have two teams shooting simultaneously, and that means we're all fighting over the same sets, the same actors. So we have to be really clever how we construct the scripts, so we don't have characters talking to each other who are in different stories. It can be done, but it's much harder. It seems like when a new executive producer comes in, a large family follows: the Taverniers, the Jacksons, the di Marcos, the Slaters. What's in store?

We're checking each character to see if this one is getting a bit tired. Are we short of people? We're looking at every character to see where we need new energy coming in. Over the next two years I think a lot of new people will come in. It's not focused on one specific family. There are a lot of areas where we can have some fresh blood. What was it like to be back after being away for so long? I'm looking at Natalie Cassidy, who plays Sonia. I knew her when she was a child. I watched her grow up.

WG: Do you ever dream about *EastEnders* characters?
LB: Frequently. It happened in '94-'95, and it took some months before I stopped doing it. I'd been back here a week and it started again. Oh boy, there goes the rest of my life.

WG: In your first tenure with *EastEnders*, how did you make your mark?
LB: As story editor, the first big story I did was "Sharongate."

WG: That's one of my as well other *Gazette* readers' favourite storylines. We did a survey, and it was in the Top Three.

LB: That's great. John Yorke was there as well.

WG: Are there any particular challenges these days?

LB: Since going four times a week, we're working on so many stories at the same time we have to make sure the characters aren't involved in too many at once. We'll be needing them at the Vic for the love triangle story, but we'll also need them on the lot for another little comic story about a budgie (Editor's note, Brit word for parakeet). It's tricky.

WG: We just saw the budgie episode (in July) on BBC America.

LB: The one going up the vacuum? (Jim Branning is cleaning his pet's cage and inadvertently sucks it up.)

WG: Yes, I thought it was one of the funniest things I've ever seen. I'm also a big Monty Python fan. It's been suggested on the AOL chat group that you should have the two pet store clerks as permanent characters.

LB: That was a Tony Jordan script. He created those characters. They were wonderful. That's one of the things he does best as a writer—when you have to do those mechanical plot devices. When something like that happens, you could have Jim just buy another budgie, or whatever. But Tony will never leave it like that. He'll always make the story device the most interesting thing in the episode, like the two guys in the pet shop. But we had a number of complaints about the budgie story.

WG: From animal rights activists?

LB: I think so. They thought we were being cruel to an actual budgie.

WG: It wasn't a real bird, right?

LB: Right.

WG: In your e-mail to me, you mentioned that you found interesting an article we ran that asked whether *EastEnders* is too violent. At times, do you think it might be?

LB: It's difficult because it depends on your definition of violence.

WG: I didn't think the budgie scene was violent. If anything, it was left to the mind like Hitchcock. You didn't see the budgie actually go up.

LB: You see a blur of feathers, which did the job. But it isn't that kind of thing. The Trevor/Little Mo storyline (spousal abuse, aired on BBC America) caused a lot of controversy. But it does force us to examine whether we were too violent. The only complaint that was upheld against us was an episode that transmitted in the UK on Christmas Day, which is the one when Trevor pushes Little Mo's face down in the plate. Did you see that?

WG: Yes, I did.

LB: It's not in itself violent like Phil Mitchell punching someone in the face in the Vic. But it was very distressing, shocking, and it upset a lot of people. It's that which provokes the complaints. The audiences have become more sophisticated now. In the old days [TV producers] used to think that if you didn't actually show the physical act of violence, it's all right, it's acceptable. You don't show the knife going in, the broken bottle, it was acceptable. It isn't anymore. The audience isn't reacting to what you're showing them in actual detail. They're reacting to the emotional reality of the scene. The problem is that a show like *East-Enders* has to go to that emotional depth to stay real. How do you do it without unduly shocking people, because we transmit here before 9 o'clock in the evening, before the watershed? What time of the day does it transmit in the US?

WG: It's actually all over the map. There are two different tiers of viewing. The BBC America episodes, which are two weeks behind the UK, used to be on at Friday afternoons at 3 p.m. for two hours of four back-to-back episodes. That Omnibus had been repeated at 11 a.m. on Sunday mornings, but that has been switched to Saturdays at 1 p.m. BBC America started about three years ago and is available by digital cable in parts of the country and by satellite services nationally. Meanwhile, *EastEnders* is currently on 20 public television stations in major cities like New York, Philadelphia, Washington, DC, Miami, and Houston. They air it at different times and different days, but generally after 10 p.m. Those episodes are two to three years behind the UK When the series launched in the US in late 1987 there were about 80 stations. What bothers me about BBC America is their failure to recognise *EastEnders'* potential to repeat its UK popularity in the US, where there are demonstrated pockets of real interest, and how they don't anything to promote it on other time slots to gain new viewers.

LB: It doesn't make a lot of sense, really. Does the time gap between BBC America and the public TV broadcasts mean that you've missed whole chunks of stories?

WG: Yes it does. I never saw the whole Bianca/Dan storyline, for example. I started receiving BBC America in May 2001. Half the cast was completely new to me, characters like Steve Owen and the Slater family. Some of those new characters like Steve, Melanie, Lisa, Jamie and Billy—have shown up on my public TV station episodes only in the last month (June). Someone has actually put together a guide of who's who guide for other public TV fans who started watching *EastEnders* on BBC America. I have to be careful how much I reveal.

LB: How do you deal with this in the *Gazette*?

WG: I walk a very thin line. Three quarters of my readership still watch via public TV and only a quarter watch via BBC America. I once ran the Christmas cast photo that the BBC distribute to the press, and received a letter from a reader who enquired why Dot Cotton wasn't in the photo—had she left the show?

LB: It's a danger for us as well. You read in the *Walford Gazette* about a character being very popular, but whom we already killed off. You think a character isn't working out well and maybe kill him or her off. And then you read the *Walford Gazette* where they're three years behind and they've just seen the character and think "this one's amazing, fantastic," and we've already killed them off.

WG: I still won't generally reveal major UK developments, but I made an exception in the last issue when I ran the story that Mark Fowler was leaving the Square because I felt he was such an important character, and besides he'll be on public TV episodes for at least another three years. Why did you originally leave *EastEnders*?

LB: When I left *EastEnders* in 1995 I wanted to take a different path. I wanted to do film drama for a while. Now I've come home.

WG: When you came in as series producer this past January, did you know all along that you would be made executive producer?

LB: It was always intended, a kind of an elaborate hand-over period. The show is bigger than any of us. The danger is when you bring in a new executive producer, it becomes like a new reign—change everything. The thing is, it works. If it ain't broke, don't fix it. So we thought we'll just work together for a few months, really get to see it a bit. And then gradually ease in and take over the job. In a way, nobody has even noticed.

WG: I think it's interesting that most of the past executive producers had previously worked on the series in other capacities.

LB: I think it's always happened like that. People always come back to the show. It's like home. The cast often feels the same. They'll go away for a bit and do other things. And even though they may be really successful in other shows, they'll still feel the urge to come back here. It's something about the history of it. What it is, the way I see it, is that in 1985 somebody put in the coal, set up the engine and set the train going. And the train hasn't stopped. In all that time, it has never stopped. You go away and do other things, but the train is still going. It's not like the programme ceases to exist because you're not there. Sooner or later you are drawn to it. You can't help watching it. The characters on the screen—they're part of your family. I just talked to Sid Owen who plays Ricky, who has just come back after a long break. He said, "It feels like coming home." But if you don't feel that about the show, it's very difficult to work on it in any very meaningful way. You have to love it, care about it, be prepared to argue passionately about these people. You have to dream about it.

WG: Do you?
LB: Yes I do.

WG: Could you tell me what the dreams are about and would you incorporate them into the show?
LB: That would be giving away far too much, but sometimes storylines turn out that way.

WG: I imagine Tony Jordan dreams about the show too.
LB: I know he used to, but I haven't had that conversation with him recently. He once said, "I dreamt of Pauline all last night. What does that say about me?"

WG: One of the things I've been in conversations with the BBC in New York is to do some kind of *EastEnders* video series. The two-handers I think would work extremely well as stand-alones.

LB: I would think that they'd do really well.

WG: My understanding is that the issue is tied up in rights issues. Is that something you're involved in?
LB: Tangentially, yes. Are there any particular two-handers you're interested in?

WG: I have a whole list. The Christmas shows, Ethel and Dot reminiscing about the war—that type of thing. Kathy confronting her rapist, Willmott-Brown. These are episodes where a viewer wouldn't need any prior knowledge of *EastEnders* to be immediately caught up in the drama.
LB: Yes, standalone drama. They are looking more favourably on that kind of thing. We did that video on the Mitchells. We're doing a new one on the Slaters. Releasing special episodes, I don't know why we don't do that. I would think there would be a huge market over here as well. It's a good idea, and I'll keep checking on those t-shirts as well.

WG: Did John Yorke give you any advice before passing on the baton?
LB: It's a difficult one. When we worked together the first time, I was actually John's boss. I was series script editor, and John was a script editor. When I left, I promoted him and made him my successor. What John always said was that I taught him everything that he knew. He usually says that when I've done something unusually devious. This time he said, "Just remember to enjoy yourself." It was good advice actually.

WG: Are there any American TV shows that you particularly like?
LB: *ER*, of course. Everybody does over here. We learn a lot from that. At story conferences, writers will often ask, "Did you see that episode of *ER*?" We're very influenced by that kind of storytelling. *24*, of course,

at the moment. And obviously *Friends*, all the unusual, quirky, exciting things. The problem is that anyone who works on *EastEnders* doesn't have time to watch much television.

WG: What was it like to work with Patsy Palmer (Bianca) away from *EastEnders* on *McCready & Daughter*?
LB: I love Patsy Palmer, and I think that Bianca has been her finest hour. I only worked on the pilot *McCready & Daughter*.

WG: What else have you done recently?
LB: The last thing was a show called *Messiah*, a co-production with Paramount, the first time I've worked with American television directly. The difference was interesting to work on. I gave a talk to a bunch of students from Syracuse University. They came to London. It was fascinating getting their reactions to watching *EastEnders*, and the difference between American television and British television. They were awestruck about how unglamorous it was—that we show ordinary-looking people, which is something I noticed again working with Paramount. That we like things to go really real, not necessarily pretty but real. I don't want to make a big generalization, but would you say that's a big difference?

WG: That is the reason why I'm attracted to *EastEnders*—that it represents real life. There has never been a serious show on American television that covers contemporary working class people. Also, Americans regard *EastEnders* as a drama, not a soap.
LB: So do we.

WG: Which is why I took umbrage to the British Film Institute three years ago leaving *EastEnders* off its list of the Top 100 British TV shows. I asked how could it win the Best Drama BAFTA award the year before and not show up at all.

LB: What was their explanation?

WG: They admitted everybody sort of takes it for granted, that it's a wall-to-wall tabloid phenomenon.
LB: Interesting. I should like to have a discussion with them.

WG: Meanwhile, *Coronation Street* showed up at No. 40.
LB: Oh no. We're far more like drama than *Coronation Street*. That's a different area. At the same time, I don't knock soaps because there are things you can do in soap that you can't do in any other drama. That's one of the reasons I wanted to come back. Drama is like edited highlights of things. You have an explosion, somebody comes in and shoots somebody, a big moment of infidelity, fall in love and get married. What we can do is all the interesting stuff that happens after the end credits start rolling—when you really deal with character, what really happens after somebody beat up somebody or something like that. You can follow that through. And when somebody in *EastEnders* gets shot, that's not just a character you've known for 45 minutes of a movie. It's a character you've known for years, everything about him and you care that much more. You can't do that in drama. That's the difference.

• • •

Mal Young: EastEnders' Guiding Light

By Larry Jaffee

(Editor's note: The following interview took place in 2003.)
Visitors to the White City, London office of Mal Young, the BBC's Controller of Continuing Drama Series, encounter a shelf of classic American television memorabilia, such as a mini *Twilight Zone* TV set and *Flintstones* figurines.

Of the latter, Young quips, as only a television executive would: "The birth of Pebbles got one of the biggest ratings ever, 60 million!"

The *Walford Gazette's* visit was a long-awaited chance to interview and thank in person a BBC executive who has been very supportive of this newspaper's endeavors in keeping *EastEnders* alive in the states.

Young oversees *EastEnders,* along with 13 other programmes. When he first arrived at the BBC six years ago, he restructured the division so that *EastEnders*, and also another popular show, *Casualty,* were at the centre of everything that was produced.

Young concurs with me that *EastEnders* is often not given enough credit as drama, and too often dismissed as nothing more than a "soap opera." The Liverpool native was well familiar with the genre, having spent 12 years, starting in the early 1980s working in every job at one time or another for *Brookside*, which launched on Channel 4 in November 1982, a few years ahead of *EastEnders*. *Brookside* was praised for tackling tough issues, such as child abuse and rape, and received notoriety for a lesbian kiss. The BBC was obviously paying attention. Nearly two years in development, *EastEnders* launched in February 1985. "Oh, I remember the night. I certainly can. You know, everyone remembers where they were when Kennedy was shot and when Diana died," reminisces Young.

"I remember where I was when *EastEnders* first came on the air, and we were very nervous, because *Brookside* in those days was very hard-hitting, very different. It was—we called it, and the media agreed with us—the "soap for people with brains," uncompromising. You know, it was good. And, you know, I used to try to make it for people who didn't want to watch TV.

"So when we heard that the BBC was making *EastEnders,* we were kind of resting on our laurels and thought they're going to take something from us. It made us much more competitive because until then we hadn't needed to be. *EastEnders*] was a soap that was going to be on a mainstream channel. We were on Channel 4, a very niche audience. And so [the BBC] enabled us to be more controversial. While they did it in the mainstream, we would write the kind of story that no one had ever done before—kill someone and put the body under the back patio. So I think actually *EastEnders*' existence made us [*Brookside*] think bigger."

Of his years working for Mersey TV, which produced *Brookside* for Channel 4, Young comments: "It was just a very concentrated amount of great on-the-job training. So 12 years later I found myself running the company and producing. I've got the job I love, but you become very insular, you think this is your world, this is the only world, and particularly Liverpool, you know, we think we run the world anyway."

While working for Mersey TV, Channel 4 gave Young a development deal to make his own shows. "So I devised a show called *The Beat Goes On*, set in Liverpool in 1960. We know about the Beatles, but what about the other 600 bands that were in the Liverpool in 1959? It was a drama about those bands. That was a big success."

Greg Dyke (BBC director-general, the highest position within the organisation), contacted Young and told him that he was setting up a new company (which was to become Channel 5), and acquiring other television production companies, including Thames and Grundy. He put together "a massive infrastructure, and he asked me to set up a drama department. That was seven years ago. Eventually my life changed over a weekend."

Young moved to London, and created for Channel 5 a show called *Family Affairs*. He also developed and pitched dramas to the BBC on behalf of Pearson. "I was here at the BBC's White City programming headquarters] pretty well every week," he recalls. The BBC offered him a full-time job, "and that was it. I felt really awful having to say to Greg, 'I'm going to leave.' He was so supportive and said, 'It's the best thing you could do. You never know, I might join you.' A year later, he did. It's just so cool. So that's how I got here."

Young relished the thought of helping guide *EastEnders*. "I made my name making popular dramas. When I got to this department, I decided to put the two biggest shows [*Casualty* is the other] at the centre. The biggest show, *EastEnders* is [made] 17 miles away at the [BBC Elstree] studio. Although it's still physically 17 miles away, it's in our hearts and minds. The trick behind a successful soap—don't employ anyone there who doesn't believe passionately in it."

Young devised an incentive plan that required the creative staff to spend two years working on *EastEnders* and *Casualty*, after which the writers, directors and producers were promised a shot at developing their own shows. The strategy has helped the BBC keep their creative staff happy with new challenges. Young believes that everyone—the employees, the BBC and the viewers—benefit from the resulting talent pool. "The lead writer from *Casualty* spawned all these other things."

Young says he's most proud of *EastEnders'* recent storylines of domestic violence and incest. So who's Young's favourite *EastEnders* character? "I probably get asked that the most throughout my whole career. I tend to diplomatically say, 'All the actors are very insecure,' so I never tell. I tend to be proud of the whole show."

Young works closely with *EastEnders'* creative team "to make sure we don't rest on our laurels. I think we've probably been through the best years in the life of the show ever, quality-wise. It's gone through ups and downs. There have been peaks before—Den and Angie were great. But quality-wise, I think what John [Yorke] and [long-time *EE* writer] Tony Jordan did in those two years, the impact on the screen of the shows, we're now building on that."

With 14 shows under his responsibility, Young admits that he's not involved in *EastEnders* on a daily basis. He's generally focused on future strategy, and every six months *EastEnders* gets his undivided attention to plan the show's direction. As an example of his involvement, five years ago it was Young's idea to cast Martin Kemp as Steve Owen as the new bad guy on *EastEnders*, based on the actor's performance in the film *The Krays*.

About four times a year, Young says he must pull rank and asks the *EastEnders* team to edit a show because it might be too violent. But he resents about the negative criticism government and watchdog agencies sometimes mount regarding *EastEnders*. "We have to be careful. TV always is about easy scapegoats. These watchdogs, these committees, these commentators, act as if we're not human beings. We care. My job on behalf of the BBC is to run their biggest chunk of drama. I wouldn't be doing my job properly if I just kind of dismissed the audience in a cynical way. You have to challenge the audience and give them the best drama possible, but you keep to the rules. Just to break all the rules all the time-no point. I'd rather put on a very hard-hitting episode of *East-Enders* that asks questions about incest. We've done it. It's much more worthy than it if was tucked away in a documentary at 11 o'clock at night. Crime's on the increase, and it's our responsibility to reflect that. So is it chicken and egg? Are we holding the mirror of society? And this is how you are. We reflect, we follow the trends."

The BBC recently conducted consumer focus group research on what they liked and didn't like about *EastEnders*. In response to whether the *Walford Gazette* may publish any of the findings, Young quips, "If you give me a lot of money! (Laughs) No. I mean that's probably the most sensitive information around, isn't it?"

• • •

Sharongate Revealed by Director Chris Fallon

By Tim Wilson

Chris Fallon is perhaps best known for directing *EastEnders'* "Sharongate" episodes, which centered on Grant listening to a certain audiotape and finding out his wife had once an affair with his brother Phil. Then, of course, all hell broke loose.

WG: How did your work first come to the attention of the powers-that-be on _EastEnders_? Did you send in a reel?
FALLON: The show has an extremely good policy of letting each new director wander around the set to gradually get to know the actors, as well as the producers, crew, and of course the studio guards, who are quite important.

WG: Those guards have been mentioned before in The Walford Gazette....
FALLON: I must have met Deepak Verma, Shobu and Sudha around six or seven days before we started taping those episodes. They didn't seem particularly suspicious or anything like that. They were simply there to do the best job they could with the material at hand—and they were well- aware that this was important material for them. They trusted Barbara to select the right director and I hope they were happy with the results.

WG: When I interviewed Deepak, he told me that he was quite proud of those episodes.
FALLON: Did he? I'm glad, because we worked hard.

WG: Which were the next episodes you worked on?
FALLON: Let's see there was the one where Cindy nearly hits her son, Steven, because she's so fed up with Ian's treatment of her. Another one which springs to mind is where Sharon first notices Kathy's engagement ring and everything starts to unravel in her mind about her feelings towards Phil.

WG: That's a very good segue into the portion of this interview which deals with "The Audiotape Heard Round Albert Square" episodes. Did Barbara Emile phone you up and say "Chris, I am entrusting you with some of the most important episodes in *EastEnders* history?"

FALLON: She didn't put it in those words, of course. But it was there in her voice, all the same. Everybody at *EastEnders* knew how crucial those scenes were.

WG: Did you know why you were the one chosen to direct them? Was it your success in dealing with Sanjay and Meena's adultery?

FALLON: Perhaps a coincidence, perhaps not. I have no idea if it factored into my being chosen. I'm just grateful to have been given the chance. I try not to over-analyze anything, I go a lot on gut instincts.

WG: What were your gut instincts when you first read those scripts?

FALLON: The scripts by Tony Jordan were absolutely terrific. They really did the job in terms of what was needed. The Sharon and Phil affair had been such a big secret for so long...

WG: Exposing the secret to all those people at the same time was a brilliant idea.

FALLON: Absolutely. And my challenge was to shoot it in a way which would put across that bizarre communal embarrassment.

WG: I hope you will regard this as a compliment: the initial scenes leading up to the exposed secret reminded me of *The Poseidon Adventure*, with a large group of people gathered in one place and this, overall feeling of dread—

FALLON: Only we didn't have Shelley Winters. We had Auntie Nellie....

WG: I can recall certain camera shots of The Queen Vic from the outside in which it looked as though it might explode at any moment.

FALLON: You've got the right idea. The build-up was directly calculated to maximize the effect of The Big Moment. My job was to heighten what was already there in the scripts—and it was already great stuff.

WG: I loved the seemingly unrelated scene which preceded the Blow Up, when Natalie and Bianca are in the convenience store. Bianca is flipping agitatedly through a magazine while Natalie chatters on and on about Ricky's ex-wife Sam. To me, that helped build up the tension. The stillness of that scene worked very well. I don't think it would have been as interesting if Bianca and Natalie had been outdoors.

FALLON: I guess you could call it a happy accident. The lousy weather also altered the bit where the party revelers form a conga line. It was supposed to snake around The Square, around the park, but we had to keep it inside The Vic.

WG: Which, in my opinion, added to the feeling of claustrophobia.

FALLON: I guess you can call it a happy accident. The lousy weather also altered the bit where the party revelers form a conga line. It was supposed to snake around the Square, around the park, but we had to keep it inside The Vic. The only outdoor scene of any duration in that episode was the one where Grant replaces the beer keg at a mate's house, somewhere in the suburbs.

WG: There were quite a few shots of Grant in his car, listening to that tape. Did it take long to do those?

FALLON: I'd say we recorded from around 9 or 10 o'clock at night through to 2 the next morning. Those shots involved more than just Grant in the car. Those shots involved more than just Grant in the car. They also involved operating the car, pulling up at the Vic, etc.

WG: How is Ross Kemp to work with?
FALLON: He's great. He's really great. When I walked into the BBC cafeteria to tell him that I'd be the one directing those episodes, he looked up from his lasagna and uttered a four-letter word. Knowing his sense of humour, I understood that he was joking. But the realisation of the work we had ahead of us was sinking in, apparently.

WG: Did he need a lot of time on his own to emotionally prepare for those scenes?
FALLON: Yes. But he never took time away from the production. He did most of his preparation in the dressing room. I remember that he took me aside to ask me to make it absolutely clear to all those assembled in The Vic to concentrate and not fool around—which they often do on taping days in The Queen Vic. This time everybody behaved, respected Ross. They rose to the occasion.

WG: Are you happy with the scene where Grant walks into The Vic and plays the audiocassette with Sharon talking about her affair with Phil?
FALLON: Yes and no. I would love to have had more time to work on that scene, from a camera perspective. The Vic is a particularly difficult set on which to move cameras about. It would have been great to have had the luxury of time and space to do more panning shots of the engagement party guests. The four cameras we had were basically trained on Grant, Kathy, Phil and Sharon. I wish I had not had to rely on cutting to the various principal characters.

WG: I can't imagine it being more effective that it was.

FALLON: Oh, it would have been better if somehow we could have contained a continuous shot of the entire group's reactions, along with some sort of tracking shot in which Sharon tries to walk away and the camera goes with her.

WG: The later scene, which took place at The Arches (Phil's garage), must have been tough to do seven minutes of dialogue before Grant attacks Phil.

FALLON: That took the most preparation in a way. Ross and Steve (McFadden, who plays Phil) were fantastic in it. And that entire scene was done in only one take, after only one camera rehearsal. They were perfect, spot-on.

WG: You're kidding!

FALLON: We already knew we had it. It was absolutely nailed on the first take. Two hand-held cameras were used—one on Ross, the other on Steve. It worked brilliantly. Those guys were great.

WG: Are hand-held cameras used very often on *EastEnders*?

FALLON: We're not *NYPD Blue*, nor do we try to be. Hand-held cameras were appropriate for use in that scene, which needed a sense of uncertainty and danger. The only lighting we used was a single light bulb in the garage. This added to the sense of uncertainty.

WG: Wasn't the fight scene shot before the scenes at The Vic?

FALLON: Yes, thank God. Because [in real-life] Steve was attacked and badly injured by some thugs. This happened on the night we were shooting Grant's car scenes and Steve was not working. I don't know how we could have done the Phil/Grant fight if Steve had already been injured. Steve still came in later on to do the engagement party scenes,

God love him! Then, of course, we had to shoot the scenes of him in the hospital when [in reality] he had actually just been in the hospital. Talk about bizarre timing.

WG: Tell us about the hospital scenes. How did you motivate the cast?

FALLON: Do you know the scene in Hitchcock's *North By Northwest* when Cary Grant is waiting by the side of the road and a car stops then leaves—before the famous plane arrives? I wanted to make scene where Kathy and Nigel wait for Phil's prognosis have the same effect...

WG: Calm before the storm?

FALLON: Yes. Gillian and Paul (the actors) are both Hitchcock fans as well. So I did not need to explain to them in-depth what I was after. Of course, that old adage of "the best laid plans..." came into play here, because I wanted to heighten the suspense by having the nurse bolt, through those double doors we had constructed. But, when she did so, the rest of the set nearly crashed down around our ears! Another problem we had was with the one wheelchair that we had on-set. It had a puncture, so it made this horrible screeching noise. No time to fix it, I guess. But it was fun to do. And Gillian and Paul were so enthusiastically up for it.

WG: The result was wonderful television.

• • •

Letter From the Set:
Words from EastEnders Scriptwriter Ashley Pharoah

Editor's note: When we requested a telephone interview in early 1993 with EastEnders scripter Ashley Pharoah, he replied that as a writer he would prefer to answer in print. So he took down the interviewer's questions and penned a reply. Soon there afterwards, Dan Abramson received the follow-ing set of answers arrived in the mail (these were the days before the Internet and email) postmarked from Borehamwood, Elstree.

To what degree is the script of an *EastEnders* episode an individual effort and to what degree it is collaborative?

An inner core of six or seven writers meet with the producers every six weeks or so to discuss the next block of episodes. All writers are encouraged to send in stories and so we arer confronted by a document the size of the first draft of *War & Peace*. These stories are thrashed around all day in a reasonably democratic way. Maybe two out of every ten get accepted.

These stories are then broken down into episodes. The writers ear-marked for the next six episodes then meet and discuss these particular episodes with the producers and editors. This is the Planning Meeting. At this stage, only the bare bones of what will happen in each episode are given so that the writer has plenty of scope to develop the storylines as he or she sees fit.

These writers come back in a week's time for the Commissioning Meeting, where they outline in more detail how they are going to deal with specific episodes. This is the stage at which sets and available actors are assigned. Then the writers disappear for or five weeks to write their first drafts, keeping in touch by phone with the other writ-ers in their block with regards to story continuity. Then the delivery day comes and the writers go the bar for a couple of days. From now on each writer works with a script editor who passes notes from the producers until a shooting script is ready.

Of the episodes you wrote, which are your favourites?

Tough one. The nature of the multi-stranded beast means that you are invariably dealing with some strands you prefer more than others. But my favourite experience was working with a director who happened to be a friend from film school. The episode's mood was given by the fact that Pauline had just come back to the Square from the sunny places of New Zealand and was taking a long hard look at her life in the urban East End. We had rain machines all over the place, beggars, greyness, even lightning (special effects) above the Square! But juxtaposed with this visual drabness we had an episode crowded with human life: Hattie discovering boyfriend Steve with another girl; Grant in trouble with some thugs; Sam dressed up as a giant piece of cheese in a supermarket. I was proud of that one.

Have you ever had a favourite scene edited out?

I can honestly say 'no'. Because of the writing process I described above you sort of know what you should be writing. Whilst you should always aim to surprise the producers and script editors and not just go through the motions of giving them what they asked for, it shouldn't really happen that a scene you write is rejected. Minor changes and tweaks, of course. Sometimes a scene has to be suddenly moved from an interior, for instance, but you have to remember we're having to produce an hour's quality television a week (*Editor's note: now it's two*) and it's definitely not the place for the precious.

Can the directors and actors make changes in each script?

They can try! There is a limit—in my experience at least—to what they can change. This isn't a movie we're dealing with where people have months of pre-production. Some of the actors have a very strong sense of their characters—after all, they have been playing them for years—and will sometimes give you advice or disagree with story-lines. This is more the role of the script-editors. The actors and the script writers tend to meet in the neutral territory of the Elstree bar. No doubt some directors find the lack of creative input a bit limiting. But, as they rule the roost in just about every other aspect of the TV and film industry it's not something I personally lose sleep about.

What are you current working on—away from Walford?

At the moment, I'm writing the third draft of a low budget (about $2.5 million) British feature to be shot in Zimbabwe next Spring. The working title is *Home for Christmas*, but the title may well change. Look out for a road movie set in Africa at Christmas time, there can't be too many of them about!

I've also just finished a screenplay for the BBC about a true-life murder and subsequent miscarriage of justice, which is very exciting.

What were your career credits before *EastEnders*?

I was educated at the University of Sussex and at the National Film and Television School, where I graduated from a screenwriting course in 1989. My graduation film, *Water's Edge*, was nominated for a Bafta (the British Oscars) in that year and went on to win several international awards, including a Silver Hugo at he Chicago Film Festival and the Gold Award at the Bilbao Film Festival.

Other film work include the screenplay for *White Elephant*, a feature set in Ghana and starring Peter Firth, shown at the Chicago and Berlin Film Festivals.

• • •

So You Want to Be An EastEnders Script Writer?
Zeddy Lawrence Tells What It's Like

By Larry Jaffee

Zeddy Lawrence was hired by *EastEnders* to inject some humour into the programme for three episodes that aired in the UK in 1995 and 1996. In retrospect, he's not sure that he succeeded, he admits.

"I was a sitcom writer and somebody at *EastEnders* saw some of my comedy-drama stuff and invited me aboard. It was a time they were trying to make it more lighthearted."

At the time, Gita was having an affair with Guppy while her husband Sanjay was back in India attending to family business. "At the end of the day, I'm not sure the storylines were that humourous. That one [Gita's affair with Guppy] was depressing."

Another storyline at the time dealt with Ted Hills and his two teenagers moving into the Square. Lawrence worked a bit on the plot development of daughter Sarah becoming a kleptomaniac, which didn't last very long nor was that very funny, he remembers.

"Tiffany hadn't been on very long. They were toying with making her a prostitute rather than just a good-time girl. She was going to sleep with businessmen for money. They decided to not go down that path and just make her a lovely young girl," Lawrence reveals, putting his brain in rewind to come up with another story that he worked on.

"It's all coming back to me—I haven't thought about it in years. My favourite bits that I wrote was for David Wicks when he was trying to get back with Carol Jackson. And then David started having feelings about Bianca [Carol and David's daughter]."

Lawrence notes the issue was based on social reality. "Something like 30 percent of people in that situation [fathers who were separated following their daughters' births] are sexually attracted [to their offspring] when they meet later in life. So we went down that line of David fancying his daughter. But there wasn't much humour there [either] to get into really," he admits. Lawrence points out that while it might not always have been funny, it was a pleasure writing for Michael French, who played David. "Everyone [at *EastEnders*] loved writing for him. I think the show goes through stages at which one character dominates the show. At that time, it was him [David]. More recently it has been Grant. David was a good one to write for."

Besides *EastEnders*, Lawrence through the 1990s was also regularly writing TV scripts for various British television series, including a sitcom called *The House of Windsor* for Granada. His soap credits include:

Byker Grove; London Bridge; The Dream Team for Sky Television, which co-starred Brian Croucher (Ted Hills on *EastEnders*); and *Family Affairs* on Channel 5.

At the time of this interview, he's employed by a website called TotallyJewish.com, for which he has conceived a comical Jewish cyber-soap called *BaruchSide* (a takeoff on popular UK soap *Brookside*), as a photo story with six new photos running three times a week. It was his idea to put a photo of Grant Mitchell up on the site to gain attention for the new feature.

Lawrence provided a glimpse of behind-the-scenes of what it's like to be a script-writer on *EastEnders*. "The writing process is two months per episode. You have to write a first draft, a second, a third and a fourth draft. You keep going back and change things. It was a good gig while it was going on. I've turned out so many episodes of different things that it's just like any other job. Writing soaps, there's so little room for your own creative input. It's like pieces of a jigsaw. They tell you what has to happen and you have to arrange it all. You're given about 80 percent of what has to happen in your episode, and you can create sort of isolated little things in your episodes, which had to tie into the other episodes. They give you a five-to-10-page document that tells you what has to happen to each and every person. All you can do is say what's going to happen to the person in the morning in the Queen Vic, what's going to happen in the afternoon in the Square. You just have to work out the order and then fill in the words.

"Everybody writing for a soap opera has a different approach, but it becomes quite formulaic. 'When are we going to make him gay?' Or, 'Is she going to sleep with his brother?' I think that is the constant challenge of soaps. [They] introduce new characters and have them play out old storylines. That's my view. While I was doing all of this soap stuff, I was also a radio journalist employed by various radio stations to read or write the news. Soaps were something that I'd get back to every couple of years."

Top 10 Uses for Your Extra
Copies of the *Walford Gazette*

1. Wrapping for an order of fish 'n chips
2. Paper airplane for transatlantic flights
3. Two Words: Paper Chase!
4. Kindling to make a bonfire for videocassettes
5. Paper-train your apricot-coloured poodle
6. Walford Oregami
7. Placemat for BBC-TV Dinners
8. Mop up spilled Churchill's Ale
9. Place it beneath an aspidistra plant
10. The crossword puzzles are great for starting arguments in pubs!

– Dan Abramson

The *Walford Gazette* was conceived as a fundraising tool for US public television stations that broadcast *EastEnders* to give something back to viewers for their financial contributions. Above: a recent pitch from WETA, of Arlington, Virgina. Below: *Walford Gazette* co-founder Dan Abramson answers phones for WLIW21, of Long Island, New York, in 1997.

PHOTO: DARREN NELSON

Larry Jaffee in 1994 at the Elstree/Borehamwood train station, north of London, after finding out that he was banned from visiting the BBC Elstree studio where *EastEnders* is made. The reason? For publishing a series of photos of an American woman who somehow talked her way onto the set with the headline "ALBERT SQUARE TRESPASSER." Two years later, a new regime welcomed Jaffee to the set.

December 1, 2003

Mr. Larry Jaffee
Publisher & Editor,
Walford Gazette
35 West 93rd Street
Apt. 1K
New York, NY 10025

Dear Mr. Jaffee:

Thank you very much for your letter about the EastEnders.

We will be sure to consider all your insights.

With best wishes,

Yours sincerely,

Rupert Murdoch

Rupert Murdoch

Media baron Rupert Murdoch said he would consider Jaffee's suggestion that News Corp. should acquire the US rights to *EastEnders* after BBC America cancelled the show in 2003. It did not. Below: In 1995, *The Times* of London quoted *Walford Gazette* co-founder Dan Abramson regarding his plans to protest over possible cancellation.

THE TIMES FRIDAY AUGUST 18 1995

Iraq gives further arms details to UN

By MICHAEL THEODOULOU

ROLF EKEUS, the United Nations official responsible for ridding Iraq of unconventional weapons, arrived in Baghdad yesterday and obtained vital new information that the Government had promised to hand over after the defection last week of President Saddam Hussein's military "mastermind".

Mr Ekeus after meeting Tariq Aziz, the Deputy Prime Minister, said he needed to assess the data before making a judgment. "Iraq has made the first presentations in two of the weapons areas — the biological and nuclear," he said, adding that he would continue his talks today with Lieutenant-General Amir Mohammed Rashid, Oil Minister and head of Iraq's military industrialisation commission.

fled to Jordan with his brother Lieutenant-Colonel Saddam Kamel Hassan and their wives, who are Saddam's daughters. Baghdad yesterday claimed the two women, Raghda and Rana, were drugged and taken to Jordan against their will.

When Iraq invited Mr Ekeus to Baghdad on Sunday it acknowledged that information he needed had been withheld, but unconvincingly blamed this on General Hussein Kamel. The admission bolstered Washington's argument that Baghdad discloses information about its weapons programmes only under intense pressure.

Before the defections, Mr Ekeus said he needed more information about Baghdad's biological warfare program-

New York battle over EastEnders

By ALEXANDRA FREAN
MEDIA CORRESPONDENT

AMERICAN fans of *EastEnders* are threatening to march on the BBC's offices in New York in a battle to keep it on their screens.

The British soap has become cult viewing in 19 cities in America, even though viewers often struggle to understand its rhyming slang and impenetrable accents. But despite its popularity, the show has lost its slot in New York as a result of the sale of its host station, WNYCTV.

Unless the BBC can find another New York station to buy it, the programme may be withdrawn completely. This is because WNYCTV effectively subsidised the programme by paying more for the rights than other stations.

Gretchen Franklin (Ethel Skinner), with whom Larry Jaffee enjoyed a close relationship the last 12 years of her life, relaxes here at her home in Barnes, London, with her favourite newspaper. Jaffee also stays in regular touch with John Altman (Nick Cotton), here in his garden in Surrey, England in 2004.

GENEVIEVE RAFTER-KEDD

Tim Wilson has interviewed for the *Walford Gazette* many *EastEnders* cast members, including Pam St. Clement (Pat Butcher). Few American fans have had the opportunity to visit the *EastEnders* studio, but Tim and Mackenzie Lambert Wood (below) are among them, as she pulls a pint at the Queen Vic.

'I Was an Albert Square Trespasser': A Photo Essay

Christine Christiano, an *EastEnders* fan from Brooklyn, refused to take no for an answer when the BBC told her they maintain a closed set and do not allow visitors to "Walford."

Christine was on vacation with her boyfriend, Simon (no, she doesn't call him "Wicksy"). They decided that they had nothing to lose and so headed for the BBC's Elstree Centre studios, north of London, where Albert Square can be found.

She would rather not say how the two of them got inside, because "a person's job depends upon my silence." But Christine and Simon did get to experience Walford, as the following pictures show.

"While in Elstree I got a few pages from one of the scripts and few other souvenirs as well. This was one of the nicer days on a very pleasant vacation," Christiano reflects.

CHEZ FOWLER — "The most impressive interior set was the Fowler's living room/dining room. There was food on the table. And, hanging on the walls, were pictures drawn by children, signed 'Vicki' and 'Martin.'"

Excerpts from the 1993 photo essay that resulted in the *Walford Gazette* getting banned from the BBC studio. Around this time, other ingenious fans still managed to get inside, such as Linda Miller Goodricke (below), who still won't say how she did it.

Walford Gazette webmaster Paul Field (left) meets Joe Absolom (Matthew Rose) and Martin Kemp (Steve Owen) with his wife Denise (right), who then ran into Shaun Williamson (Barry Evans) and Tony Caunter (Roy Evans) during their studio visit in 2000.

When WLIW21 made the decision to cancel *EastEnders*, I was prepared to auction off my cherished authentic sign, autographed by the entire *EE* cast. It was given to me in 2002 by the BBC's Mal Young as a token of the show's appreciation for all that the *Walford Gazette* had done to keep up interest in the series Stateside. Luckily, fans raised the necessary funds without me having to part with it.

WLIW TO KILL EASTENDERS

Dear *EastEnders* Fan: http://hometown.aol.com/e20launderette/index.html
After years of threatening to do so, WLIW/Ch. 21 will SHOW ITS LAST EPISODE OF *EASTENDERS* ON FEB. 26, the *Walford Gazette* has confirmed. The new programming director will keep it on if WE THE FANS CAN RAISE $29,000 BEFORE JAN 3. So please mail by Jan. 26 your checks of $50 or $100 made out to: WLIW, sent to "SAVE EASTENDERS," Park West Finance Station, P.O. Box 20631, New York, NY 10025. IF WE DO NOT HIT $29,000, YOUR CHECKS WILL BE RETURNED TO YOU with a self-addressed, stamped envelope AND NOT BE GIVEN TO WLIW. Your tax-deductible contribution will enter you in a drawing for such prizes as a telephone chat with an *EastEnders* actor. Send me your e-mail address to walfordgazette@yahoo.com to learn about a celebrity fundraiser in NY we plan to do in mid-January. If you have any questions, please call (212)366-6111 and visit the website above for updates. Sincerely, Larry Jaffee P.S., THIS IS REAL. THEY'RE NOT BLUFFING

SPECIAL VICTORY ISSUE: 'MISSION ACCOMPLISHED'

Walford Gazette

FANS REVERSE CANCELLATION!

$34,521 Raised for WLIW21 in Less Than a Month to Cover BBC Licensing EE Fee for Another Year

The Adventures of Young Grant & Phil

By A.S. Berman

The *Walford Gazette* has always run its share of the whimsical, such as A.S. Berman's occasional comic strips.

One of the fringe benefits of publishing the *Walford Gazette* is that I get to meet *EastEnders* actors. Here are five of them (from left, counterclockwise): Leonard Fenton (Dr Legg); Ricky Groves (Garry Hobbs); Sylvester Williams (Mick Mc-Farlane); John Bardon (Jim Branning) and Michael Greco (Beppe di Marco).

SEAN BORU

ANNE TRAUBEN

ANNE TRAUBEN

Deepak Verma (Sanjay Kapoor) has been a long-time mate, and contributed a foreword to my first book, *Albert Square & Me: The Actors of EastEnders*. We often stay at each other's homes. Deepak met well-known musician and massive *EastEnders* fan Lenny Kaye at a *Walford Gazette* party in 1996 (below).

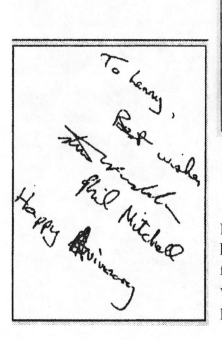

Lenny's wife Stephanie once was on holiday in Paris where she managed to find Steve McFadden (Phil Mitchell), who gladly obliged an anniversary present/autograph for her husband.

UK TV presenter Lorraine Kelly (far left) visits Manhattan's Carnegie Deli to interview Tim Wilson, Larry Jaffee and Suzanne Campbell to find out why New Yorkers are fans of *EastEnders*. Melissa Berry, of North Carolina, and Katharine Smith, of Erie, PA, wear their fandom on their car license plates.

Walford is commonly thought of as a fictional East End borough of London, concocted by *EastEnders* co-creators Julia Smith and Tony Holland. In actuality, Walford does exist – in England's Midlands, as photographed above and below by the *Gazette's* UK correspondent Elizabeth Toppin, who stumbled upon this revelation when she moved in 2002 to nearby Ross-On-Wye.

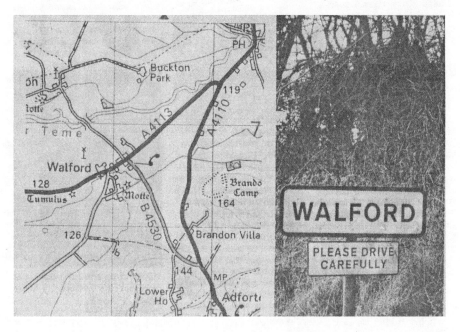

Arts, Briefly

THE NEW YORK TIMES,
TUESDAY, JANUARY 11, 2005

Can This Soap Be Saved?

A fund-raising effort by fans of the British soap opera "EastEnders" gives new meaning to the "public" part of public television. Last week, WLIW, the Long Island PBS affiliate, threatened to cancel "EastEnders," which it has broadcast since 1996. But Joe Campbell, WLIW's program manager, offered viewers an opportunity to save the show: he will keep it on if they can raise $29,000, the cost of a year of licensing the series, by Jan. 31. "EastEnders," which follows the lives of residents in a working-class neighborhood in London, has been on the BBC since 1985, and it continues to be a ratings success in Britain: its Christmas episode drew 12.3 million viewers. As an import, "EastEnders" has fared less well, so its small local audience has set out to raise the money for WLIW by planning a string of benefits. The first was held Sunday when Michelle Collins, an actress formerly on the show, appeared at the West Village restaurant Fiddlesticks, where enthusiasts paid $100 each to meet her. The benefit's organizer, Larry Jaffee, said, "Everyone there was a true fan and got to chat with her." Mr. Jaffee said that the event had brought in $1,700 and that the drive had raised $8,900 so far.　　　*KATE AURTHUR*

'EastEnders' Rides Again

Fan support and expatriate outrage couldn't save British soap *EastEnders* on BBC America in 2003. The net dropped the show — but Dish Network picked it up on PPV, cancel...

...ing some solace to fans trying to keep up with life in the fictional East London neighborhood.

Older episodes air on public-TV stations around the country, including WLIW, a Long Island, N.Y., outlet with cable carriage throughout the New York City area. When the station let it be known donations weren't commensurate with the show's license fee and that airings would end Feb. 26, fans took up the challenge. They raised among themselves the annual $29,000 license fee and then some.

Larry Jaffee, publisher of the

THE NEW YORK TIMES, MONDAY, JANUARY 31, 2005

A Reprieve for 'EastEnders'

New York fans of "EastEnders," the British soap opera about a group of working-class Londoners, have successfully raised the money required to keep the show on the air in New York for another year. At the beginning of the month, WLIW, the Long Island PBS affiliate, announced it would cancel its broadcasts of the BBC series but would stay the execution if fans could raise $29,000 — enough to pay a year's licensing fees — by today. Led by Larry Jaffee, an Upper West Side resident and the publisher of a fan magazine about "EastEnders," supporters of the series held three fund-raising events: a raffle, a viewing party at SoHo House and a get-together with Michelle Collins, a former cast member. Mr. Jaffee said the combined efforts raised $33,692, which he would deliver to WLIW today. A spokeswoman for WLIW confirmed that the station will honor the agreement to continue broadcasting "EastEnders" for a year.　　　*KATE AURTHUR*

Foreign affairs

Last exit to Walford

The Guardian

EastEnders may be in desperate straits, according to ex-viewers who have been voting with their remotes, but there is a group of fans for whom the Walford chronicles maintain a grim fascination. They comprise one of the smallest of all viewing minorities – Americans, who watch the show on 16 local cable channels dotted across the US.

To the horror of New York's Enderphile contingent, the local outlet, WLIW, plans to cancel the show on January 31 on the grounds that it can't afford to renew its $29,000 licence fee. The station took on the programme 16 months ago, when it was dropped by BBC America due to low viewing figures (informally estimated at 6,000). The New York fans, some of whom had been watching since it debuted in America in 1987, didn't take the BBC's action lying down, picketing its Manhattan headquarters and wearing teabags as protest badges. To no avail – EastEnders was shunted ...

America showed current ones.

Now, though, even this is at risk. Deciding that old episodes are better than none, a cabal of fans have vowed to raise the cash themselves. "We have a multi-tier strategy," says Larry Jaffee, editor of a long-running Manhattan-based fanzine, the Walford Gazette. With its unstinting loyalty to both Enders and virtually all things Brit (one issue even swoons over Dean Gaffney), the Gazette puts to shame the naughty British press.

One of the tiers was a fund-raising evening, which took place last Sunday, raised $1,600, and featured former Walfordian Michelle (Cindy Beale) Collins. "Michelle empathised, and said she'd make some calls when she got back to London." Jaffee also hopes to persuade fellow an Elton John to do a benefit

Current

After San Jose win, imported soap faces showdown in NYC

The drama will keep New York fans of the cockney soap opera *EastEnders* enthralled until Jan. 31: Can devotees of the long-running BBC series raise the dosh it takes to keep it on the telly?

Larry Jaffee, a New York journalist with a sideline of publishing the *EastEnders* fanzine, *Walford Gazette*, predicts the ordeal will come to a happy ending. For now, however, he's irked with the local station. WLIW, which plans to cancel *EastEnders* unless its devotees contribute $29,000 to cover the whole BBC licensing fee.

Jaffee is leading a fundraising campaign on behalf of the show, sending e-mails and postcards to New York area fans and organizing special events with some from the cast. As of last week, he had collected checks totaling $11,340.

The primetime soap opera, set in a working-class London, is to celebrate its 20th anniversary on the BBC next month, but stateside fans have reason to be concerned about its continued availability in the U.S. The digital cable channel BBC America dropped *EastEnders* in 2003, citing poor ratings. The cancellation came just one week before Dirty Dea — a lying, cheating scoundrel from the soap's early days — was to make a comeback. *EastEnders* buffs protested, but in vain.

Viewers in San Jose, Calif., had better luck persuading their pubTV station to reinstate *EastEnders*. KTEH dropped the show in May 2003 and received "relentless calls and e-mails from fans" throughout the summer, said Ken Patterson, traffic and continuity coordinator...

Just a sampling of the kind of press coverage about fans privately raising nearly $35,000 in January 2005 to keep *EastEnders* on public television in the New York area. The *Walford Gazette* led the effort.

The *Walford Gazette* publishes a brand of advocacy journalism that serves as a platform for disenfranchised *EastEnders* fans in the US. As respected *Vanity Fair* columnist James Wolcott wrote in his blog: "The publisher of the *Walford Gazette*, Larry Jaffee, is the best friend on this side of the Atlantic that *EastEnders* has ever had, a tireless evangelist for the show fighting for its availability on public television and cable despite setback after setback."

IV
ADVOCACY

BBC America Pulls Plug; EE Fans Revolt!

By Larry Jaffee

George Bernard Shaw once quipped that Britain and the US were divided by a common language. Another difference between the two countries, if you were to ask BBC America, is an appreciation for *EastEnders*.

Simply put, we were blindsided by the sudden announcement on the BBC America website the evening of September 25, 2003 that two days later would be the last episode of *EastEnders* to air on BBC. To be honest, I'm not all that surprised. We knew that the channel did hardly any on-air promotion for *EastEnders*, and by its own admission absolutely none since January and February when BBC America claims that it ran more than 500 30-second commercial spots that promoted *EastEnders*. Fans who watch more than just *EastEnders* on the network cannot recall *EE* commercials anywhere near that level. I challenge BBC America to produce the logs to support the claim.

The reason why *EastEnders* never achieved the level of ratings that BBC America wanted is simply because it did an extremely poor job promoting it. BBC America's assertion that the audience fell 70 percent after a lead-in from its popular *Ground Force* does not address promotion; that is a scheduling issue.

Within a week of the cancellation more than 10,000 people signed an online petition calling for BBC America to reinstate the show. For several weeks following the announcement, the Bethesda, Maryland-based channel stopped answering its telephones because of the deluge of complaints. Press on both sides of the Atlantic have picked up on the cancellation story. Unfortunately, BBC America is not bowing to the pressure we've exerted.

Droves of fans are canceling their subscriptions to satellite and digital cable TV services that carry BBC America. And it's not just us common folk who have our knickers in a twist over the cancellation. In support of the show's American fans, Wendy Richard (Pauline Fowler) wrote to her BBC bosses, including Director-General Greg Dyke to complain. Michelle Collins, who played *EastEnders'* Cindy Beale, tells the *Gazette*: "I'm quite shocked and surprised really. It's a bit of a shame, isn't it?"

In addition, I received an e-mail of support from respected journalist James Wolcott, who's a contributing editor to *Vanity Fair* magazine: "I'm really peeved about BBC America's decision because I just began getting the channel a couple of months ago, and besides, most of their programming is pure fluff—it seems like every time I turn it on it's either a gardening show or a house make-over show or a *What Not to Wear*. I'll be happy to put my name on any petition or write a brief note to the powers that be. It's particularly maddening with Dirty Den making his return!"

BBC America's mission is supposedly to bring "the best of British television to the US." *EastEnders* is the longest-running, most popular series in BBC television history, typically attracting 15 million to 20 million UK viewers four times a week in prime time. It is the British equivalent of *Friends* or *Everyone Loves Raymond* in terms of viewer popularity. It's a perennial winner of Best Soap Opera awards by various sponsoring organizations and publications, and in 1997 even won a BAFTA (the UK equivalent of the Emmy) as Best Drama. That sounds like "Best of British" to me.

BBC America's failure to promote *EastEnders* in any kind of meaningful way suggests at best a management team that brought with it from the UK some sort of a prejudice against a programme that is often dismissed in Britain merely as a "soap," and at worst a marketing department completely devoid of any creativity, at least when it comes to the goings-on at Albert Square.

Consider how it never crossed the minds of BBC America to mention to the press or viewers that Steve McFadden, who starred earlier this year in a segment of *Murder in Mind*, also is *EastEnders'* Phil Mitchell. Or how two of the current castmembers appeared in this year's hit movie *Bend It Like Beckham*.

In order to grow *EastEnders'* audience—one would assume this to be the network's goal—BBC America needed to pique the interest of viewers who tune into BBC America's other drama and comedy programming. It had done this effectively with the upper-class rural contemporary drama *Monarch of the Glen*. But would-be *EastEnders* fans were never given a taste of the show's rich tapestry of emotions and personalities that populate the fictional Walford.

Without promoting it regularly during its other shows, BBC America inexplicably was setting up *EastEnders* for failure. It didn't always seem that way. For example, in a January 2000 press release commemorating the series' 15th anniversary, BBC America president Paul Lee stated that "*EastEnders* has become a phenomenon on both sides of the Atlantic. Who would have thought that a British soap opera—where no one has money or plastic surgery—would have captured the hearts of so many of our American viewers?"

What has transpired since then? Well for one thing, BBC America's potential audience has grown significantly, as more local cable TV systems deployed digital infrastructures, thus creating larger channel capacities. An estimated 35 million households can now receive BBC America either through digital cable or satellite services like DirecTV. Many customers signed on for these new services expressly for *East-Enders*. Hence, even without on-air promotion, *EastEnders'* audience was bound to grow.

When *EastEnders* made it to commercial television via BBC America, albeit a fledgling niche in a 500-channel universe, its fans thought that they would finally be rid of the incessant threats of cancellation if membership goals aren't met. What *EastEnders* fans have learned is that advertising-dependent commercial cable television is as an uncertain environment—if not more so—as the constantly financially struggling, non-commercial PBS world. *EastEnders* on public television is going through significant trials and tribulations of its own lately, with cancellations this year in Philadelphia, San Jose, Dayton, OH, and Plattsburgh, NY.

Some history: First introduced to American viewers via public television stations in 1988, *EastEnders* was never picked up nationally by PBS, and subsequently only 50 stations carried it the first year. By the fall of 2003, 16 stations were left and by 2010 only nine. The public TV stations broadcast *EastEnders* episodes that are three to four years behind the UK storyline, whereas BBC America's episodes were two weeks behind the UK.

EastEnders fans do have a track record of getting such decisions reconsidered. Last year, bowing to viewer complaints, BBC America within three weeks reversed a decision that would have left *EastEnders* only on Friday afternoons. On public television in the past decade, viewer complaints forced station executives in St. Paul, MN, San Jose, CA, Buffalo, NY, Denver, CO, and Raleigh, NC to reinstate the programme. Buffalo's WNED ended up killing it two years ago after a year-long reprieve, while San Jose's KTEH enjoyed a 10-year run after the first cancellation but again pulled the plug on *EastEnders* this past January.

BBC Americas CEO Mark Young, with whom I met on 2003 October 12 in London for over an hour, said that video on demand (VOD) was being considered to fill the void, but as of 2010 it still hasn't launched. BBC America announced a VOD service in 2001 that was to have launched in early 2002, but it never materialised.

It wasn't lost on *EastEnders* fans that the timing of the BBC America cancellation was particularly poor, two weeks before the character Den Watts was set to return to Albert Square after a 14-year absence, during which he was presumed dead. It was another example of how management failed to care about the *EastEnders* fan psyche. And the very last shot of *EastEnders* aired on BBC America, further adding insult to injury, was a glimpse of another character, Lisa, whose disappearance six months ago fuelled speculation of foul play at the hands of her former boyfriend Phil.

So the question remains, why can't this British crown jewel find a home in the former colonies? After all, it's available in some 50 countries, the latest being Ukraine.

• • •

Interview With Mark Young, President & CEO of BBC Worldwide Americas

By Larry Jaffee

LONDON—Not taking "no" for an answer, my persistence paid off and yielded an interview on October 14, 2003—two weeks after BBC America's cancellation of *EastEnders*—with Mark Young, who serves as president and CEO of BBC Worldwide Americas. A man with several titles, Young is BBC Worldwide's managing director, GMBD (Global Marketing & Brand Development) and managing director, EMEIA (Europe, Middle East, India and Africa).

Our meeting of more than an hour was cordial and frank. As you will see from the following, I asked the tough questions, and while Mr. Young's answers may not have been always satisfactory, at least he responded. I accomplished what I set out to do—have someone of authority at the BBC hear me out.

WG: I think it is very important for us to establish a dialogue. I realise reversing the cancellation now is a very difficult thing to do, but I can't not try. I don't know, maybe it's the American way. I think it's something that has to be done. After all, everything I've done is to support the BBC, really. I just wish that they maybe the

Bethesda office consulted with me a bit more about promotional opportunities. For example, *EastEnders'* current cast includes two actors who were in *Bend It Like Beckham*, which has been a huge hit in the US That was a great promotional opportunity that just passed. I wonder if it wasn't done because the cancellation decision had been made quite a long time ago, maybe in February when the commercial spots stopped. *Bend It Like Beckham* was a hit late spring theatrical release. Did someone at BBC America think, "*EastEnders*, it's history. There's no point in promoting it at this stage."

MY: That's not how it happened. It is a recent decision and it was off the back of the performance of the programme from January onward.

WG: Well, that's my point. In February, the spots stopped, according to [BBC America vice president of programming] David Bernath in the on-line chat. How could the ratings increased if there was not some promotion after February—between February and, say, September?

MY: I think you have to look at what happened in the previous six months. We did promote the shows at the beginning of the year, and there was absolutely no uptake in audience as a result of that promotion. You know as well as I do that if you try your best to promote the show, you spend money on it and nothing happens, then you probably have got to come to the conclusion that that form of promotion is not going to raise the audience awareness that you want.

WG: Well, we didn't see very much evidence of promotion to begin with. I mean I recall seeing a couple of spots, but it was certainly not the type of attention that *Ground Force*, *What Not To Wear* and *So Graham Norton* get on a continuing basis. Could you please be more specific regarding exactly what weeks and how many spots ran in January and February.

MY: We ran 500 spots around our highest-rating shows, things like *Changing Rooms, Absolutely Fabulous, Monarch of the Glen* and *What Not to Wear*. So it was a fully-fledged promotional campaign using the best programmes that we have to try and drive the ratings.

WG: Getting back to the cross-promotional opportunities that I think were missed. Why didn't BBC America run commercials for the *Murder in Mind* episodes that starred Steve McFadden and Michael Greco, both popular *EastEnders* actors? *Red Cap*, which stars ex-*EastEnders* actor Tamzin Outhwaite was promoted quite significantly in the summer, but *EastEnders* was never mentioned. Do you agree that kind of cross-promotion could have been done?
MY: No.

WG: Why?
MY: I think in working with talent, you've got to be really careful about how you use an actor to promote a programme. And they go through life whereby they establish themselves in *EastEnders* and then they decide that they want to change. They come out of *EastEnders* and go into *Red Cap*, or they go somewhere else and they're trying to create a new persona for themselves. And so from a talent point of view, they don't always want the audience to be harking back to them as whatever that character was in *EastEnders*. And so it becomes difficult to do a generic promotional campaign around an actor or an actress who has moved on from *EastEnders*. It proves really difficult to do.

WG: I mean I hate to sound crass, but at the end of the day doesn't BBC own the actor in the sense that they could basically do what they would like....
MY: That's not crass. That's wrong. We don't own the actors; they are, in fact, free agents and we're grateful for the work that they do for us

and we work with them and we pay them a decent whack for the job that they do and then they go off and they do another job.

WG: Well, in the case of Steve McFadden at least, he was moonlighting with *Murder in Mind*. I mean he was going back to *EastEnders*. In his case, I certainly think there was a missed opportunity there. I can't imagine he would have objected to BBC America running a commercial for *Murder In Mind* saying he was on *EastEnders*, which is paying his mortgage. Wasn't there also a chance for cross-promotional opportunities with the public television stations that run *EastEnders*? When I watch on WLIW in New York, the first thing you see is "BBC America presents..." It seems to me that from the beginning, public television stations and BBC America have viewed each other with suspicion and competition when they should have been embracing each other and using each other for cross-promotional opportunities. *EastEnders* fans really don't care who's putting it on; they'll watch wherever. Fans took subscriptions with DirecTV and with the digital cable services expressly for *EastEnders*—not just for the vast array of channels they offer.

MY: I don't know of any cross-promotion that occurs across rival television groups. So it's not that we don't want to do it; it's just that television is such that it just won't happen. You've got to break the paradigm in television in order to do it. The PBS stations will say, if you go and talk to them, why should they suggest to their viewers that they should watch *EastEnders* on BBC America? They want to retain as much audience as possible. And so they're never going to direct you to watch a rival channel.

WG: I have been receiving e-mails from people who are dropping en masse their digital cable and their satellite services specifically because of this cancellation. Does that trouble you that American subscribers are dropping their service because of this?

MY: It troubles me only if subscribers drop the service because of a change that we've made, but it doesn't mean to say the decision wasn't the right decision. Clearly the reason that we're making the change is because we believe that the channel ratings will improve as a result of doing it. And, therefore, whilst we may well lose a number of our *EastEnders* audience, the whole point of doing this is that we believe that we'll gain more of an audience as a result. I think there are other programmes on BBC America which I think *EastEnders* fans will find of equal value. So I hope they won't decide to drop their subscription to DirecTV and the others.

WG: Obviously there's been a groundswell of support for *East-Enders*. Did you underestimate the complaints?
MY: No. When we changed the schedule last year, there was an equal level of disquiet at what we'd done. So I think we knew when we decided to pull *EastEnders* off the schedule that there would be at least as much disquiet as we received last year. So I don't think we've underestimated it. I'll ask you a simple question. If you've got either a television programme or a part of your magazine which is delivering only a tenth of the audience that your best programme is delivering, and if when you go into a programme you lose 70 percent of your audience and when you come out of that programme you go up 80 percent, what would you expect us to do?

WG: Well, it's a fair question, but I would suggest that BBC America needed to do things differently, such as cross-promote, and perhaps *Ground Force* wasn't the best choice to couple with *EastEnders* (i.e., no synergy between audiences). Another thing I wondered was why *EastEnders* was never mentioned in the programming highlights distributed weekly by e-mail to the press. It doesn't cost anything to take a sentence or two in an e-mail that's already going out and say, "Oh, by the way, *EastEnders* won Best

Soap in the National Television Awards in the UK It was an opportunity for television writers to find out about *EastEnders*. Why wouldn't that be done?

MY: Because when you supply information to media in that way, your intention is to provide them with sort of material that they're going to pick up and use. And our experience over the last five years on BBC America is that although *EastEnders* is a fantastic programme, although it's got a loyal audience, although it's won numerous television awards in the UK, for whatever reason, it's not a programme that the journalists have shown any interest or inclination to pick up on. And after a while, you know as well as I do, that if you receive information that you believe is irrelevant to you as a journalist, then it reduces the credibility of the balance of the information that you're passing to them. And so it becomes in a way counter-productive to have something there that they don't want to receive. We have over the five years tried to create a market for this programme in numerous different ways, and almost whatever we do it does not seem to have an effect on the audience.

WG: Could you please tell me a few of the ways?

MY: [BBC America senior vice president of strategy and communications] Jo Petherbridge has told you a few of the ways. Dave Bernath's told you a few of the ways. [BBC America president] Paul Lee told you... I do not know the details to the extent that you would want them in order to report them.

WG: The only thing that they've talked about recently is the spots that you mentioned in January and February. There also was a promotion three years ago for the 15th anniversary asking viewers for their favourite episodes. BBC America put together a nice press packet for that. Since then, there's been absolutely no evidence of—as far as I know—any serious kind of marketing push other than what we've talked about before.

MY: We've tried to promote *EastEnders* in the most effective way possible and whenever we've done it, we haven't seen a noticeable uplift in the audience. And we've come to the conclusion that it is one of those programmes that has an incredibly small, but incredibly loyal audience. BBC America can only stay in business if we deliver an acceptable level of ratings. It's a commercially funded channel and now that we're on daily ratings, it's important that we maximize the rating on the channel, and *EastEnders* just doesn't do that. So we know that we've got a loyal audience that is upset, and we're sad about that. But we believe that we will put BBC America as a channel at risk if we didn't address programmes that were underperforming in ratings terms and put the schedule right.

WG: I'm just curious what the ratings were on the two weeks that it's been off. Do you have any idea of that?
MY: I don't. I'm going to America tonight. I'll go to the ratings then.

WG: In November 2001 there was a press release from BBC America announcing a video-on-demand service that was to launch in the first quarter of 2002, but never did. It's interesting that *EastEnders* was selected as the first programme.
MY: It was selected as the first programme because it has a relatively small, but incredible loyal audience—exactly the sort of programme that should work well on video-on-demand. Over the course of the next year we're going to re-focus our efforts with the on-demand and see whether or not we can create a VOD service that could include *EastEnders*.

WG: This specific service was supposed to be launched in the first quarter of 2002. What happened? Why didn't it materialise?
MY: Because *EastEnders* is a soap that is on four times a week, it is technically expensive to make the full service available. I mean you can

watch *Fawlty Towers*—from memory it's 13 episodes in total. It's not expensive in technology terms to make those 13 shows available. If we make 13 *EastEnders* shows available, then in three weeks' time you'd be out of date. So you need to constantly renew any soap on a VOD service and that becomes expensive to fulfill and if you don't get the flow-through, then the video-on-demand provider sees it as an inefficient use of his bandwidth. We're still working with all of the VOD suppliers in the US to try and get a video-on-demand service for *EastEnders*.

WG: Is one reason why you wouldn't try to quicken the pace of the VOD service is because it could be perceived by the loyal fans that it was just a ploy to cancel the programme and get them to pay for it? You probably would gain a lot more revenue through that type of transaction than you would from your current advertising.

MY: Video-on-demand is not yet there in the States in strong numbers. If we were going to do that as a ploy to transfer our loyal audience to a paying subscriber audience, it would probably be in our best interest to keep *EastEnders* for another nine months, despite being inefficient in the schedule, until the video-on-demand had finally taken off. That's the best guarantee that we're not doing this for monetary purposes; we're doing it because it's in the best interest of the channel.

WG: Have you heard that numerous tape trains have been established with UK viewers recording *EastEnders* and sending over tapes to US fans? Any reaction to that?

MY: Well, you're not going to get me to condone what some people would view as piracy. But on this occasion, I think it's entirely legitimate for a loyal audience to source its programming. I'm not condoning it, though.

WG: I also understand that there might even be a website that's uploading episodes that can be downloaded.

MY: If individuals are having tapes delivered to them by friends in order to satisfy a personal desire, then that's one thing. If somebody is taking a tape and uploading it and making it generally available, then I've got a problem with that. And that does infringe not only on our rights, but also the rights of the actors and the talent in *EastEnders*. There's a very fine line. I can understand the audience's desire to do it.

WG: How about in terms of another broadcast entity in the States picking up the rights to *EastEnders*? I mean, for example, Bravo is now owned by NBC, so they have deep pockets, and it's sort of a niche channel. Is that something the BBC would consider?
MY: The fact that it's been on BBC America does not stop us from trying to sell the programme elsewhere.

WG: So is there an effort going on right now in light of the cancellation?
MY: It's a continuing effort to maximize the value that we get for all of our programmes.

WG: It also occurred to me that DirecTV, which is now losing subscriptions, might be a candidate since Rupert Murdoch is about to acquire the service. I realise there's a long contentious history between Murdoch and the BBC. But in one sense, *EastEnders* might be the olive branch that could put some of your differences aside.
MY: We haven't got a problem with Murdoch at all. We would treat him not only in relation to *EastEnders*, but any other programme, as a perfectly acceptable international partner for the programme. Some of our biggest deals were done with News Corp.

WG: How about in terms of the availability of videos? Only three VHS titles were released in the UK, and there's the new Slaters

DVD. None have been made available for the US market.
MY: We looked at that. It's the same issue with video-on-demand. In order to satisfy the requirements of a serial, we'll broadcast two hours of video a week, 104 hours a show, whatever the figure is, and that's a hell of a big commitment.

WG: I'm thinking in terms of specials. *EastEnders'* **Christmas specials have always been very exciting, and could stand alone, as have the "two-handers," such as Dot and Ethel reminiscing about the war. A two-disc DVD set for** *Coronation Street* **was released in the US earlier this year and included the first five episodes and a documentary about the show's 40th anniversary.**
MY: If we believed there was a market for an *EastEnders* video or DVD, then we would do our best to support it. There's a critical mass of videos that you need to believe that you can sell in order to justify their inclusion in any catalogue. There isn't a policy of not distributing *EastEnders* on DVD. There is a policy that whatever we do, we do commercially and we do it in a way that we believe will allow us to be able to sustain the market across a number of years.

WG: As for that critical mass, do you have a number in mind for *EastEnders?*
MY: It wouldn't be *EastEnders* specifically; but we would have to believe that we can sell more than 5,000 units.

WG: The BBC's lack of promotion for the public TV stations is also one of the things that has disappointed me. *EastEnders* **made a decent launch in 1988 initially on 50 stations. They had a press event in New York and brought over a couple of the actors. Fifteen years ago was the last time any kind of effort was made by BBC Sales to instill some sort of awareness or excitement about** *East-Enders.* **It bothers me that BBC America has coined this phrase**

about how the programme didn't "resonate" across the Atlantic. How could it not resonate if it's on 15 years later on major cities like in New York, Los Angeles, Miami, Houston, Seattle, Minneapolis? I mean obviously, like you've said, there has been a loyal audience. Fifteen years sounds like it resonates to me. And these are cash-poor stations that have to make the very hard decisions that you do. These viewers typically pay $75 for four issues of my newspaper.

MY: I'm really pleased that *EastEnders* works for these individual PBS stations. We're trying to extend the reach of *EastEnders* through individual PBS stations this year as much as we were trying last year or 15 years ago.

WG: I hope you're right about that, given all the recent cancellations.

MY: You can't force a PBS station, and we wouldn't want to. We're grateful when they want it.

WG: Any parting words?

MY: Look, we had to take *EastEnders* off of BBC America. We know that there's a loyal, but, we believe, a small audience out there who are going to feel disadvantaged as a result of that. That's not going to make us put *EastEnders* back on BBC America, but I think what we should do is try and work with you in the *Walford Gazette* through direct marketing and look at video and VOD over the next six months.

WG: I know that you're responsible for things other than BBC America. How much of your day is occupied by BBC America matters?

MY: Well, over the last three weeks, a little bit more than the previous three weeks I probably spend a day a week. I'm responsible for all of our operations in the States, all of our operations in Europe, Middle East,

India, and Africa, children, music, and businesses globally. So it gets at that proportion. I'm a channels man. I used to be managing director of BBC World. I launched BBC Prime in Europe.

WG: Thank you for hearing me out. I didn't necessarily think you would say to me, "You're quite right, we made a terrible mistake, I'll put it back on next week." I just wanted to make sure you see the big picture.

• • •

Still Brassed Off

By Larry Jaffee

I was hoping to report in this issue that stateside *EastEnders* fans were going to have some new way of accessing current episodes of the series either through a new network home or a video-on-demand service. At press time, neither had materialised, but a BBC America spokeswoman assures me in a somewhat patronizing tone, "I'll be the first the first to know."

Following my appeal in the last issue, on Dec. 1, 2003 I received a written reply from Rupert Murdoch that he would "take into consideration" my suggestion that his News Corp. acquire the US rights to *EastEnders* for its newly acquired DirecTV satellite service and perhaps its FX cable network.

Since then I have not luck getting in touch with either Mr. Murdoch or DirecTV's new head, Mitch Stern, to reiterate how DirecTV and other digital cable/satellite TV services are losing scores of subscribers because of *EastEnders* fans who have cancelled their subscription as the result of BBC America pulling the plug on *EastEnders* last September. But I plan to be persistent with both News Corp. (and BBC

America, for that matter) because I believe this is a legitimate business opportunity. The day after picking up the last issue of the *Walford Gazette*, I met with Mark Young, CEO of BBC Worldwide Americas, who thought might have some news for us by February. Obviously that passed, and Mr. Young has not returned my calls or e-mails to find out what is going on.

But I must share something that happened during our lunch. The day before, the trade magazine *Television Week* ran a letter from me regarding a short piece the publication ran the previous week regarding a protest that some New York fans mounted in front of the BBC offices on Third Avenue. The reporter called Jo Petherbridge, BBC America's senior vice president of communications, for comment about the protest. "We know Larry well," she sighed to *Television Week*. (I found the statement amusing.) She went on to explain about how the show never performed even when led in by the channel's highest rated show, *Ground Force*, the protest's turnout was small, and besides the New York location is a sales office that has nothing to do with BBC America.

My published letter to the magazine stated that it's nice to see BBC America is amused by our protest, but that does not explain why the network chose not to promote the series, and all that BBC America proved was there's little synergy between a dramatic serial and a home improvement show.

Reading my letter, Mr. Young commented: "Fair point." I immediately exclaimed, "Fair enough to put it back on?" to which he replied, "No, of course not." It's obvious they are not willing to admit that they made a mistake, and did not give *EastEnders* a fair chance of succeeding.

But at the same time, BBC Worldwide realises that it would be foolish to not take advantage of a diehard audience willing to pay for its favourite show. It's for that reason that I doubt they would ever sell the show to another party such as News Corp. for fear of cannibalising any kind of subscription service. Mr. Young mentioned that one option being considered by BBC Worldwide to fill the void is a

DVD-R subscription service. Who knows if it will ever materialise? Obviously the BBC has the far bigger problems these days than current *EastEnders* episodes not being on in the US In late January the BBC's chairman and director-general both resigned following a British judge's report that the BBC erred when it let a radio news report over the air that suggested the Blair administration "sexed up" the case against Saddam Hussein to justify Britain's involvement in the war against Iraq, resulting in the eventual resignation of the BBC's top executive, Greg Dyke.

In any case, Mr. Young told me that Mr. Dyke was aware of my meeting (prior to his resignation) with him in November and was in fact in New York that day. Too bad he didn't join us.

• • •

An Appeal to Rupert Murdoch

November 24, 2003

K. Rupert Murdoch
Chairman and CEO
News Corp. Ltd.
1211 Avenue of the Americas
New York, NY 10036

Dear Mr. Murdoch,

I would like to introduce myself. I am Larry Jaffee, a business journalist concentrating on the media over the past two decades, who has a novel side business: publishing a quarterly newspaper about *EastEnders*. Hopefully, you've heard about BBC America's cancellation of *EastEnders*. In a way, this might be an opportunity for your News

Corp., which as you stated in your recent annual report to shareholders is about to acquire DirecTV.

You might not be aware of how DirecTV is currently losing scores of subscribers—others are downgrading their service—specifically because of BBC America's action. They're also cancelling or downgrading from the Dish Network, as well as the various digital cable services from the likes of Time Warner, Comcast, et. al. I have received over 100 letters to that effect, some of which have been published in my latest issue of the *Walford Gazette*.

I would like to suggest to you that is a microcosm of the opportunity here for your company. I don't have to tell you that one of the reasons your satellite business Sky has been so successful around the globe is exclusive programming.

In addition, I thought your US cable network FX could always use the kind of loyal audience that *EastEnders* is sure to deliver. Adding *EastEnders* to the FX programming schedule would ensure that many of the former digital cable customers, who are city dwellers and cannot install a satellite dish because they the required line of sight, could once again see their favorite series.

While he might have been very well humoring me, Mark Young, president and CEO of BBC Worldwide Americas, told me that BBC Worldwide would be open to talking with News Corp. about *East-Enders*.

It goes without saying, that the BBC could learn plenty from the marketing acumen that your Fox network continually demonstrates. And I'd also like to point out that it was BBC America's failure to recognise obvious marketing and cross-promotional opportunities that led to *EastEnders'* demise on the network.

I am fairly certain that *EastEnders* has been a program that you have coveted, at least in the UK As you know, this past summer BSkyB's Tony Ball proposed that the BBC be forced to divest its most popular shows—I'm assuming he included *EastEnders* among them—and make them available to its commercial competitors. Here's a way to achieve that in the world's biggest TV market without the government intervention that's sure to come up on a few years during the Beeb's charter renewal process.

I realise that there is a lot of acrimonious water under the bridge between News Corp. and the BBC, the latest dispute being over their decryption of Fox programming internationally.

I am wondering whether *EastEnders* US rights might be a way that you can help each other out and perhaps the series could be a bargaining chip in your continuing negotiations.

At the same time the BBC obviously doesn't have a clue when it comes to maximizing *EastEnders* in the States, while I have full confidence that your organisation would be creative and inventive in ways that BBC America and public television stations (which have broadcast *EastEnders* since 1988) have not.

This is because making money is not second nature to these institutions, which are first and foremost dedicated to providing public service; News Corp. and its various subsidiaries obviously don't have that problem or those kind of restraints. True, BBC America is a 50/50 joint venture with Discovery Communications. This partnership, which by the way, was renewed in 2002 for another 10 years (and won't expire until 2012), may very well work in other programming categories, such as science and documentaries, but leaves much to be desired in the entertainment category. When was the last time a British Airways or Virgin Air commercial ran on BBC America? The answer is never; its commercial time is filled by per-inquiry, direct-response spots for household goods.

Frankly I'm not all that surprised by the cancellation. By BBC America's own admission, it did absolutely no on-air promotion for *EastEnders* since February. Without promoting it regularly during its other shows, BBC America inexplicably was setting up *EastEnders* for failure. BBC America's assertion that the audience fell 70 percent after a lead-in from its popular *Ground Force* does not address promotion; that is a scheduling issue.

Thank you for your time, and I look forward to hearing from you.

Sincerely yours,
Larry Jaffee
Publisher & Editor, *Walford Gazette*
cc: Peter Chernin, Lachlan Murdoch

Editor's post-script: A few weeks later, I receive a letter (reprinted in photo section) from Mr. Murdoch, saying he would "consider all [my] insights." I never had any further dealings with him, the BBC struck an EastEnders *subscription deal instead with Dish Network, and News Corp. a few years later divested DirecTV.*

• • •

FANS REVERSE CANCELLATION— WLIW21 Keeps on *EE* for Another Year After $34,500 Raised in Less Than Month

By Larry Jaffee

I thought, "Not in my backyard. No way."

That was my reaction to the anonymous phone call I received in the third week of December from someone who said she "had it on very good authority that WLIW was planning to cancel *EastEnders*, and perhaps maybe there's something you can do about it?" She hung up.

Still feeling a little guilty that not enough was done two years ago to save *EastEnders* on WHYY in Philadelphia, I figured the problem there was that no one stepped up to mobilise the community. It clearly needed a local person supported by other fans to spearhead any effort to save the show.

And still feeling a bit punchy over the BBC America cancellation in September 2003, I thought we had a better chance of saving WLIW because a public TV station would have to respond to money. A commercial TV network like BBC America is motivated by ratings and advertisers; there was little *EastEnders* fans could do to affect either of those things.

Despite the commercial vs. public TV differences, there was a parallel in the situations that led to the programming decisions at both WLIW and BBC America. In both cases, a relatively new programmer had arrived and had little interest in *EastEnders*. Obviously, killing the series was on "a to do" list, considered by others at the station/network, but until then no one ever got around to it.

I can't say I was entirely surprised by the WLIW news since they hadn't made any attempt to fund-raise around the show in any kind of meaningful way since the previous December [2003] when Leonard Fenton (Dr. Legg) flew in from London into a blizzard and the live pledge was postponed for a taped, not-as-effective segment the next week.

WLIW has had other bad luck when it brought in *EastEnders* actors for live pitches, such as competing against Monica Lewinsky being interviewed by Barbara Walters, or Al Gore giving his concession speech. But that was in the past. We needed to deal with the here and now.

Complicating the matter at hand was the tsunami tragedy, which dominated the news the week before we launched the campaign. Given the Southeast Asian catastrophe, saving *EastEnders* in New York seemed trivial in terms of philanthropic support. I realized that it wasn't the greatest time to be asking for money, but I was confident that most people could see that the one thing had nothing to with the other. But it was never an issue of either/or; fans could decide to support both causes if they were so inclined.

Fuelled with the knowledge that local fans in Minnesota, North Carolina, California and Colorado had managed to reverse *EastEnders* cancellations, I had little doubt we could win. Fortunately, WLIW programme manager Joe Campbell provided an opening by offering to allow the fans come up with the $29,000 to cover the BBC's annual license fee on our own.

But we had one huge disadvantage: WLIW refused to alert viewers of the programme's cancellation. We were literally on our own, bringing new meaning to the station's often-repeated promo station breaks as being "member-supported." I knew I had at my disposal the *Walford Gazette* database of approximately 1,200 names and addresses of fans in the New York area, including 621 who subscribed via WLIW.

At the same time, the *Gazette* was only one of probably 10 *EastEnders* thank-you gifts that WLIW had offered to contributors in the previous eight years. It just seemed patently unfair that the station wasn't giving fans the benefit of the doubt, and one last chance to show how much this programme meant to them. That's how it was saved by KOCE in San Jose in the spring of 2004 (although sadly it ultimately pulled the plug in the fall of 2007). WLIW's obstinacy to not let viewers know about the cancellation decision, and give "one last chance," made me even more determined to prove them wrong.

Pumped up by a soundtrack in my mind playing John Lennon's "Working Class Hero," Patti Smith's "People Have the Power" and Bob Marley's "Get Up Stand Up," I knew we needed nothing less than a multi-tiered strategy: one or two direct-mail postcards to the *Gazette* list pleading for cheques to come in immediately; the local newspaper, trade press and national media, all of which I thought would recognise the story as a classic David vs. Goliath media story, and any publicity would tip the odds in our favour; possibly a celebrity benefit concert with someone of the stature of David Bowie or Whoopi Goldberg, both New Yorkers whom I had reason to believe were *EastEnders* fans; a "meet-and-greet" with an *EastEnders* actor; mobilising the online *East-*

Enders community to help get out the word of our plight; an auction of rare *EastEnders* collectibles, including my Albert Square street sign autographed by the *EastEnders* cast; perhaps a major corporate contribution or two; and a benefit screening of rare episodes.

We had the good luck that Michelle Collins (Cindy Beale) was already in New York for a screening at the Museum of Modern Art of a film she starred in, *The Illustrated Mum*, which had won an International Emmy the previous November. With two days' notice, we managed to pull together an event for Michelle on 9 January, in which we raised $1,600 from a group of ecstatic fans.

But ultimately it was the postcard, and its follow-up, that was responsible for the lion's share of the cheques made out to WLIW that packed my P.O. box nearly every day for over three weeks. My job experience early in my career editing columns by fund-raising copywriting expert Herschell Gordon Lewis (also known as the maverick schlock filmmaker) came in handy when writing the postcard copy in which every word counted. Also it didn't hurt that we promised to give the money back if we fell short of the targe.

My guess was that if we convinced about 300 of the 1,200 postcard recipients to give us $100 apiece, we would easily hit $29,000. (Thanks to several large contributions—one for $2,500, two for $1,000 each and 31 cheques from $200 to $450 each—the average donation did turn out to be about $100 when taking into account the number of cheques for $50 and under.) Responses were coming in from people in all walks of life. Retirees, lawyers, a professional fund-raiser whose firm ironically has several PBS affiliate clients, doctors, and a Queens-based real-estate landlord.

The New York Times picked up the story, and we were able to receive additional financial support from *EastEnders* fans who weren't on my list. These included individuals like TV Guide writer Ileane Rudolph; Peter Bloch, the long-time editor-in-chief of *Penthouse* magazine, who was quoted in *The New York Observer* article about the campaign;

and a high-powered Wall Street law-firm partner, who sent directly to WLIW's offices two certified letters each containing cheques of $500 earmarked for *EastEnders.*

As I went about trying to get celebrity and media support, I felt almost like a combination of Sir Bob Geldof and Rupert Pupkin (Robert DeNiro's delusional character in Martin Scorsese's *King of Comedy*) in equal doses. Convinced that David Bowie was an *EastEnders* fan who watched via WLIW (based on his quote in the autobiography of British DJ Goldie about how ecstatic he was that his friend Goldie had landed the part of Angel "but it'll be 19 years before" he'd get to see him because the States' episodes are so far behind the UK), I called a friend of mine who had given David Bowie's wife Iman yoga lessons years ago (he once participated). Hearing the urgency in my voice, she parted with the phone number and address.The only problem was that the Bowies moved four years ago, the concierge of the St. Regis on Central Park South informed me. I dropped off a package at his management company, and spoke to his assistant, who seemed skeptical about my motives. Other associates of the musician whom I knew through being a music journalist, told me I was going about it correctly, but cautioned that he was still recovering from his health problems of last September, and that in any case they had little influence over him regarding something like this.

Whoopi Goldberg apparently told talk show host Graham Norton last year when he taped his show in New York that she was an *EastEnders* fan, and I recall a *TV Guide* interview years ago when she said the same thing. I left countless messages for a disc jockey on WBAI who I knew would know how to get to Whoopi's current Broadway show publicist, and even tried to get on the air. A package was dropped off at the theatre where Whoopi was performing, but we never heard back.

I called my friend Bob Tulipan, whose company Traffic Control Group arranges visas for internationally touring clients the likes of

Sir Elton John, to see if the musician would consider doing a benefit show, assuming that he might have a soft spot for *EastEnders*, perhaps a warm-up gig to his long-term Las Vegas casino engagement. Bob never did hear back from Elton's people. But Bob was able to arrange a private screening at Soho House, the New York branch of his trendy British social club, at which I decided to show "The Return of Den Watts," which was broadcast in the UK soon after the aforementioned BBC America cancellation.

Fellow fans in the online community immediately dashed off several DVD-Rs and tapes containing several requested holy grails. Luckily, one DVD-R and one VHS tape offered good enough quality even when blown up on the club's movie theatre screen. To see *EastEnders* on a big screen absolutely brought chills to all 35 of us who were at the screening, which put us over the top money-wise with a few days to spare. After checking several legal opinions as to whether the BBC could consider the screening copyright infringement, I threw caution to the winds, believing that the benefit would safely fall under fair use, especially since the proceeds ultimately would pay off the BBC.

I had even more ideas that basically couldn't be tapped due to a lack of time. If David Bowie or Elton John weren't available, I'd enlist professional musician and genuine *EastEnders* fan Lenny Kaye to headline a music benefit, and I'd fill up the bill with other Brit expat musicians, who still have some following among rock circles. I thought I'd make an appeal to some of the British fashion designers living in New York, like Stella McCartney and members of Soho House NY, in hopes that they might be missing the goings-on in Albert Square and would like to see the return of Den Watts.

Completely maddening was the inexplicable sheer indifference regarding the campaign on the part of BBC Worldwide, whose responsibility is purportedly to sell BBC programmes to the US public TV stations, but obviously they gave up long ago trying to make *EastEnders* a success in this country. Since they would be the beneficiaries of such an effort, one would think they'd take a bit more interest in seeing us succeed.

Also somewhat disheartening has been WLIW not being able or willing to admit that perhaps it has been going about *EastEnders* the wrong way all these years. At the 18 January 2005 WLIW Community Advisory Committee meeting in Plainview, Long Island, WLIW management explained that the cancellation decision had been made "to best serve the audience and station goals."

In 2003, *EastEnders* generated $12,468 for WLIW after six days of on-air fund-raising, and in 2004, $11,805 after ten days. I asked rhetorically, "Then how is it possible we were able to collect more than $18,000 in less than two weeks without any on-air promotion whatsoever?" When I suggested we could work together to maximise the *EastEnders* audience for WLIW's gain, I was told by an advisory board member in no uncertain terms that I should just worry about the 31 January deadline.

Similarly, when I tried to get Dr. William Baker, who heads WLIW parent public station WNET/Thirteen, to listen to my view that perhaps Thirteen (the nation's largest PBS affiliate) might be a better home for *EastEnders*, I was told this was solely a matter for WLIW to handle.

Looming on the horizon was what effect the potential loss of a New York outlet would have on *EastEnders* for the rest of the country. When the series was in danger of being dropped nationally in 1995 (when WLIW saved the day by picking up the show from the defunct WNYC—a true lifesaver, and all credit to them), the BBC talked about the need for a New York-area station to make *EastEnders* viable elsewhere on public television in the US, especially since the New York market paid a heftier license fee than other markets. A BBC source said the loss of WLIW would not be a good omen for *EastEnders'* future in America. In addition, public TV stations next year must abide by FCC rules requiring close-captioning of all programmes. *EastEnders'* weekly doses might be cost-prohibitive, the source surmised.

Perhaps it was *EastEnders'* uncertain future for all US residents that was partly responsible for the 18 contributions (of a total of 307) from outside the New York area, including an extremely generous $1,000 gift from the Minnesota EastEnders Fan Club. Jean Brooks, who empathised with our plight and saw it as foreshadowing what the Twin Cities could soon face, thank you!

My heartfelt appreciation also goes to:

- Carolyn Weinstein, *EastEnders'* company manager, who gave us for auction autographed cast member cards, as well as two copies of the *Radio Times*, one signed by Leslie Grantham (Dirty Den) and another by Nigel Harman (Dennis Rickman). Carolyn also provided a letter certifying the authenticity of my Albert Square street sign autographed by the *EastEnders* cast, which I was prepared to auction via eBay. As it turned out, the highest bid was way below the minimum, therefore held onto it. As one interested bidder noted, "You never know when you're going to need it again" [for fundraising purposes].

- Jan Austin, the biggest *EastEnders* fan I know on the West Coast, who was invaluable in tapping her network of *EastEnders* collectors.

- Soho House New York's Jo Addy and Carrie Snitcher, who both showed great hospitality at our benefit screening. Carrie, by the way I learned, once was the girlfriend of Paul Nichols (Joe Wicks).

- Nathaniel Roberts, the proprietor of Fiddlesticks, who hosted several of our events.

- The following companies provided complimentary DVD boxed sets that were auctioned off: New Video (*Monty Python Megabox*); First Run Features (*The Up Series*); Blue Underground (*The Allan Clarke Collection*); BBC Video (*Coupling: Season 3*); and Sony Legacy (*The Clash: London Calling 25th Anniversary Edition*).

As publicity mounted on both sides of the Atlantic (including an online endorsement from *Vanity Fair's* James Wolcott), I realised that this campaign could turn into my "15 minutes of fame," epitomised by a NY1 Time Warner Cable news report on 28 January about all of Google's new features when I caught a glimpse of my name being Googled on the screen.

I look at myself as sort of an *EastEnders* advocate, representing a constituency of thousands of US-based disenfranchised fans, not taken seriously by the BBC's powers-that-be, who for the most part are faintly amused by our enthusiasm for their creation. They wonder why we're not rather watching *Desperate Housewives* or the latest Hollywood reality TV fad. Rest assured, I will continue to lead that mission, and hopefully wake up Auntie's honchos at Broadcasting House in London to the attractions of this would-be lucrative export.

. . .

EastEnders Fans Reverse Cancellation, Once Again

By Larry Jaffee

EastEnders will remain on WETA, the public television station that serves Maryland, Virginia and Washington, D.C., through 2008, though it came very close to biting the dust. This marks the second time in two years that *EastEnders* fans reversed a decision to cancel the series by privately raising the money to cover the BBC's licence fee. The WETA fans put together more than $50,000 entirely on their own.

WETA never acknowledged on the air that it had decided to cancel the show; nor has it mentioned that it has been renewed—as was the case with WLIW in New York in January 2005. The latest effort was spearheaded by Washington lawyer Michael Gordon, who contacted the *Walford Gazette* in June 2006 once he discovered WETA's plans to pull the plug on *EastEnders*. A core of fans materialised, and once again proved the power of the people. Among them was Judy Hallett, a professor of classics specializing in Latin language and literature, who has taken over from Gordon as spokesperson of the successful effort.

"This is a very nice victory. Michael was very unsure that we were going to make it [the 15 January deadline to raise $50,000 in about six weeks]," Hallett told the *Gazette* about two months after the series was saved. "I had no doubt once I met the other *EastEnders* fans—true believers—even after [WETA] upped the ante [requesting the fans to come up with the second year's licence fee]. I knew we had to stay positive. We had nothing to lose," she said.

Hallett agrees that having *Washington Post* columnist John Kelly write about the fans' plight might have caused WETA to consider the cancellation decision a bit more seriously, but she also wonders if the reason Kelly paid attention to the story in the first place was because the journalist was interested in what she taught. "Kelly wanted to know why a classics professor is an *EastEnders* fan," Hallett explained. Other newspapers and media outlets in the UK, including *The Mirror, The Sun, Metro* and *Sky News*, also covered the story, and BBC Radio interviewed Gordon.) Hallett says it's important for the fans to stay together and "energized," but she still doesn't know if WETA's management has learned at all from what has transpired. "WETA needs to be a better listener. They're so unaccountable," she adds.

Washington fan Mary Ellen Stroupe, who financially supported the campaign, praised the fan group's leadership as being "very professional and organized." The end result was "fantastic. I thought it was well worth it to support the effort, although I think it was extortion [on WETA's part, especially to demand the second year]. The fans left no stone unturned. No phone call unmade."

• • •

BBC Gives Peggy Online Sendoff US Fans Can't See; BFI Disses EE Again

By Larry Jaffee

(Editor's note: The following was published in 2010.)

The BBC is sending off Peggy Mitchell in style. Barbara Windsor announced nearly a year ago that she would retire from playing the popular character that has been so central to *EastEnders*, and her last episode will air in the UK on 9 Sept. 2010 (US public TV broadcasts are six years or more behind what BBC1 airs, so we'll have Peggy a good bit longer.) The official BBC website did a great job coming up with various online features under the umbrella "GOODBYE PEGGY MITCHELL," but the problem is—with the exception of YouTube clips of some classic scenes—they can't be accessed outside the UK I really can't think of a good reason why the BBC feels it needs to deprive American fans of seeing Ms. Windsor explain in an interview how she feels about leaving the job she's had for 16 years, or what are her personal favourite Peggy moments. We also don't get to see Peggy's greatest "slapdowns" with various other characters.

Meanwhile, a feature article in the June issue of *Sight & Sound* magazine sounded promising enough. Published by the British Film Institute (BFI), the article "The New Golden Age of British TV Drama" some 3,000 words and four pages later did not have even one mention of *EastEnders*, which this past spring took home the BAFTA award for Best Continuing Drama Series.

The article, written by BFI curator Mark Duigid, focused on the perception that the US produces better drama, shows like *Mad Men* and *The Wire*, and *The Sopranos* before them, created and nurtured by American pay cable networks like HBO.

Duigid's *EE* snub is not completely surprising, considering the BFI's

dismissive attitude of soap opera in general and *EastEnders* in particular. A decade ago, *EastEnders* didn't even rank among the BFI's poll of
the 100 Best British TV Programmes; it finished No. 132 (*Coronation
Street*, No. 40). In fairness, all the BFI did was tabulate the industry's
choices. Ballots were given to 1,600 programme makers, performers,
writers, technicians, executives, critics, academic analysts, historians,
activists and archivists.

And mind you, *EastEnders'* poor showing in poor showing in the
BFI TV 100 came three years after it won in 1997 the Best Drama
award (not Best Soap Opera) from the prestigious British Academy of
Film and Television Arts (BAFTA).

A recurring theme at a September 2000 public discussion at the
National Film Theatre to review the poll's results was the glaring omis-
sion of *EastEnders* from the list. An industry panel and audience members at the event concurred that the series is so easily taken for granted
as the result of its omnipresence in the tabloid-driven British media.
Or could it be a snobbishness that can't fathom that a serial could be
anything other than 'lowbrow'?

John Yorke, current Controller of BBC Drama Production, comments: "Historically 'soaps' have tended to be excluded from these
things. I lose no sleep!" (Maybe not over *EE* not getting respect, but
perhaps over the constant threat of government budget cuts?)

Former *EastEnders* writer Andrew Collins, currently film editor of
the BBC-published *Radio Times* weekly magazine, had a lot more to
say: "I read that article with interest, as it shone a rare light of positivity
on British TV drama, and countered the raving pro-Americanism that
characterises much writing here about TV drama. (I am an unashamed
fan of the best US TV drama too.) I had never considered any prejudice
against soaps at the BFI until you mentioned it. You do still encounter
critical resistance, because soap is still regarded as practical, populist,
schedule-filler, used by broadcasters as a guarantee of regular audiences,
hence its heavy marketing on all the big terrestrial channels. Because I

no longer watch *EastEnders* I am unable to comment on its current quality. But certainly when I was there, in the early part of the decade, some brilliant writing was being produced, under huge pressure. And had been since the start. I still rate the two-handers and, in Dot's case, one-hander, of Tony Jordan. The fact that he has moved from *EastEnders* to writing and producing big populist BBC drama like *Life on Mars* and *Hustle* probably means he will continue to struggle for critical kudos. Critics will always focus on one-off drama on TV here. Or even big fiveparters like *Criminal Justice* or *Five Days*. The event stuff. Soap just rolls on, critically unnoticed and unloved, three or four or five nights a week, and is watched by millions of people. I don't take it personally."

The BFI didn't always view soap with such derision. In 1987, it published *Public Secrets: EastEnders and its Audience*. And in 1981, as part of the BFI's *Television Monograph* series, a group of academics studied *Coronation Street*. Both books examined television's role in society and the reasons behind soap popularity.

For better or worse, *EastEnders* is the closest we can get on our home screens on both sides of the Atlantic to the kitchen-sink realism of the "golden age of British drama," circa early 1960s.

Favourite Beatles Songs of The EastEnders

Dirty Den: "Good Day, Sunshine"
Frank: "Tax Man"
Kathy: "Lady Madonna"
Dot: "When I'm Sixty Four"
Colin: "You've Got to Hide Your Love Away"
Lofty: "I'm A Loser"
Rachel: "Please, Please Me"
Hattie: "She was just seventeen*"
Mandy: "She Came In Through The Bathroom Window"
Mark: "I'll Cry Instead"

* We know the song is entitled "I Saw Her Standing There," but that way the joke doesn't work

– Dan Abramson

V

FANDOM

Growing Up With Barbara (Peggy) Windsor in England

By Estelle Lazarus

Barbara Windsor
c/o Peggy Mitchell
EastEnders
Albert Square
London E20, UK
Dear Barbara:

I have been watching *EastEnders* since it started in New York way back in 1987. When you arrived on the scene I was delighted. You brought a touch of glamour to the cast and a somewhat biting tongue.

Most of all I was happy to brag to my very good friends down at Tea & Sympathy, our only authentic English restaurant in this fair city, that not only did I go to school with you but we were also very close friends for a while. I think we were about nine years old at the time and we attended Church Street School in Stoke Newington. We were in Mr. Coward's class and I believe also in Mr. Lugg's class. I am not sure how I remembered these names from all those years ago. But now I am writing to you some of the past is coming to the forefront of my ever-waning mind.

I lived at 35 Stamford Hill, which was on the main road opposite all the stores, not far from Stephen's Department store. If I am correct you lived in a prefab in Bouverie Road and I thought you were so lucky that you had your own house. I know we both visited each other's house to play. In those days, kids of our age went everywhere by ourselves. If my memory serves me right, I also recall that you went to Madame Bahannas dance school (I am not sure if that is the correct spelling).

149

Once, again I envied you because I wanted to go to a dancing school too, but circumstances prevented me. Another thing I think I was too shy. I had been an extra in films when I was six to seven years old and I wanted to be a movie star.

Well, you achieved what I wanted you appeared in several movies, shows, television but during this time I was not envious anymore just proud that you had made it and that we had been friends. I don't remember when and how we lost touch. Maybe it was when we went to different high schools. I remember we had a friend named June (I can't for the life of me recall her last name). Another friend of mine was Marion Malinskey but I don't know if she was your friend too.

In any event, when I was not quite twenty years old. I emigrated to the United States, to find fame and fortune. Achieving neither, I am still here; I didn't even get married.

At one point, I worked as a personal secretary to several celebrities. One of them being Anthony Newley, who I know joined the cast of *EastEnders* last year for three episodes towards the end of his life. His character has not reached New York yet, as we get the series about two years later. It really saddened me when I found out he passed away this past spring, as he was a very nice person and I had enjoyed working for him even for such a short period.

While working for Tony here in New York, it was during his Joan Collins period, he and Joan had a party to which I was not invited but you were. We spoke on the phone and at that time you said you remembered me. We said we would try and meet but a couple of days later we met by accident at the offices of Weissberger & Frosch, attorneys for many celebrities I had to pick up some papers and you were there, of course, on business. You were going back to London so we never really got to talk at length. By the way, Tony was in New York with Leslie Bricusse (and Yvonne) his co-composer, for the Broadway opening of *Stop The World*.

Since that time obviously we have not met, but one day if you come to New York, perhaps we could meet and have a cuppa or more at Tea & Sympathy. Or, if I get home (as I still call London after all these years) we could see each other there. I haven't been to London in four years but hope to go again sometime. My Mum now lives in Finchley.

Please let me hear from you so that we can reminisce. I also think we know many people in common. For instance, I am good friends with Shirley and Don Black of *Born Free, To Sir With Love, Sunset Boulevard,* etc. Also, after being a secretary for a few years I graduated to becoming a publicist for several years, as well as managing a recording studio.

As it happens it was just yesterday when I was at a taping of a show about New York-based *EastEnders* fans, the director, David Cumming of September Films, told me that he was going to interview you this week in London and that you were recording an album.

Hope to hear from you soon, let me know either way if you remember any of this.
Best regards,
Estelle Lazarus
New York, NY

• • •

Angie Watts Found in Florida!

By Melissa Berry,
Western North Carolina EastEnders Fanatics President

Ahhh! The joys of air travel! I woke up the morning of March 13th to fog and drizzle. Naturally, the flight out of PTI was delayed and when we landed, I hit the concourse in Charlotte running—they had already been boarding my connecting flight for ten minutes! But I made it! Chest heaving, I handed my ticket to the attendant—I was going to Miami to meet Anita Dobson!

When I got to Miami, it was 87 gorgeous degrees outside! Thirty minutes later, I was pulling up in front of the hotel right in the middle of South Beach and one block from the Atlantic! Life was good! The hotel is a 1939 art deco classic that is owned and has been restored by renowned fashion designer Todd Oldham. Beautiful potted orchids are everywhere and the ambiance has a very eclectic feel.

About 7 p.m. that evening, Chris Mitchell, the producer of *East-Enders Revealed* rang me and asked if he could "pop over for a chat." Within minutes, he was there, in a t-shirt, khakis and BAREFOOTED! Chris filled me in on the filming that had taken place that day, and told me they had just returned from filming on the beach, where he said Anita became a bit emotional. (The bits they were filming dealt with Angie's life since leaving the Square.) The he told me about the next day's schedule and my part in it all. First, Anita was going to be shopping in Bel Habour for a dress for Liza Minnelli's wedding in New York. Then they were going to be filming our Ange "driving around Miami" in a rented Cadillac.... or pretending to be driving, I should say! Then about 5 in the afternoon, myself and a few new *EE* fanatic friends would be gathered in the hotel restaurant gabbing about *EE*, and in would walk Anita!

Then came the bad news.... Chris didn't want me to see Anita before the actual filming. He said the "surprise element" wouldn't be there on film if we had met prior. So, we struck a deal: Chris would put in a word for me with Tony Jordan so that I could get on the *EE* set in August, and I would stay out of sight until the next afternoon.

Jim, Jan and Dayle and I met at the hotel about 3 that afternoon. We sat out on the patio and talked about our favorite programme and got to know each other. I said it then, and I repeat it now: it doesn't matter where I go, *EastEnders* fans are the GREATEST bunch of folks around.... so easy to talk to.

About 5, Chris showed up and asked us to "hide" in the outside restaurant of the hotel! The film crew was hot on his heels and Chris asked us some questions and let the four of us work off each other with our replies. This was the segment they would air in the UK He says that Brits have a hard time believing that *EE* has such a large following here in the US and that's what they are all interested in hearing about.

Right in the middle of our impromptu chat, who should walk down the steps, but Anita herself! I immediately ran over to her and gave her a big WNC *EE* FANATIC hug! We introduced ourselves, and then I made the comment that the bar was ten feet away from us and that Angie should be behind it pouring us a pint! Anita enthusiastically agreed, and asked the hotel staff if they could accommodate us! Within minutes we were on bar stools and Ange was behind the bar making us all "shandy's"! (half beer and half lemonade!) Oh, the stories she told us! For instance, Willie (Ethel's little pug) was infamous for farting (Anita's exact words). She said that many times they would have to stop shooting a scene because they couldn't breathe! She also told us that she chose all of Angie's wardrobe and that we would be surprised at how small the *EE* set actually was.

Anita told us that all the beer in the Vic was real but the liquor wasn't and how sometimes the extras in the scenes would be wobbling in the background from too much ale! She told us that Roly was an amazing dog, so well behaved and acted on cue—much better than even some of the cast at times. Other anecdotes included when Angie was contemplating an affair with Tony Carpenter, the producers wanted her to kiss Tony in the Vic. Anita said she informed them that Angie wouldn't **** in her own house! (she very discreetly whispered this to all of us!) and she would have no part of it!

She said she doesn't watch *EastEnders* any more due to her busy schedule, but she did mention that had it not been for *EE*, she doesn't think she would ever have met her husband, Brian May (formerly of the rock group Queen). She said that being in Miami and filming this episode of *EastEnders Revealed* has been the closure that she and viewers alike needed to end hope of Angie ever returning to Albert Square.

Filming was over, but was it the end? Not a chance. Anita sat around with us for about two hours! We talked about everything! She told us how nice everyone had been in Florida. She told us she never managed to find that perfect dress for Liza Minelli's wedding but that if we saw any footage of it, she would be dressed in either red or blue!

She told us that earlier that week, the BBC had surprised her with her own episode of *This Is Your Life* and that so many of the cast (past and present), such as Letitia Dean, Leslie Grantham, Gillian Taylforth, Gretchen Franklin and Pam St. Clement to name a few had been the subject of the show.

Anita is so sweet and so amazingly easy to talk to. Within minutes, I felt as if I was talking to an old friend. She posed for countless pictures as she looked through my *EE* autographs and other memorabilia that I had brought along. She signed autographs, and she was amazed at the things we remembered about the early years of the show. Her favourite memories being those of Den giving her the divorce papers on Christmas Eve, and the episodes filmed in Venice when Den found out she had been lying about being ill.

I told her that I had some mail for her from fans here in the States who wanted her to know how much they enjoyed her work on *East-Enders*. She wanted to see them immediately! She read through some of them, and I saw tears in her eyes as she put them away. She told me she would read them on the plane going home. I told her that I only thought of the idea to collect them the night before I left and that I was sure there would be more when I returned home. She made me promise to send them to her, and I most definitely will. I had taken some of our WNC *EE* club wear with me to give to her. Two t-shirts (Brian had to have one too, after all!), a tote bag and a cap. She put the cap on and said she would wear it on the plane home! I apologized for having only large sized t-shirts, but told her that I HOPED she would wear it at least ONE night to sleep in. She turned to me and said: "I love big t-shirts to sleep in!" I thanked her for being so sweet about it, and she said: "You don't believe me, do you? Melissa, I WILL wear this to sleep in!"

And you know what???? I believe her!!!!!!!!!!!!!

• • •

Cindy May Be Long Dead, but Michelle Collins Remembers Her EastEnders Fans in New York

By Tim Wilson

Whilst lathering up in the shower on the morning of January 9, 2005 another of those brilliant ideas came flashing through my already over-burdened pea-brain.

The very fact that this occurred as I was in deep recovery from severe jet lag following my return from London 10 hours previously struck me as something of a miracle. However, the idea turned out to be a direct tie-in to the impending NYC arrival of one of my all-time favourite *EastEnders* actresses, Michelle Collins (Cindy Williams Beale).

Michelle, thanks to Larry Jaffee, the *Gazette's* editor supremo and chief spearheader of the "Save *EE*" 2005 campaign, had graciously accepted an invitation to make a personal appearance at an Irish pub in Manhattan named Fiddlesticks in order to help raise some funds for our cause.

I was extremely excited at finally getting the chance to meet Ms. Collins in person. We had actually met once before over the British TV airwaves when I provided a question to be answered by her for a short-lived BBC morning programme of dubious quality entitled "Open Air."

It was a quite amiable question, really: "Why is it that virtually all of the male characters on *EastEnders* are henpecked (and in some cases, cuckolded) by the female characters?"

Ms. Collins was seemingly neither amused nor charmed by my question. She didn't skip a beat, and shot back with: "Well, Tim from New York City, USA, why SHOULDN'T we get to play strong women? That's how they are in the East End, anyway. Soaps in this country revolve around strong women, actually. Soaps are about conflict and high drama, and strong women characters are great at providing that. Is it any different in America? Well? I thought not!" Her feisty retort signaled to me that she and her character Cindy were perhaps not all that different!

I couldn't wait to meet this lady in the flesh, especially since I'd heard such great things about her over the years from Larry as well as mutual friends such as *EE* scriptwriter Tony Jordan and actresses Gillian Taylforth and Pam St. Clement. So I was determined to make my dicey/dodgy idea a reality when we finally would meet that night-and prayed it wouldn't have an adverse effect on our honored guest.

I staggered off in the freezing cold to Fiddlesticks, still jet-lagged but obviously gathering up enough adrenaline to keep the fatigue at bay for at least the next few hours.

I was greeted there by Larry, who left to collect Michelle from her hotel. and we met to discuss plans for the event with Nathaniel, the owner of Fiddlesticks and an all-around swell guy whose graciousness and generosity towards our endeavour should never be underestimated.

I told him I had an idea, and wondered if could he help me out with it. "There was this song, y'see, called 'The Bitch Is Back'," I informed him. "It was played on the Queen Vic jukebox as Cindy made her stunning reappearance back there in 1997 or thereabouts. I think it was performed by Elton John. Do you have a tape or CD of it that we could play when Michelle arrives?"

Nathaniel replied there was this great new innovation called "downloading," and he definitely could have it played when needed.

And, sure enough, the song played on the sound system as Michelle arrived. She heard "The Bitch Is Back," looked up and with typically sublime timing, cracked: "Is that intentional? Because I certainly hope it is."

"Result!" as the Brits are fond of shouting after something finally goes right. Not only was Ms. Collins chuffed at the gesture of playing "The Bitch Is Back," she whispered to me at the end of the night "It's the LITTLE touches which make the difference!"

Michelle looked absolutely fantastic. She was accompanied by her movie star-handsome Welsh fiance Parry Cockwell, as well as an English woman friend who's been residing in NYC for several years.

They were, of course, warmly greeted by all of us who were lucky enough to attend this terrific event. She sat down for a bit and various attendees walked up to her and introduced themselves.

For someone who seems so extroverted on the surface, Michelle, like many actors, is actually a bit on the shy side. She was charmingly reluctant about participating in a formal, *Actors Studio*-like Q&A session hosted by Larry, adding, "I'll probably run out of things to say!" She never did, of course, once the informal questions started flinging in from the audience. She flipped through an *EastEnders* anniversary photo book, which *EE* devotee Lizzie Yacoubian handed her to autograph. It was like a stroll through memory lane for Michelle.

"Wow, I've never seen this book before—so many great photos!" She came across a photo of Cindy holding her baby twins Peter and Lucy. I asked her if she'd seen the show recently and she said she hadn't. I informed her that the show had very recently brought on a gorgeous little 13-year-old actress to play Lucy, who was definitely intended to become a Mini Cindy. Michelle was tickled by that.

"I couldn't stand working with those babies!" she laughed. "All they did was scream and puke! I guess they gave me plenty of experience when the time came for me to raise my own little girl, Maia, though!"

Michelle thumbed past a photo of Carol Harrison (Louise, Tiffany's mum), and Lizzie and I remarked on the amazing facial resemblance they share. "You could be her slightly younger sister," I innocently offered.

Ms. Collins lovely eyes suddenly transformed themselves in a squinty picture of mock fury and she hissed, "SLIGHTLY YOUNGER?"

I realized Ms. Harrison was probably nowhere on this continent let alone in this pub and quickly modified my opinion, "Uhhhhhh.... I meant BABY sister!" Michelle grinned and admitted she and Carol were actually good friends and frequently went out socially. "She's a very nice lady," said Michelle, "albeit a maneater!"

I told her about our "Open Air" experience. She thought that was very funny, adding "I'm a lot less like Cindy now. I guess we were a lot alike then in some ways. The writers were uncanny in being able to incorporate our own personalities into the characters!"

I reminded some of my other friends there who were at the event (like Lizzie) that Michelle was not just a former *EastEnders* actress, but a huge star in the UK due to her leading roles in the series *Sunburn* and *2,000 Acres of Sky*, as well as television films such as International Emmy-winning *The Illustrated Mum* and *Can't Buy Me Love*. The latter, in which she played the wife to Martin Kemp (Steve Owen), attracted nearly 8 million UK viewers.

Michelle agreed that if Martin had been on the show at the same time as she was there would have been amazing chemistry. I suggested a Steve/Kat/David/Cindy/Mel storyline would have helped the show get ratings comparable to the Den/Angie days. "I think you could be right!" she agreed.

She remembered sitting in a car on the set of that TV movie and telling Martin that the show's higher-ups never even told her that her character was being been killed off in childbirth. He filled her in about how they staged a fiery car explosion so his character could never return—the BBC apparently doesn't take kindly to actors leaving *EE* to do other things—look at poor Tiffany! Martin capped the story off with "Perhaps we'd better be careful in this thing!"

Michelle told us she was on her way to Los Angeles later in the week to meet a very high-powered agent recommended to her by her own very high-powered

London agents. It was at that moment that I came up with another brilliant idea (no shampoo required this time): she should be added to the cast of that massively popular new US series *Desperate Housewives*. She has the perfect look, she's the perfect age and she could be a big asset. Michelle gasped, "YES—that show just started going out over in England. I'd LOVE to be in that."

At the Q&A session hosted by Larry, which Michelle reluctantly agreed to do after overcoming her initial shyness, I brought up *Desperate Housewives*. I declared my intention of campaigning to get her on that show. After all, Cindy was the original Desperate Housewife! Michelle openly supported my idea, claiming it would be a great way to introduce herself to the mainstream American audience.

This exchange at the event turned out to be picked up somehow by the British media but it made it sound like she was making an overt pitch! Michelle doesn't have to make overt pitches for anything, career-wise—if it would happen it would happen through her talent, vivaciousness and all-round fabulousness.

I asked her a LOT of questions, so much so that I did feel at one point I was hogging the event a bit. I asked her about the "duf-duf." "The what?" Michelle asked with a puzzled look on her face. I explained that that was what we here in the US *EE* fan community used to describe the tom-tom sound at the end of each episode—was she excited when Cindy got a camera close-up followed by the "duf-duf?"

"Ohhhhhh, WE called it the 'dun-dun!' Yeah, it WAS pretty exciting. All of us loved being able to get that but it was also considered a big responsibility because we were the focus of that episode's cliffhanger. Actually jealous feelings got started up as to who would get more 'dun-duns' than others! Some NEVER got 'em!" She said the last bit with a wicked smile. We all laughed.

I asked her if she'd seen the episodes containing Cindy's funeral. "They never even told me she DIED! I was in Portugal shooting *Sunburn* and didn't even get a phone call about it by the BBC or anything. And I was still working for the BBC! Thanks for letting me know, fellas! I was a little miffed by that. Oh, well. No, I didn't get to see the funeral episodes, either. I hear for those they brought on my poor mum as well and a sister I never even knew existed!"

I told her the episodes were very good in that they really explained the essence of Cindy via her mother Bev and sister Gina—Cindy was never some brazen hussy out to destroy men, she was simply craving the love she sought and wasn't able to get from her roguish daddy Tom. I reckon he looked a lot like Ian MacShane—I certainly would have tried to bring him on as stunt casting if I was producing *EastEnders*.

"Ooooooooh, good casting, Tim," Michelle responded. "And, yeah, I agree with that character assessment of Cindy. The press made her out to seem like this insatiable slapper because it suited their purposes but there's a reason she fell hard for both Wicksy and David. I strongly suspect they reminded her of Daddy!" She giggled a bit at this.

Another fan asked which actors did she like working with the most and which ones did she not like to work with—Michelle demurred on the latter, adding. "Oh, that wouldn't be nice so I'm not saying."

I suggested Adam Woodyatt (Ian Beale) but Michelle sternly rebutted, "Absolutely not, Tim. Adam was really good to be with—we had a great chemistry as actors as well, and it showed."

She told us she loved working with Michael French (David), but was totally baffled by someone (probably me) who followed up by declaring that there are many on the Internet who are totally enthralled by the way David chewed on his toast. "That sounds rather kinky!" she exclaimed.

One bit of *EE* casting trivia probably none of us knew about was that Michelle could have been an original cast member if Julia Smith had seen fit to cast her as Punk Mary, Annie's mum. However Ms. Smith and co-creator/writer Tony Holland both wanted Mary (real name Theresa) to be Walford's initial fish-out-of-water on *EE* so it was decided that Mary should hail from the North of England. "Needless to say I'd have been a very different Punk Mary!" Michelle surmised.

The Q&A session ended and Michelle went off to have photos taken outside Fiddlesticks by fans as well as by some of the British press. One of them was taken on top of a New York yellow taxicab! She was asked by one compatriot to have her photo taken with some Union Jack bunting. She refused flat-out and I initially thought she'd rejected the idea as being too corny. I later found out it was because it is considered extremely dodgy to pose near representations of the Union Jack these days because it would be equivalent to supporting the BNP (British National Party), an extremely nationalistic, racist political organisation. She's a smart cookie, that Michelle—don't mess with her, fellas.

Now, on to my campaign to get her onto *Desperate Housewives*, the phenomenally successful ABC TV series. I've dashed off a letter to the series' creator/writer Marc Cherry. I look forward to that 10 percent commission someday, Michelle.

• • •

My Dinner With Wendy—
Star-Struck Fan Remembers to Curtsy

By Sherry Lehman

(Editor's note: The dinner described occurred in 2000.)
A few short weeks ago, a group of hardy, longtime *EastEnders* fans were invited to dine at the well-regarded Indian restaurant Dawat in Manhattan with Wendy Richard, our own Queen of *EastEnders*; that is, our own Pauline Fowler, Mistress of the Launderette, dispenser of service washes and much ancient wisdom and Albert Squarean lore.

Come sit here with me, I'll put the kettle on. Yes, the one, the only,

Wendy Richard, famous from *Are You Being Served?* and of course, known to us as the wife of the late, lamented Arthur Fowler, and mother of three of Walford's most shining lights.

The restaurant chosen for this occasion was not your East End curry takeaway, or Ian's chippie, oh, no, mon frère, this place was even fancier than the one where Carol and Bianca dined on a girls' night out, that time they almost got picked up by two young blokes.

At about 5:30 someone called out "There she is!" and we scurried to our seats. As Wendy and her companion John came in, I just had to do something, so I walked up and shyly presented her with the (now wilted) flowers I had brought. (It might have been better if I had waited until she got herself settled, as she had no choice but to put the flowers on a ledge behind the seats). And, speaking only for myself, I had the urge to curtsy, as if in the presence of the Queen. As she accepted them she asked my name and gave me a hug! I was over the moon! She appeared more petite than on TV, and looks years younger! Her "looking" older on TV is evidence of her acting ability—the way she totally inhabits the character of Pauline Fowler. After all, what many of us like most about *EE* is the fact that the show is not full of the plastic-looking overdressed characters we see on US television.

At one point, Wendy admitted she just had to step out for a cigarette, or two, and a few of us joined her, even those not smoking. Outside she told us several funny anecdotes. I regret not having the "bottle" to ask her about "our 'Chel," and if she still keeps in touch with Susan Tully (who so many of us miss).

Wendy gave us all our choice of two terrific signed photos. In one she is dressed up like a glittery rock star, and I wanted to make some remark that would show her how well I knew the show, so I said 'Gee, Danny Taurus wouldn't know how to handle you if you looked like that?' [OK, lame, I know, but you try thinking on the spot!]

Best of all, when she bade us farewell, after several hours of fine food, pleasant chat, and really delicious deserts, she and John walked out to our spontaneous applause and standing ovation, and the rest of the diners wondered what honoured and beloved personage they had just been privileged to see.

Next visitor to our shores? David Wicks? C'mon Larry and Tim: Get busy!

• • •

Pam St. Clement Stayed At My Hotel!

By Suzanne Campbell

In December, WLIW/Channel 21 of Plainview, NY, hosted its winter fundraising drive. I was fortunate enough to be invited down to New York City to participate. Pam St. Clement (Pat Evans) agreed to fly across the pond to help roust up *EastEnders* fan support for the station. Rumour had it that, surprise of surprises, Ms. St. Clement would be staying at my hotel, which would be quite the Happy Coincidence (for me, anyway), almost too good to be true.

I came back to the Hotel Excelsior late Tuesday evening after an after-hours meal at NorthWest (where I also happened to run into Buckaroo Bonzai himself, Peter Weller). Imagine my surprise when, as the doorman at the hotel opened the door, I saw the Grand Dame herself, Pam St. Clement (elegantly wrapped in a beautiful full-length white coat), checking in at the front desk.

As my husband patiently waited by the elevator admiring the Christmas tree, I made my move. Sauntering over to the front desk, I asked one of the desk clerks about attaining tickets to *The Rocky Horror Show* at Circle in the Square and/or *The Nutcracker* at Lincoln Center. While the clerk told me about the theatre brochures across from the counter that I already knew about, I tuned in to Pam and her conversation with the other desk clerk.

Not that I was eavesdropping (she was staying on the eleventh floor), but one cannot help but be a bit curious standing arms-length away from someone they've cherished watching for over 10 years on their favourite show. I was aghast to hear her name mispronounced by the hotel staff. Rather than publicly flogging the erroneous employee, I waited for my moment.

As Pam turned my way, I knew my moment had arrived. Deep breath..."Excuse me Ms. St. Clement? Pam St. Clement?"

"Why yes I am" (look of surprise on her face). "I'm Suzanne LaFrance and I write for the *Walford Gazette* and it's such an honour to meet you!" "Oh! It's nice to meet you!"

After several moments of light conversation (me in a semi-daze in which I'm sure my face was three shades of red, I realised that she must have been jetlagged, and let her go. After saying hellos to Tim Wilson, who was accompanying her to the hotel from the airport, I said my good-byes.

The next night we drove out to what seemed like the farthest reaches of Long Island to the TV station. Once there, we went through the standard "how to take a pledge" training, then settled into the Community Room to wait our turn for a shift in the studio.

Unfortunately, Al Gore's concession speech/George W. Bush's victory speech interrupted the scheduled *EastEnders* marathon. Other than a few callers insisting on talking to Ms. St. Clement herself—which wasn't possible—the fundraising went quite smoothly. As Pam walked into the studio, fans bristled with excitement, eagerly awaiting her presence.

Once in the studio, Pam and Laura Savini, the WLIW on-air host for the evening, chatted during breaks between programming. She also auctioned off several autographed t-shirts and, much to the viewers' delight, an authentic pair of Pat's earrings, big and sparkly as one would expect. The final prized items for the evening: two autographed *EastEnders* scripts for episodes not yet seen by US audiences. I'm proud to say that I took the winning bid for the bigger script. I didn't tell the chap on the phone that he was bidding against me.

The highlight of the evening was the Q and A session between Pam and Ms. Savini. Larry Jaffee, my husband J.D., myself and all the other *EastEnders* fans present that evening were invited to be in the studio while the interview took place. Pam chatted with Laura about *East-Enders*, about the differences and similarities between her and her alter ego, Pat and about Pam's involvement with animal rights activism.

Upon the completion of the interview, fans flocked around Pam, showering her with autograph requests, photo opportunities and Christmas presents. She was gracious, poised and warm, letting everyone have their moment.

We drove back into Manhattan, an ice storm nipping at our heels, safely deposited back to the Upper West Side. As we waited by the elevators, who should stroll in behind us, but Pam. She seemed to have had a lovely time that evening. She asked of our culinary plans, to which she seemed surprised and a bit interested that food delivery was still an option. I gave her the name of the pizza parlor and we parted ways for the evening. The next day when we upgraded our room to a suite, the bellhop escorted us and our luggage to the elevator and pushed eleven. Happy Coincidence.

• • •

Well, Hey Y'All!"Alfie Moon's Tarheel State Adventure

By Claire Meyerhoff

(Editor's note: The following occurred in August 2009.)
Just like the dashing Alfie Moon, North Carolina EastEnders fans met Shane Richie as he dashed, literally, across the United States. Richie and *EastEnders* co-star Josie Lawrence were on their last leg of the BBC's

"Around the World in 80 Days" celebrity challenge, raising money for the BBC Children in Need Appeal.

Their North Carolina fans dashed as well, on a steamy August evening, converging in Fayetteville from all parts of the state, and from even more exotic locales like Cleveland, Ohio. More than thirty fans gathered at Fayetteville's Mash House Restaurant and Brewery, waiting several hours before the BBC crew's arrival. This gave them plenty of time for much-needed *EastEnders*-centric conversation and to do something that North Carolina *EastEnders* fans are famous for: raising money.

A fast whip-round of a red hat netted the handsome sum of $510, and plans were made on how to present the donation to the dynamic duo of Shane and Josie. Just as they finalized their plan, the BBC crew's mega-bus pulled into the restaurant parking lot. Since they were gathered on the outdoor patio adjacent to the parking lot, the fans were able to witness one of the greatest events in state history; the moment Alfie Moon stepped onto North Carolina soil. And they went wild.

"Well, hey y'all," Shane Richie greeted the crowd, with his best "Alfie does an American" swagger. By his side was the lovely, gorgeous, witty, fabulous and extremely friendly British actress/comedienne Josie Lawrence, known to many for her appearances on *Whose Line is it Anyway*. In another time and dimension, known as Albert Square in 2009, Josie plays the artsy femme fatale Manda Best.

"You don't know me then, do you?," asked Josie, absorbing the mind-bending fact that US fans are living in Ye Olde Walford. Shane picked right up on this, wondering out loud what the fans knew—and what they didn't.

(Attention to those who cannot tolerate spoilers; continue reading at your own risk.)

"So you haven't seen Kat and Alfie get married then?" asked Shane. "Oh, there's so much to come!" he teased.

Even though they'd been traveling America's highways for eight days, including stops in Atlanta and Memphis, where they dressed as Elvis impersonators (that's what a reporter understood them to say), Shane and Josie happily answered a barrage of questions. They also had many of their own questions for their North Carolina fans.

"Who are your favorite characters?"

"Do you get *Coronation Street* here?"

"What's the big one over here, "*The Young and Restless?*"

This last question prompted the fans to give a quick lesson in the ways of US TV ("that's a daytime soap! It's not the same!!!") and the harsh realities of being an *EastEnders* fan in the United States.

"Shane and Josie truly seemed taken aback," said longtime UNC-TV viewer Rosemary Buerger of Fayetteville. "We let them know the fans raise upwards of $50,000. a year here in North Carolina, and they were really amazed by that. I think it was then that they probably realized that this wasn't your ordinary fan base."

While North Carolina *EastEnders* fans are generous with their contributions to UNC-TV, they're also known for their southern hospitality. At one point in the evening, Shane expressed a bit of worry over an impending hurricane, Mary Duke Barnwell offered him accommodations at her home in Wilmington, North Carolina.

"Ah, you'll be my Kat for the night," replied Shane, with that Alfie Moon grin. "Just a little more red lipstick, darling!"

Shane stayed in what seemed to be quasi-character, cheeky-Alfie mode, but when a fan tipped her red hat to him, uncovering a wad of cash, announcing that it was for Children in Need, Shane was quiet serious. "This means so much," he said.

Shane, Josie and the BBC crew spent several hours with fans at the Mash House. They took care of "official duties" including exchanging gifts (Shane and Josie brought autographed signs; fans presented *EastEnders* shirts they had signed), taking photos, signing autographs. Yet, they also spent a large part of the evening "off camera" just chatting with everyone, sampling some American food and beverages.

After their US trek, Shane and Josie were set to board a cargo ship back to the UK

"I'm the only woman with twelve men," said Josie. "I better grow a mustache."

On November 20, Shane, Josie and five other teams of British celebrities will head to BBC studios to find out which team raised the most for the BBC Children in Need Appeal.

• • •

London Actor Waits for His EastEnders Break After Brushes With Numerous Castmembers

By Larry Jaffee

English actor Peter Kosta knows dozens of actors who have been on *EastEnders*. He wonders whether his chance will ever come. We met at a Morningside Heights café near Columbia University in New York when the actor was on holiday in New York in late February. We discussed his theatre career, which has involved many brushes with such thespians as Michael French (David Wicks), with whom he once shared a dressing room, and Nicola Stapleton (Mandy Salter), whom he met when she was promoting Peter Pan at a function where Kosta was playing Roland Rat. "We had an immediate rapport."

And his CV includes an appearance in the British TV series *Sunburn* (1999), which starred Michelle Collins (Cindy Beale), whom he knew when they were both starting their careers and working at a London call centre. "A few years later, she made it big in *EastEnders*. When I auditioned for *Sunburn*, there was Michelle, and we chatted about the old days," he said.

"All of these connections always cross my mind. Yet I've never been in [*EastEnders*]! I've never got a chance to play a part. I've auditioned a couple of times [at *EE*] for various things, but never got anywhere. It's just amazing when I look at my life, how often I crossed paths with *EastEnders*. I'm not complaining."

Kosta is also friends with Harry Landis (Felix Kawalski)—Walford's one-time local barber. "I know him (Landis) very well," says Kosta, who has watched *EastEnders* religiously since the very first episode. He once picked up a charity contribution from Wendy Richard (Pauline Fowler) at her home, where he caught a glimpse of her ceramic frog collection. Kosta played Puss to Debbie Arnold's Princess in the pantomime Puss in Boots. She was April Branning in *EastEnders* (1995–1996). Another friend of his, Pamela Cundell, played *EastEnders'* Nora Swann, the ailing mother and grandmother of characters Mike Swann and Dawn Swann, not yet seen on public TV in the US "[Nora] died [in February 2006]; they killed her off after five episodes."

Another new character, Shirley Carter, who arrived in Walford in December 2006, is played by Linda Henry, who was Potiphar's contin-ued on next page continued from last page wife to Kosta's Potiphar in Joseph and the *Amazing Technicolor Dreamcoat*.

Kosta notes that he sees Ross Kemp (Grant Mitchell) "all the time on the Kings Road" in Chelsea, where Kosta lives. At Pinewood Studios, he's also met John Altman (Nick Cotton), whom he called "a lovely man," when he was promoting the fabulous musical adaptation of *Fanny Hill* by Ed Dixon, which was presented at the York Theatre in New York.

Like most actors, Kosta has a regular job between acting opportunities, making travel arrangements for transatlantic college exchange students, which allows him to periodically visit New York. When he was in college, Peter knew Pam St. Clement (Pat Evans) quite well. "I'll always be eternally grateful to Pam for suggesting a song cycle of four Greek songs, which I've used to audition. It's got me jobs." Actor Dennis Waterman, star of the original UK series *Minder* and father to Hannah Waterman (Laura Beale), also went to Kosta's college. Shane

Richie (Alfie Moon) is starring in a new remake of *Minder*. "When I was on a national tour of *Happy Days*, the musical, Shane Richie was dating a member of the cast. He came to my birthday party when we were in Manchester." Also in the cast of *Happy Days* was Stephen Dean, the brother of Letitia Dean.

Yet another *EastEnders* connection for Kosta is through Elaine Lordan (Lynne Slater). "I just finished a Christmas show called *Cindefella*, in which I played an Ugly Sister, with Elaine's cousin Kevin Lordan playing Cinderella. He's a very popular drag artist. The girl who played the fairy in *Cindefella* also was a great friend of Barbara Windsor's. When I was in *Cindefella* there was another show running parallel to us in this same little theatre. The young dancer there plays the barman in the [E20] club." And before he became popular in *EastEnders,* French shared a dressing room with Kosta in the "real *Cinderella*, a pantomime in Nottingham."

"Kenneth Williams, one of the *Carry On* team, was a great friend of mine. Of course, he was a great friend of Barbara Windsor's (Peggy Mitchell). Another dear friend of mine, Helen Pearson, who was in three episodes of *EastEnders* in 1990 playing the character April McIntosh, is now one of the leads in [UK soap] *Hollyoaks*." April is described on this fantastic resource within Wikipedia of minor *EastEnders* characters as "a market trader whose livelihood was under threat in 1990 when Walford Borough Council threatened to demolish the Market."

The last time Kosta auditioned for an *EastEnders* part was when they were introducing a Greek Cypriot family, which would have been perfect for him because he's of Greek Cypriot heritage. "My friend Peter Polycarpou got the part, was only in three episodes and never heard from again," says Kosta. In February 2006, Polycarpou appeared in *EastEnders*, playing Yanis Pappas, father-in-law of character Carly Wicks. Kosta notes the only Cypriot who sometimes appears is Mr Papadopolous, who owns the launderette. "He's made the odd appearance. Also, doesn't anyone own a washing machine? That's one of *East-*

Enders' anomalies. The guy who owned the B&B would even bring the laundry over to the launderette."

Sometimes Kosta's civic activism allows him to rub shoulders with *EastEnders* alumni. Edna Dore (Mo Butcher) served on the Save London's Theatre Campaign committee with him. Michael Cashman (Colin Russell), now a Labour politician, was treasurer of British Equity when Kosta was on Equity Council and became a friend. "He is now a member of the European Parliament and I'm still on Equity Council," Kosta adds, with a laugh.

On that same council, he became acquainted with Susan Tully (Michelle Fowler). Michael Leader, who plays *EastEnders'* recurring milkman, is also "a great friend" of his. I tell Peter I've talked to Michael on the phone, and he was reluctant to do an interview for fear of repercussions by the powers that be. "Probably after this interview they wouldn't bother to interview me for anything. Oh well, I'm too old to worry about it. You get to the point where you don't really care any more," he says philosophically.

• • •

Anna Scher: She Launched Many An EastEnder

By Larry Jaffee

Researching the backgrounds of *EastEnders* actors, especially those younger than 50, one name keeps popping up: Anna Scher. Her acting school in the London neighbourhood of Islington provided training for numerous young thespians, many whom ended up having a drink at the Queen Vic.

Here are just some of the names: Susan Tully (Michelle Fowler); Sid Owen (Ricky Butcher); Gillian Taylforth (Kathy Beale); Adam Woodyatt (Ian Beale); Patsy Palmer (Bianca Jackson) James Alexandrou

(Martin Fowler); Natalie Cassidy (Sonia Jackson); Martin Kemp (Steve Owen); Sylvester Williams (Mick McFarlane); Troy Titus-Adams (Nina Harris); Brooke Kinsella (Kelly Taylor); Judith Jacob (Carmel Jackson); as well some of the more recent, such as Phil Daniels (Kevin Wicks) and Jake Wood (Max Branning). It's a virtual who's who.

Reached by telephone by the *Walford Gazette*, Scher is humbled by the success of her former students, some of whom she still is regularly in touch, such as Taylforth, an Islington resident. "We recently had a reunion drink," says Scher, who notes that she's no longer associated with the school that long bore her name and she ran for 35 years.

Scher was ousted from the school in 2000, following a breakdown. But four years later she resurfaced with a new drama programme, dubbed "Anna in Exile," for youngsters set up in a church a few streets away. Her old school, which also grew into quite a successful talent agency, has been re-christened as The Young Actors Theatre.

Although she started out herself as an actress, Scher realised that she received much more enjoyment being a teacher, and launched the school in 1968. "Improvisation is a staple of the work," she explains, as to why her young students have gone onto greater things. "It produces very natural actors."

Scher remembers when *EastEnders* began in 1985, the producers sent around to her school casting agents to observe the classes to find new talent. "Sometimes they would like someone, but it was not quite the right fit for the part they had, so they'd write a part," she adds. "They would watch the actors, and several people made it," she says. For example, Cassidy immediately impressed all who saw her as a 'YP' (young professional), even as a 'tween (she was 11 when she made her *EastEnders*' debut). "We called her a 'second Kathy Burke,'" reminisces Scher, referring to the highly regarded British actress. "Everyone thought, What a fantastic girl!"

Since the 1970s, some of the young actors who were discovered at Anna Scher ended up in *Grange Hill*, the BBC kids programme, whose alumni includes Todd Carty (Mark Fowler) and Tully. "That was the first generation," Scher looks back on those years fondly.

Tully told the *Walford Gazette* in 1995 that she "used to pay Scher 50 pence per lesson to study acting," and that she was still in touch with her former teacher. Patsy Palmer told the *Walford Gazette* in 1995 that Scher herself told her she won the part of Bianca. "The school is a brilliant place for young people to learn about acting. Anna is a wonderful person and the school is an excellent place for kids to really use their emotions and imaginations. It doesn't push them into a career. In fact, the kids there are not allowed to do commercials until they are sixteen. Pretty good policy, I think. Commercials can make kids a bit to spoiled and rich before their time."

Young actors must realise that success is hard to achieve, Scher emphasises, and she urges them to have "other qualifications to earn a living." While Taylforth studied at the Anna Scher Theatre School, she also worked as a secretary before being cast on *EastEnders*.

In the book *EastEnders: The Inside Story*, two pages are devoted to how series co-founders Julia Smith and Tony Holland visited the school on 13 July 1984 to find some talent for the cast. (The series debuted 19 Feb. 1985.)

"The Anna Scher Theatre is in North London. Anna is a pushy, vital Irish woman who takes her adrenalin neat. Unlike a lot of drama schools, where the students are admitted, ironed out and then sent to the outside world as 'actor' all looking and sound like one another, Anna's school cashes in on what the students already have, themselves. She doesn't flatten their personalities or accents even. On the contrary, she encourages them to use them. Her students aren't taught how to act, they're helped to dig in themselves and be. Just the sort of non-acting acting that we were looking for. Every so often the school has an 'open evening.' Julia and Tony had been invited to attend such an evening. They invariably start with a warm-up session that consists of a lot of hand-clapping and a sing-along, during which the audience is encouraged to participate. Then the class split into groups, and various improvisations are staged.

"Not all the participants in the class are new. Frequently old students will drop by just to keep their hand in. On the night that Julia and Tony were there, Judith Jacob had been as good as ever. Susan Tully had been very impressive. Natural and unaffected, she had expressed hidden depths of emotion inside herself. There was a third person who had caught their attention. Gillian Taylforth, a stunningly attractive blonde, slightly older than most of the others. But it wasn't her looks, or the range of her acting skills that had drawn them to her. It was her voice."

Martin and Gary Kemp thought so highly of Scher, based on the eight years of training they received from her when they were kids, that they went back to her for private lessons for a few months after they were already cast to play the Kray brothers in a feature film. Remembers Martin Kemp in his autobiography *True*, "I walked out of Anna's that first day with mixed feelings of excitement and fulfillment that I hadn't felt in years.... She taught me important lessons for life. Her big saying was never forget your three P's—Professional, Punctuality, and Point of Focus."

Losing The School

A 2004 article in *The Guardian* detailed the "Kafkaesque" situation in which she warned to not use her own name for any rival acting programme she might be considering.

According to the article, Scher was not offered her job back, but in September 2002 she was invited to return to the school to teach two classes a week. The following December she was offered the opportunity to continue to teach if she agreed to an 86-point plan from the new school's chairman.

Among her objections, according to *The Guardian*, was this stipulation: "The method of delivering the drama is to be controlled by the director under the overall authority of the trustees. The content of classes must follow the object of the charity, namely education through drama for young people. Classes cannot be used as blackboards to advance issues such as peace studies, discrimination studies, or the like." Scher was steadfast to not do anything different from how she'd always done things. "I said, 'No way, read my lips, there is no way I'm going to sign this.'"

The training that Williams received while a student at Anna Scher inspired him to start his own acting school in 2001, Characters, as he explains on his website. "I wanted to create something that had the feel of a club, but the qualities of any well renowned Drama School, like for instance, Anna Scher's Theatre, was a club, but had the discipline and educational value of a good school."

Since leaving *EastEnders*, Williams has taken active steps to regenerate inner-city London by starting a drama school and an actor's agency that encourages arts and positive creative action in deprived areas that has also extended to other cities around England. "Anna would take kids off the street. Her legacy could never really be forgotten," Williams sums up.

• • •

British Dramatist Hanif Kureishi [Wrongly] Sees No Link to EastEnders in His Work

By Larry Jaffee

Hanif Kureishi has been one of Britain's favourite dramatists for the past two decades, as novelist, playwright and screenwriter. He recently received excellent notices for his screenplay for *Venus*, a cinematic tour de force for Peter O'Toole, who was nominated but criminally overlooked for a Best Actor Oscar. Venus reunites director Roger Michell

(*Notting Hill*) with writer Hanif Kureishi (the pair also worked together on *The Buddha of Suburbia* and *The Mother*).

In 1995, following a BBC screening in New York of *Buddha*, Kureishi granted a telephone interview to the *Walford Gazette* that has gone unpublished until 2007. The *Buddha* began as a novel, a coming-of-age tale from the perspective of a transplanted Pakistani teenager who grows up in early 1970s London under the corrupting influence of his best mate, who ends up becoming a David Bowie-like superstar. The novel was made into a BBC television miniseries but never broadcast in the US The *Walford Gazette* thought it was time to publish this interview, in view of the recent Oscar connection.

Walford Gazette: At the press conference you said that PBS thought The Buddha of Suburbia was "too rude" for American television. Do you see a parallel with the controversy that followed PBS airing Armistead Maupin's *Tales of the City*? I understand that production money was available to produce a sequel to *Tales of the City*, and US public television would not support it (the series subsequently surfaced on pay TV network Showtime years later).

Hanif Kureishi: That's what I was told, and the reason why they wouldn't show *The Buddha*. The advertisers and the TV company had been disturbed by the Maupin thing. *Tales of the City* was incidentally made by Working Title, which *made My Beautiful Laundrette*.

WG: Getting back to *The Buddha*, David Bowie composed the great soundtrack for the miniseries and it was released as a CD in the UK (eventually also released in the US).

HK: I think he was disappointed that the soundtrack album he released didn't do better, but I think he was very pleased with some of the music he produced on the album. I was interviewing Bowie for *Interview* magazine funnily enough, as we were just finishing shooting *The Buddha*. This was in London. We have many things in common. He grew up in the same town in the [London] suburbs as I did. He had been at the same school and had the same teachers. So we started chatting about that, and we started to meet. I asked if he would be interested in doing some music and he agreed immediately. He said he had never done a soundtrack before.

WG: You directed the film *London Kills Me*, and I was curious if you were planning to do any more directing?
HK: Well, I work in lots of different writing areas. I write short stories, screenplays, novels. It's quite a lot to do. Directing is a different art. Although I enjoyed doing *London Kills Me*, I think I'd rather work with other people. I like the collaboration working with other people like Stephen Frears (*Sammy and Rosie Get Laid, My Beautiful Laundrette*) or Roger Michell (*The Buddha of Suburbia, Venus*). Collaboration means a lot to me. With the writer and director together it's sort of like the mad king—there's no one to control or argue with. I don't have plans to direct, but I may do it. There's so much writing I want to do at the moment that I can't see that I could commit that much time to it.

WG: Isn't your new project is about a cabdriver?
HK: Yes, it's set in the north of England. It's about a cabdriver whose son becomes very religious. It's based on a story called "My Son the Fanatic" that was published in *The New Yorker*.

WG: I am actually a son of a cabdriver. My father has been driving in New York for the past 20 years.
HK: Oh really, how interesting. I bet he has some great stories.

WG: He does—everything from getting robbed, helping to deliver a baby and having celebrity passengers like Derek Jeter. I was curious to know whether you followed *EastEnders* at all.

HK: It's on in my house, but I don't really follow it. It's kind of early for me. I'm not really watching TV at that time. But yeah, it does have a big following in England. I find it miserable, and prefer *Coronation Street*. It's funny, more camp.

WG: Does your work have anything in common with *EastEnders*? Themes like maintaining cultural identity in contemporary England, arranged marriages, etc. show up in both.
HK: Maybe, I hadn't really thought about that.

WG: I know in the UK it's considered to be a soap opera. But here in the US, we think it's a serious drama.
HK: (somewhat incredulously) *EastEnders* a serious drama, really? I wasn't aware of that. I think soap operas are different. They just sort of go around and around. I never really thought about it.

WG: I don't know if you this, but Antonia Bird (who at the time had recently made the controversial British film *Priest*) was an early director of *EastEnders*.
HK: Yeah, she directed my first play in 1979. She's a good director. I haven't seen *Priest* yet, but I've known her for a long time.

WG: When you set out to write a screenplay sometimes it ends up taking a different form. For example, Stephen Frears originally thought *Sammy and Rosie* was a TV film.
HK: *Laundrette* was originally made for television. There's a close relationship in Britain between television and cinema because movies in Britain aren't very expensive so they're not far away from television. There are not big stars in England like there are in America. So writing for television or writing for a theatrical release are not different in my mind. I write the same way. My style doesn't change. *My Beautiful Laundrette* was shot on 16mm film made for TV, and it was released in

theatres everywhere. I don't really make a distinction that way. I don't know how you could because my work is mostly about character.

WG: No big-budget sets, then?
HK: My stuff is always cheap.

WG: One difference between Britain and the US is that we don't have a Channel 4 that would finance smaller films. I wouldn't be surprised if a lot of American filmmakers go to Channel 4 seeking funds.
HK: Yeah, I'm sure. There are very few places to go in Britain for films. That's absolutely right. The two main places are Channel 4 and the BBC.

WG: Do you have to be careful when you work with the BBC? I think in one of your books you mention that it had become too reactionary, that they're constantly censoring material.
HK: We had a good time at the Beeb doing *The Buddha of Suburbia*. They took out one shot, which was two or three seconds. They otherwise didn't take anything out, and left alone nudity and an orgy, and allowed us to say f#@k, sh%t and c$#t all the way through, and we never had any trouble. They get a little bit nervous with their broadcast, and the newspaper s attacked the BBC and *The Buddha* a bit. But it got great figures, so that calmed them down.

WG: So is it like the American model—that ratings are what counts?
HK: The BBC is also predicated on quality drama and progressive drama and doing neat stuff. But a bit of controversy does them good as well.

WG: You wouldn't temper any criticism of the BBC in fear of biting the hands that feed you, in the sense that there aren't many places to go?

HK: The BBC has always treated me really well. They're a bit stodgy and conservative sometimes and old-fashioned, but they know that.

WG: I was curious if you heard from Roland Gift [lead singer of the 1980s British band Fine Young Cannibals, who had a featured acting role in *Sammy and Rosie Get Laid*]. I saw him acting in an Edinburgh fringe production of *Romeo and Juliet* about six years ago.
HK: That was the last time I saw him actually. I wondered what happened to him. He hasn't made a record since then, has he?

WG: I was also curious if you had read Nick Hornby's book *High Fidelity* since you're also a record collector.
HK: I read about it but I don't read much contemporary British fiction. It's difficult when you're writing that stuff yourself to read other people's fiction because you can't afford to get their voices in your head. So I keep away from that stuff. I read American writers though, Salinger, Roth, Bellow, Flannery O'Connor, Walker, Kerouac, Ginsberg, Burroughs. Hemingway, Carver. I've always particularly loved American short-story writers.

Post-script: Soon after speaking with Kureishi, I interviewed then-East-Enders producer Jo Ward, and told her about my theory that his writing and Walford have much in common. In addition, early EastEnders director Antonia Bird directed one of Kureishi's first plays at the Royal Court Theatre. Ward, who served as co-producer of Bird's controversial film Priest, replied: "He was probably horrified at you comparing his work to EastEnders."

VI

REVIEWS

VHS Review: 'The Mitchells: Naked Truth'

By Larry Jaffee

The ultimate "two-hander" (*EastEnders* episodes that feature only two characters), *The Mitchells: Naked Truth* finds Grant and Phil in the Queen Vic after closing, saying the things that the brothers have always wanted to say to each other.

Ostensibly an excuse to make some ancillary money for the corporation, the hour-long video has enough revelatory moments to keep any *EastEnders* fan's attention as the bruvvers look back through flashbacks at the nine years they have graced (more like menaced) Albert Square.

A few of the memorable tidbits that spout from the boys who are obviously just looking to wind each up:

- Phil: their mum and dad really wanted Grant to be a girl
- Grant: he wanted to join The Old Bill (police) if he hadn't enlisted in the Army
- Phil: he thought to enlist in the armed forces" for a second
- Grant: he's the better dancer of the two; Phil says he looked like a "deranged pigeon" on the dance floor
- Phil: both he and Sharon made the first move
- Grant: Phil hasn't paid his bar tab. The latter two points may be intrinsically linked. Phil never really has been the same since Grant found that cassette of Sharon talking to Michelle about her affair with Phil while Grant was locked up, and played it for the entire Vic crowd on the night of Kathy & Phil's engagement party.

But then again Phil had always been a moody sod, obviously lonely, perhaps explaining why he hooked up with the likes of Nadia for some companionship. But it doesn't explain why he's doing his best to destroy his marriage to Kathy.

Thoreau's line about "men lead lives of quiet desperation," despite the radical change of scenery (austere New England vs. cockney East End), certainly describes Phil's downward spiral as a drunk. Sure, domestic life (i.e., married with children) is not a piece of cake. There are always diapers to change, meals to feed, mortgages and bills to be paid, kids to take to school, garbage to be taken out, laundry to be done, etc. But that all obviously goes with the territory. In the storyline, Phil never is given the chance to explain what's eating at him, the video provides that opportunity, but we're still left wondering if Sharon really meant that much to Phil. She certainly meant that much to Grant, who has been so desperate to be a father and have a real relationship with a woman that after his brief period of mourning he decides to spread around his brute cheer (and sperm?).

In any case, personally, I always thought the "I married the wrong brother" storyline was a trite device worthy of American soaps. Grant is quite aware that his brother is an alcoholic, and he reluctantly pours him drink after drink because he figure he's safer at the Vic than some other pub. Beware that the programme's flashbacks and montages flash some "spoilers," in which we find Grant in particular having sexual rendezvous with several female characters unfamiliar to us (the UK is two years ahead), so I won't ruin it for anyone. The video climaxes with Grant and Phil's already infamous stripping a la *The Full Monty* to the 1970s disco tune "Kung Fu Fighting," reprising the duo's act one inebriated night (they reminisce) in some pub before they arrived in Walford.

At just the moment that they drop their drawers, in walks an aghast mum Peggy, who wants to know what all the racket is. She thinks what they doing is plain silly, but realizes that it's been such a time since they've both been so gleeful. For me, the stripping was humourous, but what really sent me laughing was Grant's request for Phil to hit him following Grant's admission of lusting after Kathy. Phil, already on at least his third drink, hits him hard. Grant, dazed, says "I can't believe you hit me." Phil reminds him that he asked for it. "But I can't believe you hit me," Grant replies, adding that his older brother shouldn't be thinking that he knocked him out or anything, that it was a lucky punch. Phil's like, "Yeah, whatever."

It's a testament to these two actors, Ross Kemp and Steve McFadden, that they're as believable as brothers. In a serial like *EastEnders*, characters are usually able to develop only as far as the scriptwriters allow. We've always figured that Grant and Phil to be carrying some mental baggage, but rarely find out how they evolved into their current states. *The Mitchells: Naked Truth* was released only in the UK, meaning that it will be unwatchable on American TV sets. But resourceful online fans will be able to purchase the tape from various British Web sites and then have it transferred to the US NTSC transmission standard. It's also interesting to note that *The Mitchells: Naked Truth* is only the second official *EastEnders* video to be packaged by the BBC. (The first dealt with the *Den & Angie Years* and was reissued under a different name a few years ago.)

A final editorial comment: The *Walford Gazette* on several occasions has pleaded to the BBC's video and licensing executives to consider an *EastEnders* home video series for North America, only to be pretty much ignored, which is a shame considering that there's obviously a market for such material. Why haven't more videos been available for *EastEnders*, which is the BBC's most popular, longest-running programme in its history, especially given the BBC's marketing acumen of recent years (e.g., *Absolutely Fabulous, Keeping Up Appearances, Are You Being Served?, Red Dwarf, Teletubbies*, et. al.)? Sure a soap opera requires some tinkering and repurposing of previous material, but Granada never has had a problem coming with videos for *Coronation Street*.

• • •

DVD Review:
Peggy First Emerged in 'Sparrows Can't Sing'

By Larry Jaffee

As Barbara Windsor leaves *EastEnders* after 15 years of playing Peggy Mitchell, I thought it would be fun to take a look at her first major show business success, as co-star of the 1963 British film *Sparrows Can't Sing*, which I was able to watch on my multi-format DVD player via a PAL disc I bought from Amazon.co.uk. The movie opens with a young Babs sitting in a window sill, singing her heart out to the whole world or no one in particular about life's disappointments. You can see the opening scene on YouTube.

Everything we love about Peggy is reflected in what seems like a younger version of her. One wonders why the *EE* creative team never made use of Windsor's singing voice. (She recorded an album. The camera then scans down to various East End slices of life, capturing the sights and sounds of a cockney neighbourhood not unlike Walford, and it was filmed in the real East End borough of Stepney. The story settles onto Babs' character Maggie finding out that his errant husband Charlie has come home after two years at sea. Meanwhile, Maggie, mother to a baby and another toddler, has set up a new household with a bus driver named Bert, who's also married to someone else. A few years behind and not affluent enough to reflect the coming "Swingin' London" scene, this tight-knit community seems to know everyone's business and is quick to protect its own (e.g., Maggie). Charlie's reemergence causes waves in the hood. Apparently he and the missus have had a stormy relationship, and one assumes when the heat in the kitchen became too hot Charlie signed up for a two-year merchant seaman stint. Now he's back to claim his woman, and pick up where they left off.

Charlie walks the dramatically changed streets with his suitcase, packed with gifts from his travels. Surveying what looks to be a casualty scene from the Nazi blitz during WWII, he asks, amazed, "Where are all the houses? This used to be my street." Many houses, including Charlie's former residence, have been cleared out for high-rise apartments, signifying London's changing appearance. Building tension, the first half hour of the movie deals with Maggie's relatives and friends trying to shield her from Charlie, who's not having much luck locating his spouse. At one point, he knocks on the flat of a large West Indian family with the sounds of calypso filling the room, whose jovial head, a dead ringer for Patrick Trueman in his younger days, produces not the Maggie who Charlie is looking for. It's all fairly light-hearted and comical.

Behind another door another ethnic group is engaged in a dance class. Charlie visits her employer, a Jewish caterer and his mother, who claim that Maggie doesn't work there any longer, and they're unaware of her address, not fooling anyone, the least being Charlie. The scene reflects the East End's once Jewish flavour, and again the city's cosmopolitan melting pot. Charlie ends up back at his old stomping ground—the pub—where he no doubt caused more than one drunken disturbance, and he gets more reactions from the punters, "Oh no, here we go again." When Charlie and Maggie finally do reunite, she attempts to fend off his romantic advances, gently protesting that she wasn't counting the days he was going to return from his journey. On a second impromptu encounter on the street, while Maggie is pushing a pram holding their daughter, she cracks almost immediately when an over-the-moon Charlie surmises he's a dad.

Even Maggie doesn't believe her brief claim that Bert got her pregnant while Charlie was at sea, a testament to Windsor's range of emotions within a few seconds. Despite feeling a little guilty over how good Bert has been to her and the babies, Maggie's ambivalence about the entire situation lasts less than two minutes when it's obvious she still has strong feelings for her errant spouse despite his drinking and womanizing. She's still not over Charlie, no matter what fireworks are in store for the combative couple.

As often happens in *EastEnders'* Queen Vic, the love triangle reaches a showdown at the pub when Bert unexpectedly makes an appearance. He realizes that he's powerless, and comments to a bystander that he was planning to go back to his wife any way. Among the extras in the last pub scene were the notorious East End gangsters, the Kray brothers, with whom Windsor was friendly in real life at the time. (More *EastEnders* trivia: Martin Kemp a/k/a Steve Owen co-starred as Reggie Kray in the 1990 film The Krays with his brother Gary after their 1980s hair band Spandau Ballet ran its course. They recently wrapped up a reunion tour.)

Sparrows Can't Sing was based on a play, whose director Joan Littlewood also directed the film at a time there hadn't many female directors. In her 1998 interview with the *Walford Gazette's* Tim Wilson, Windsor marvels how "*Sparrows* somehow captured people's imaginations." Windsor tells how she was brought over to New York for the 1963 premiere for publicity, and appeared on *The Tonight Show* with Johnny Carson. "I was really feted and it was a marvelous experience all the way round. The reviews were fantastic. It was this cockney film that opened at some little artsy cinema and caused quite a buzz."

Windsor is right about the reviews. *The New York Times* singled her out for playing the "pint-sized wife with all the perkiness and eccentricity of a bouncy English sparrow."

The New Yorker called the film "a smasher.... a hurly-burly of sight and sound, we're swung from dock to slum to park to pub on the whirling wheelpin of East London." Its critic Brendan Gill wrote: "Not a moment strikes me as unnecessary." When it debuted theatrically, *Sparrows Can't Sing* was also notable for using subtitles for American audiences. A few weeks after it opened at the Manhattan art house cinema, some viewers complained the cockney dialect was too difficult to understand. Some even suggested dubbing over voices the British voices with American actors, but the film distributor wisely decided against that approach. Wrote *The New York Times'* critic Bosley Crowther: "This isn't a picture for anyone with a logical mind or an ear for the English language. The garble of Cockney spoken here is as incomprehensible as the reasoning of the characters who speak—and that's profound."

• • •

Michelle Collins: Life After Cindy
Play Review: 'Rattle of A Simple Man'
DVD Review: 'Two Thousand Acres of Sky'

By Larry Jaffee

(Editor's note: The following was published in 2004.)

Michelle Collins is among a fairly small group of *EastEnders* actors who have gone onto other memorable roles on British television, others being Martin Kemp (Steve Owen), Tamzin Outwaithe (Melanie), and Ross Kemp (Grant Mitchell).

Although known primarily for creating Cindy Beale, Collins' other telly credits that have demonstrated her versatility for drama include two series of *Real Women* (BBC1), *Daylight Robbery* (ITV), *Uprising* (ITV); three series of *Two Thousand Acres of Sky* (BBC1), the two-part series *Perfect* (ITV); *Lloyd and Hill* (ITV), *Ella and the Mothers* (BBC1), *Sea of Souls* (BBC1), and *The Illustrated Mum* (Granada/Channel 4). Of course, none of these have hit US television screens.

And like many other *EastEnders* castmembers, Collins also has enjoyed a successful London theatre career, the latest being a West

End run this spring of *Rattle of A Simple Man*, in which she played an unapologetic prostitute named Cyrenne, who brings home a nervous, first-time client, Percy (played by Stephen Tompkinson, perhaps best known for the film *Brassed Off*).

But even as the programme for the play notes, "As Cindy Beale in *EastEnders* she created a memorable character that the public either loved or hated and which established her reputation for play tough contemporary women who also have a touching vulnerability."

That description easily fits Cyrenne, the embodiment of early 1960s swinging London with her hip mini-dresses and penchant for records by Dusty Springfield, whom she (and Collins) physically resembles. (Collins, in fact, would like to play the late singer in a biopic film.)

Cyrenne likes the independence that comes with her chosen profession. But it's the adoring attention from Tompkinson's 40-something virgin that brings to the surface the unhappiness over her lifestyle and the shame that it has brought to her family.

Although they still haven't consummated the purpose of Percy's visit over the course of the play, Cyrenne is willing to take a chance on running away with Percy, and the audience comes away with the feeling that this relationship—even though they couldn't be more different— might successfully turn out to be a loving long-time couple.

Like Cyrenne, Abby—Collins' character in *Two Thousand Acres of Sky* (recently released in the UK on DVD)—is also hopeful about escaping her depressing environment, this time working dead-end jobs and in a housing estate bringing up two kids alone. *Two Thousand Acres of Sky* is precisely the kind of engulfing drama that should be running and promoted on BBC America.

Abby is convinced she must leave London when her 9-year-old son's school principal calls her at the grocery store she works as a clerk about her son bullying another boy. Her boss tells her she can't leave to take care of the situation; Abby tells him he could stuff his job.

Abby then comes across a newspaper advert from the small Scottish island of Ronansay looking for a family with at least two children so that they can keep their school open and continue to receive government funding. The too-good-to-be-true opportunity also comes with a complimentary house.

The only catch is that Abby must also have a husband, for which she drafts best mate and neighbour Kenny, a would-be rock star, who already serves as something of a father figure to her son and younger daughter. Kenny is amenable to the charade—even sort of likes the idea. He is sort of a slim, guitar-toting version of *EastEnders'* Nigel, a sweet bloke—not entirely smart, not entirely stupid—with a heart of gold but who every once in a while says the wrong thing at the wrong time.

Kenny's miscommunication with the island's gossiping ferryman, Gordon, about how Abby would do anything for her kids is a case in point. Kenny innocently dropped that Abby worked in a "tapas bar"; Gordon thought he said "topless bar," resulting in Abby having to convince the small community that she was not a prostitute. (Americans are often thought of not understanding the British vernacular; it's funny to think that a Scotsman can't make out what a Londoner is saying.)

Two Thousand Acres slowly builds during the first four episodes, as Abby, the kids and Kenny getting acclimated to their surroundings—sort of the like the Fresh Air kids from the big city. But early on, it's obvious that Alistair, the good-looking local fisherman, has caught Abby's eye, and his reciprocal wayward glances suggest that the feelings are mutual. The only problem is that Alistair believes Kenny is Abby's husband. In the fifth episode all hell breaks loose, thanks to a visit from two of Abby's friends from London, Jackie and Donna, both whom can't understand why she's moved to the middle of nowhere.

Jackie is engaged to be married (for the third time), and she lets on that she doesn't really love her 60-something fiancé, who loves to give her nice things and is good with her children. They later celebrate Jackie's hen night (British bachelorette party) at the hotel.

It's in these scenes where *Two Thousand Acres'* writing really shines. The girlfriends get to be catty, daring to say to each other all the things that they've always thought but never expressed.

Like Abby, Jackie thinks Alistair is gorgeous, and propositions him to spend the night. Although flattered and tempted, Alistair turns her down, perhaps because he's afraid of what Abby might think. Jackie then turns her attention to Kenny, who she thinks quickly sizes up as the only other male around worth shagging, even if she never quite fancied him before. Kenny has been grappling with celibacy since Abby has made it clear that although they're best mates she doesn't think of him that way. Therefore, it's not surprising that he succumbs quickly to Jackie's advances.

The next morning Jackie shows up in the hotel's restaurant in search of a cup of coffee just wrapped in a sheet and a hangover, while Kenny sheepishly scampers back into the room once realising they're not alone.

The entire island is convinced Kenny is a cheating cad, and Abby is furious at him for not being more discreet. As Kenny is about to board a ferry and leave the island for good, Abby comes clean that they're not married. She's sorry that she lied but if Kenny goes, the whole family goes. Abby prevails, having won over the island with her integrity intact once again.

In the first episode, Abby figures out that the island already decided on another family. Making an impassioned plea with the locals about how she was trying to improve her childrens' lives, they get to stay (partly because the other family turns out be religious fanatics). In any case, it's show-stopping scenes like these that demonstrate Collins' ability to carry a programme.

On the two-disc DVD release's extras, Collins explains how the series was devised with her in mind, and how rewarding it was to seen it borne out from the treatment stage. It's clear that she truly relishes playing Abby. Maybe it has something to do with Collins being a single mom of a daughter in real life.

There are two more series of *Two Thousand Acres of Sky*, which gets even more complicated now that Abby and Alistair are able to share their true feelings for each other and Kenny is still feeling like a third wheel.

According to the official BBC website, All the exteriors are filmed in south west Scotland. The majority of the interiors are filmed at Elstree studios, which must have been interesting for Collins since she spent so much time there for *EastEnders*.

While other British TV series have delved into the city vs. rural lifestyle differences (e.g, *Ballykissangel*), perhaps the show that *Two Thousand Acres of Sky* is most like is the US's *Northern Exposure* (1990-1995), whose protagonist was Joel Fleishman, the New York doctor who's forced to move to a small Alaskan town of Cicely because they paid for medical school.

The similarities in character types between the two shows are uncanny. Douglas, the pseudo mayor of Ronansay, recalls Maurice Minnifield, the ex-NASA astronaut who is Cicely's founding father. Cicely's good-looking single dude Chris is matched by Ronansay's fisherman, Alistair. Cicely's romantically frustrated pilot Maggie O'Connell has a Scottish counterpart in Carolyn; both attractive single women even sport short hair (at least Carolyn's a redhead).

Next up for Collins is co-starring with Martin Kemp in an ITV drama *Can't Buy Me Love*. The project is to begin filming in September and due to air late this year or early next year. Based on a true story, it's about a guy (played by Kemp) who makes out to his wife (played by Collins) that he's won £9 million on the lottery. The whole lie snowballs out of control, and he ends up buying houses and cars. The script has been written by Tony Jordan, long-time *EastEnders* head writer. Collins tells the *Walford Gazette* that she's especially looking forward to it because she has not previously worked with Kemp.

• • •

Book Review: 'Kathy & Me' by Gillian Taylforth
Bloomsbury Publishing, 1995

By Dan Abramson

Devotees of that great lady known as Kathy Beale will have a field day reading the memoirs of her non-fictional persona, Gillian Taylforth. The book, titled *Kathy & Me*, deals at length with the terrible scandal that she unfortunately was involved in last year (and which we at the *Walford Gazette* have been too classy and dignified to deal with at length in these pages).

However, the true intellectual reward from this book derives from the insights it provides into the mind of Ms. Taylforth, and the fact that she does not seem to understand just how marvelous a performance she has been giving now for over a decade as Kathy.

Taylforth—who is too modest for her own good—seems to be under the impression that "*EastEnders* is just a soap opera," and that Kathy Beale is no more than a nice lady who used to sell fruit and now runs a luncheonette.

Repeatedly through the book, she makes light of her own talents and of the collective artistry that has gone into the creation of Kathy. Referring to the central incident of Kathy's onscreen life, she states that "I didn't actually do any research—as some of the others might have, such as meeting and talking to people who had been raped—because there wasn't time. One week I was raped, the next week I was getting over it, and the week after that we had moved on to a new plot line."

Personally, I found this paragraph to be a colossal shock because I am of the opinion that Gilly/Kathy's recovery from that violation over the next few years was one of the finest jobs of acting ever recorded on television. There was the matter of Kathy's decision to prosecute the rapist against the advice of a humane police woman, who warned that the effort to prosecute might prove to be a more horrible experi-

194

ence than the rape itself. (This turned out to be true—and Taylforth's communication of Kathy's need to do so in order to continue to be her niece Michelle's heroine was a scene of gut-wrenching brilliance.)

Following the rape trial, I seem to recall many months of story-lines involving Kathy's literally kicking out of bed Pete, her husband of two decades, her emotional castration of that unfortunate fruit & veg fellow named Laurie, and her eventual happy one-night stand with the ex-cop and publican, Eddie Royle. There was then an even-better subplot involving Kathy's friendship with Eddie and his fiance, the tall, willowy Irish lady named Eibhlyn, and Kathy's Good Samaritan emotional support of Eibhlyn after Eddie got murdered. And then there was Kathy's involvement with Disa O'Brien, that unwed teenaged mother who had been raped by her stepfather. I could go on and on.....

The fact that Ms. Taylforth does not look back on these as significant events growing out of the rape (and does not seem to fully understand how beautifully she emoted in those plotlines) is mind-boggling. Either she is the greatest intuitive actor of all time or the writers and directors at Elstree have done a good job of manipulating a mannequin.

Further puzzlement derives from the fact that the actress' real-life childhood memories are so fundamentally different from the fictional early years of Our Kath. It was carefully spelled out early on that Kathy had been an abused child who was raped-and-impregnated at 14 and then forced to give birth and put the unwanted child up for adoption.

Taylforth describes her own early working-class family where everyone adored each other and the most savage punishment was to be grounded for a week. No doubt Gilly is telling the truth about her own childhood. My question is where in the hell does she derive the emotional resources and intellectual experiences that make her so astoundingly convincing as Kathy?

Just what a truly great novelist or screenwriter could do with this concept of a happy lady who does not understand her gifts as a tragedian! Since Taylforth apparently wrote this book to help pay off the legal fees that derived from that scandal, let's hope she does get to sell the, screen rights as well. In fact, this would be the perfect first movie role for Letitia Dean, who just stopped portraying Sharon.

• • •

CD Review: Barbara Windsor

By Suzanne Campbell

A combination of big band and ensemble jazz, melodic romance and smooth torch, Barbara Windsor's self-titled album is a must-have for *EastEnders* fans.

A sparkling, colourful collection of catchy pop standards, this album will please viewers of all ages. Ms. Windsor's voice is equal parts chanteuse silk, snazzy big-band gusto and pop-friendliness. It is a collection of songs spanning several decades, songs I recall my parents playing on their old turntable in vinyl form. Songs that many sang along to on their transistors in the 1970s and still hear in the piano bars of today.

On the fan-curiosity side, Dame Windsor's album will be a fine addition to any *EastEnders* collection, which we all have, be it large or small. For those who are just starting to collect *EastEnders* memorabilia and merchandise, what a great place to start.

This album captures a refined song-stress we never knew lurked behind the brassy surface of Peggy, the tough-as-nails Mitchell matriarch.

One of the highlights of the album is the swinging rendition of "They Can't Take That Away from Me," a duet sung with singer Joe Longthorne, "the spirit of show business decanted into a dinner jacket." Oh, to have Peggy break into this one at the Queen Vic Karaoke night—wouldn't that say it all to the Mitchell naysayers. If they could manage to pick their jaws up off the floor.

In addition to this, the album boasts duets sure to stir giggles of gleeful surprise from *EastEnders* fans. How often does one have the opportunity to hear Peggy and Phil Mitchell (Grant McFadden) sing James Taylor? Not to mention her rousing, flamenco-flavoured rendition of "The More I See You" with Mike Reid (Frank Butcher). It's pure gold, babe.

Barbara Windsor's album is more than a fan-based must-have, however. Her vocal stylings are both fun and elegant. The instrumental arrangements are full-bodied and well-conducted. You'll find yourself remembering scenes from some of your favourite movies.

"You Made Me Love You" recalls *Hannah and Her Sisters*, and who could forget lunch with Rupert Everett in *My Best Friend's Wedding* when "I Say a Little Prayer" begins? I dare you not to tap your feet along to "You're Nobody Till Somebody Loves You."

Ms. Windsor is no stranger to the recording industry. She can be found on soundtrack recordings, and in the early 1960 hit the charts in the US with the title song from the movie *Sparrows Can't Sing*.

Her latest release is an enjoyable album, full of familiar standards known worldwide, peppered with Barbara Windsor's own distinctive panache through each number.

• • •

Soap Bubble: 'Dot's Story'

By Tim Wilson

As I sat at my desk writing this review, I had the No. 1 American soap *The Young and the Restless* playing behind me as audio wallpaper. A 45-year-old mystery had been unearthed—a leading character (Kay Chancellor) had at long last realised that another leading character (Jill Foster) whom she'd been at loggerheads with for over 25 years was, in fact, her long-lost daughter.

This revelation, besides being laughable considering the characters' long and twisted history, was played with as much eye-rolling and scenery-chewing as is humanly possible of actors (and that's saying something). However, it indirectly informed me once again why I love *EastEnders*, the No. 1 soap in Britain (okay, it alternates with *Coronation Street* for that honour) so much: because there are many instances on *EE* where there is truthful, heartfelt acting inspired by a good, emotionally honest STORY.

Which brings me to *Dot's Story*, an *EastEnders* "soap bubble" that was broadcast on January 2, 2003 on BBC-1 in a time slot normally reserved for a regular *EastEnders* episode. BBC America, in a typical display of ungenerous programming policy, chose not to show this one here in the US, as they didn't with *Ricky and Bianca* or *Nick and Ashley* [*editor's note: the latter as in Cotton; Ashley was Nick's son*]. It is true that these "soap bubbles" are somehow considered a separate entity to the show itself because they are not shot with *EE's* regular crew. Whatever the reason, BBCA won't show these and those of you who subscribe to this premium cable channel should feel cheated.

I was lucky enough to actually sit down and watch *Dot's Story* as it was being broadcast in Britain during my annual month-long visit to the UK With my feet up on the table and a heated-up Marks & Spencer prawn curry meal in my lap, I lapped it up.

I apologise in advance for revealing "spoilers" that were contained within the episode but I somehow doubt that BBCA, realising the wicked error of their ways, will suddenly say, "Gee, our audience might like to see *Dot's Story* and why don't we just run it."

Dot's Story is quite refreshingly simple, really. Dot (the consistently brilliant June Brown) has been lured from her sister Rose's sickbed in Liverpool by a strange Welshman, Ewan, who gets her to travel to Wales with him to visit his mother, her Auntie Gwen. Long-term *EE* viewers must remember Auntie Gwen as having been the lady Dot stayed with in Wales when she'd been evacuated there from Walford during World War II.

On the train to Wales, Dot begins to recall her time in Wales, and we get the first of many flashback sequences. In them we see a young Dot, probably eight or nine years old, being accompanied on a train to Wales by her mother, a chain-smoking, dead-common harridan, along with several other children. Young Dot (Tallula Pitt-Brown) is a LOVELY child—she's got dark hair, dark eyes and actually looks like a child movie star. She could even be the only slightly less beautiful younger sister to Elizabeth Taylor's Velvet Brown in *National Velvet*. Talk about wonderful casting—I absolutely believed that this kid would grow up to look like June Brown's Dot, and that sort of thing doesn't happen half as often as it should.

Anyway, poor little Dot isn't chosen to go home with any families on the railway once they arrive because she appears to be the only little girl, and farmer families would prefer boys to help with the farming, wouldn't they? This was the first time my eyes misted over watching this, darn them.

But then Auntie Gwen and Uncle Will arrived. It turned out they weren't REALLY Dot's aunt and uncle, they were just fortunate enough to show up late and then reluctantly (at least on Will's part) agree to take on little Dot, much to the nasty mum's satisfaction since she'd get paid for the privilege. Gwen and Will make a mighty fine couple—she's small and attractive in a very warm sort of way and he's handsome in a rough-hewn, Welsh Gary Cooper sort of way. Mumsy gets her pay and swans off, leaving a confused and frightened Young Dorothy behind.

The story returns to Dot in the present, who goes with Ewan to the farm to see Auntie Gwen. It turns out she's far more ill than he said—in fact, she's dying. There's a very sweet nurse looking after her who shyly but rather obviously hankers after Iwan and vice versa—one gets the distinct feeling they'll live happily ever after together no matter what happens. Auntie Gwen sees Dot and turns away—she doesn't want her there. Why did she run off without saying goodbye and never keep in touch?

Here's where the story, for me anyway, got a bit muddled no matter how enthralling it was. It had been established on *EE* (and then mentioned again in *Dot's Story*) that Dot had returned to Wales for a bit when she was a young woman in the summer of 1953.

Remember Dot's recital of that Dylan Thomas poem at Lynne's hen-night dinner? Dot remembered hearing it on the radio when she was in Wales in '53. But it was the young child Dot who actually ran away from the farm (and Auntie Gwen) back in '43 or '44. Her reason for doing this was certainly consistent with the basic, ongoing characteristic of Dot, which has partially defined her all these years on *EE*: her deeply felt religious faith. We find out the "truth" via a flashback.

One night on the farm Young Dot took the family dog for a walk. She took the dog off its leash (or lead, as they call it in Britain) and he fell into an animal trap and had to be put out of his misery by Uncle Will and his shotgun. Dot ran home in agony and wished Uncle Will dead. And death is exactly what happened to Uncle Will later that night—his truck went into a ditch and he was killed as a result. Dot was inconsolable and felt as guilty as anyone ever could. In her mind, it really was her fault that Uncle Will was dead. And so she packed her things and somehow got on a train headed back to London.

Back to the present—Dot and Auntie Gwen achieve a major understanding and reconciliation after all has been revealed by a still guilt-ridden Dot. Auntie Gwen, it turned out, never had a clue why Dot left the farm as a child and never got back in touch-except, mmmm, that time she came back in '53?

Sorry I keep harping on it, but that IS a bit of a plot hole, isn't it?

Did Dot go back to the farm in '53 when Auntie Gwen was off visiting relatives in Scotland or something? But no matter. The very sight of June Brown playing Dot as she faced her past and life-long guilt was sheer beauty to watch, and the actress playing the now-old Auntie Gwen was not far behind her in quality.

In an extremely touching deathbed scene Gwen has Dot on one

side of her and her son on the other and they all hold hands. It is made implicit that it is all right for her to die now because she has both her "children" with her, and she does die. Dot's eyes filled up with tears and so did mine. Dot was, however, obviously grateful that she got the chance to unload the burden she carried for so long and to then be comforted by her beloved Auntie Gwen before her time had come. And a bit more of her faith had been restored in the process by Gwen assuring her ("silly child") that wishing someone dead doesn't prompt God to make it so.

It's been disappointing to me that *EastEnders* has so far chosen not to refer to the events that unfolded in *Dot's Story*. I'm hoping they still have the chance to do so with Dot's faith being challenged once again following a recent physical attack by someone claiming to be from a children's charity. I hope they do. This could only enhance Dot's story, which I hope goes on for some time to come.

She is truly one of the great soap, no, make that DRAMATIC characters of all time (even though she is also one of the most deliciously comedic), and June Brown deserves a truckload of BAFTAs and Soap Opera Awards and everything else for her portrayal year after year.

Having met and interviewed her, I'm very aware of her deep commitment to her character, and wondered how she thought *Dot's Story* turned out. I found myself at the BBC canteen bar a week or so after it had been broadcast and felt tremendously privileged to congratulate her when she suddenly appeared at lunchtime. I kissed her on both cheeks, said hello and congratulated her, and all she did was greet me, look towards heaven and give me a very demure Dot-like smile. That said it all for me, and I didn't need to prod her for a comment. She had a good right to be proud.

Dot's Story was a New Year's treat no matter its faults and it showcased a truly great actress who fully deserved a one-off special of her own. Hey, how about *David's Story* next time, BBC? And BBCA, why don't you run the special show—perhaps in a marathon, along with the others?

• • •

TV Series: 'Barry' Finds Work in Extras

By Kent Gibbons

"Are you havin' a laugh? IS HE HAVIN' A LAUGH?" The preceding quote, well-known to fans of HBO series *Extras*, showed up this week in the funny pages. The comic strip "Get Fuzzy" to be precise. Spoken there by an orange tomcat wearing a Manchester City Football Club cap, in response to a question about whether everyone in England is "foppy." Answer: "No, there's a few blokes in Sheffield who aren't complete spanners."

It certainly demonstrates the power of a potent catchphrase—even a catchphrase from a fictional (fictitious?) television show. A show within a show, if you will, starring Ricky Gervais.

Extras is the latest TV series by Gervais and writing and acting partner Stephen Merchant. Like Gervais and Merchant's original *The Office*, it's destined for a two series lifespan, although like *The Office* it might get a one-off special to wrap up storylines.

Otherwise, the recently ended run on HBO saw the last original episodes. And, unfortunately for digital cable subscribers who get HBO On Demand, for some reason it's been removed from the current on-demand lineup, while the long-dead relic Comeback Kid remains. So it's *Extras* on DVD or nothing for now.

The first season introduced us to Gervais, who works as a movie actor playing non-speaking parts and dreaming of stardom. Merchant, as feckless agent Darren Lamb, and Ashley Jensen as Gervais's fellow sad-sack actor Maggie Jacobs, also were regulars. For me, and maybe for most *EastEnders* fans who watch *Extras*, the highlights of Season One were: A) Ross Kemp's guest role in the first episode, lampooning his own acting aspirations, and B) Shaun Williamson's recurring part as an unemployed actor willing to do whatever odd job Merchant, the agent who likes to unplug his phone, has for him to do around the office.

Sadly, no *EE* principal has a guest bit in Season Two. So the highlights are: A) Williamson and Merchant's Laurel and Hardy act and a notable solo Williamson-as-Barry moment when he's just given an impassioned speech about holding firm to your standards as an actor, only to see his pockets spill out with food he's pocketed for free from the crafts table; and B) David Bowie's impromptu ballad inspired by Gervais's character's big sellout.

Basically, Andy Millman (Gervais) has an idea for a true-to-life, working-class sitcom. It gets embraced and then corrupted by the evil BBC and turned into the kind of program *The Office*'s creator would never tolerate: vulgar jokes, a laugh track and the lame catchphrase the factory supervisor played by Gervais (wearing thick prop glasses and a curly prop wig) has to utter at least once a show. Millman stands up for himself once, egged on by "Barry," whose own version of history is he stood up for himself at *EastEnders* and got fired for it. (In the first season, Kempner is credited with having left the show for a packet of cash at a rival network, an example "Barry" tried to follow and got fired for his trouble.)

One of the best jokes in the whole series is that Gervais's character, Andy, is the only person who ever calls Williamson by Shaun. Everyone else, especially Merchant, calls him Barry. HBO's own *Extras* site identifies the character as "Barry." Williamson's *Extras* bio—which truly reads like a bad *Playbill* CV—notes: "He appeared in several TV shows before landing the part of 'Barry Evans' in *EastEnders*. He regularly appears in cabaret and a Soul Band. He is a versatile and accomplished stand-up comedian, singer and after-dinner speaker. Subject of *This Is Your Life* October 2001. He hosted a live daily quiz for ITV1."

Barry's in every episode of Season Two. He's kind of the equivalent of Gervais and Merchant's podcast foil, Karl Pilkington, whose round head and thick ways turn jokesters Ricky and Stephen into howling straight men.

Extras lures extra special guest stars, like Kate Winslet, Orlando Bloom and Ian McKellen, who against type, as Kemp did. But often it's a painful exercise—Patrick Stewart poking fun at his own sense of self-importance, for example, in the first season was overly broad and unfunny. Daniel Radcliffe, by contrast, was funny this season around as an oversexed young geek, before his truly shocking starring real-life role in *Equus* on the London stage, in which he apparently bared all.

The formula also worked beautifully when David Bowie guested in Season Two's second episode. Gervais had the brilliance to convince Bowie that if he were appearing on the show, he had to sing a song about Andy. Again, thanks to the HBO *Extras* website for some lyrics: "The little man who sold his soul...sold his dreams/The clown that no one laughs at/He sold his soul for a shot of fame/ Catchphrase and wig and the jokes are lame/He's got no style and he's got no grace/He's banal and facile/The little fat man with the pug nose..."

Imagine this sung in a bar, amid Andy's friends and at least one keen rival, while Andy watches from a nearby banquette. Truly wincing. *(Editor's note: It's especially enjoyable knowing that in real life David Bowie is an* EastEnders *fan.)*

And, as *The New York Observer* neatly pointed out before the first (of six) Season-Two episodes aired the debut this season included a Gervais scene that was the equal in poignance to anything in *The Office*. After Andy capitulates, wears the wig and glasses, does the catchphrase, agrees to do anything to get his sitcom on air, his best pal Maggie (played by Ashley Jensen) finally accepts his invitation to attend the premiere episode's filming. After he does his horrid catchphrase, and leaves the stage, and the scene continues. Andy goes offstage but is able to seek out Maggie in the audience.

She looks at him and wanly gives him congratulations because she can't hide her disappointment/ bewilderment. Andy smiles back. Then silently nods his head in shame, for several seconds. Roll credits.

A Brit friend of mine loved the bit in Season Two's final episode when Maggie goes home with a guy she thinks might be Mr. Right—only to find his parents in the living room, playing bridge and more than willing to offer her advice on contraception. Me, I howled at the scene in which Gervais's character catches both Merchant's and Barry masturbating on the job—inspired by a picture of a nude woman in one of those souvenir pens that slide an image back and forth. Another great Merchant-Williamson moment involved a badly botched pick-up attempt at the same bar where Bowie tickles the ivories. Merchant spots two unattended women who also don't have drinks in their hands, and nudges Williamson and says, "you know what to do next." Turns out Barry's best idea is to chastise them for freeloading.

Another came when a punter in the pub recognizes Barry—as the guy who cleaned out the gutters at his mum's house. Merchant, as his agent, is outraged and not receiving his cut of the proceeds.

Variety reported that Gervais and Merchant had confirmed there would be no third season of *Extras*, but that a BBC spokeswoman said they did plan to write a sendoff special.

Here's hoping Barry—who reportedly wanted *Extras* to continue with him in it—gets the girl, or a steady job, in the end.

Favourite Movies of Albert Square Residents
Available on VHS from Nigel Home Video

Grant: *One Flew Over the Cuckoo's Nest*
Sharon: *First Wives Club*
Pauline: *The Perils of Pauline*
Kathy: *Diner*
Nigel: *Debbie Does Dallas*
Phil: *The Mechanic*
Michelle: *The Graduate*
Geoff: *Goodbye, Mr. Chips*
Mark: *The Wild One*
Ruth: *Highlander*
Doctor Legg: *Fiddler on the Roof*
Tiffany: *The Amorous Adventures of Moll Flanders*
Natalie: *Clueless*
Ricky & Bianca: *The Stupids*
Dot Cotton: *Les Miserables*
Ali Osman: *Taxi Driver*
Roly: *Lassie, Come Home*
Mr. Opidopoulous: *My Beautiful Launderette*

– Dan Abramson

VII

EPILOGUE

How EastEnders Saved Our Marriage

By Lenny and Stephanie Kaye

(Editor's note: This article was first published in 1994.)

Is there no one immune to the charms of EastEnders? Patti Smith Group guitarist Lenny Kaye and wife Stephanie reveal the true ties-that-bind. Lenny's comments appear in plain text, Stephanie's in bold.

We're caught up on *East*, as we call it fondly. We must be in pretty good shape as a couple these days. Sometimes it wasn't so easy. We'd be six weeks, eight weeks behind, sorting madly through mislabeled tape boxes, episodes tangled and out of order, trying desperately to catch up and renew the flickering embers of our relationship, reclaiming the rhythms of living together. But even in the darkest hours before the dawn (and the pubs don't open till 11!); we had *East*.

We've come a long way from Reg Cox. Arthur, Den and Ali first entered our living room, kicking in the door of Reg's council flat. Episode One and I was sure our marriage was brown bread. Dead. Reg was. Have to admit Lenny was the one who heard about it being aired on our PBS station, and taped the first three-hour marathon to get us started; l wasn't so sure. When I was in England, I'd gotten hooked on *Brookside* during an especially juicy rape storyline.

That was in '86. We were in Ol' Blighty long enough to get to know PC tea, so I figure maybe we were a bit nostalgic for life in the Square: fry-ups for breakfast, daily tabloid in the morning, Stephie off to see crop circles in Glastonbury while I worked in a Finsbury Park recording studio. But used to American detergents like *All My Children* or Luke and Laura's *General Hospital* with their expensively coiffed monotypes, we were unprepared for the depth of characterization, the realness of East End life, and the slice-of-life characters that could've been you or me. Like Den and Ange.

Like Den and Ange? We were Den and Ange. All right, I'll admit it. I have Luke and Laura's wedding on tape. In my defense, we'd just gotten our first VCR, and we were still in the bliss part of wedded. I thought the sun shined out of Lenny's jacket; Luke and Laura were forever. I forget what happened. I think Laura just disappeared on poor smarmy Luke, only to reappear without him as a tarty perfume heiress in prime time. Illusions shattered; life goes on. He wanted to go on tour; I wanted to go on vacation. He wanted a motorcycle; I wanted a boat. He wanted rice and beans at the Puerto Rican joint on First Street; I wanted brunch in Soho.

Yeah, and if you don't get what you want, sometimes you get what you need. I think that's why they call it male and female: two for the price of one. The thing about *East* is how well its inner family give-and-takes (and sometimes live-and-shakes) mirror your own inner dynamic as a pairing. Certainly Steph and I have played out that legendary episode devoted exclusively to one of Den and Ange's battle royals, upstairs and downstairs at the Queen Vic, but there's also a little of Frank and Pat, Ricky and Sam, Ali and Sue, Lofty and Michelle, Den and Michelle, Clyde and....

Right, so I'm blowed!... to find out we're actually two characters and this script is not being directed the way I'd written it. Where's [*EastEnders* creator] Julia Smith when you need her? Had I pulled a Michelle and married my own ill-fated version of Lofty? Was Lenny actually going to leave the Square to become a handyman in a children's home? Nope. We both stayed put, slagging it out a la Den and Ange, Lenny was doing some of his Jack-the-lad routine, and I spent a lot of time with me mates in New York boozers, legless. About the time the Butchers took over the Vic, I realised we were living in two different soaps. Often for months the only time we were actually was when we were catching up on *East*. We joked that it kept us together, but could we survive the loss of Den and Ange....?

Personally, we found we were able to weather the missing Watts, the disappearing Simon and the reappearing Cindy, Pat's attempt at the cab company's summer that you worked and I stayed at home to mind our very own Vicki/Annalea) while Frank fumed, and the you-can-count-on-it reappearance of Nick Cotton. That must've been when my ne'er-do-well buddy Larry (*Editor's note: not me*) spent three months in the basement. Parallel lives, or great minds run in the same gutter.

Remember when Mandy stayed with Kath? How 'bout Dot's flat after Nigel's birthday party, or the Vic after the fire, or my house after Larry? Yeah, Larry (Lenny's best mate) flooded the basement with my washing machine hose, burnt holes in the couch, was involved in a fender bender while borrowing my car and broke my daughter's new Walkman while attempting to change the batteries. And that was just the first week. At least he didn't try to poison me.

Wrong analogy. Not Nick's mum, but Ethel to my Dot. Friendship is truly like marriage. Anyway, that's all bits and bobs in the annals of true love. What greater adoration can man have for woman than to turn a blind eye when she forgets to tape Den's penultimate murder scene—as my wife did when I was out of town (on the lam)? Was this a way of telling me that I didn't have to perish for Den's sins, that Christ symbol of *EastEnders,* and a symbol to all of sacrifice to a yobbish ideal?

Who knows what archetypal characters lurk in the subconscious urging us to do this and forget to do that. Maybe a call to the Good Samaritans...? But I did it. The unconscionable, the indefensible, the ultimate injustice... I watched it, alone. And I forgot to tape it. Every other petty crime in our marriage pales in comparison. He could have it all: the house, the kid, the dogs, the VCR, the (sob) *East* tapes. I deserved nothing. I could get myself a little flat somewhere, maybe a job in a Laundromat, I could start smoking again...

And maybe I could get a job in the Arches. We all have our happy endings.

He forgave me! But did I forgive him? A year later I'm in Paris

prowling Montparnasse with my friend Sabine. I prattle on and on about the state of my marriage. I need a sign, Sabine. This month is our thirteenth anniversary. I sigh, looking beyond Sabine's concerned face to the neonpink and bug-light yellows of the Place Pigalle. My eyes are drawn to an outdoor table. To someone I recognise. In Paris! It must be an old friend... "Phil" I scream. "Phil Mitchell!"

I have the autograph to prove it. My anniversary gift. Thanks babe. I love you. I guess *EastEnders* really does keep us together. I love you too, honey. Now let's see if *EastEnders* can keep Pauline and Arthur together.

• • •

Gooseberries:
How EastEnders Saved Our Marriage (Again)

By Stephanie Kaye

(Editor's note: This article was published in 2005.)

EastEnders is never better than during its half-hour riveting duets. Well, we finally had our own. We were going at it hammer and tongs, or is that tongues? Granted, it was quite a bit longer than the usual tidy half-hour, but surely the fine editors at East could have pulled out enough cinematic moments to rival Den and Ange's proper old flap, the Dot and Ethel reminiscences, or the Steve and Matthew psychological thriller. In the end it was a tear-jerker a la Bianca's good-bye to Ricky. We decided to split up. "Ba-dum-bum-bum."

The next episode was expectedly dull by comparison. It lasted about five months, and we were decidedly between juicy plot lines. Natalie and Barry are moving back home, Sonia's Italian beau dumped her, Pat and Roy are in money trouble again... ho hum. We lived apart but not much had changed; we still watched *EastEnders* together. Sometimes we even kipped down together after. Just like those episodes when you kind of wish something big would happen, but it's all so cosy nonetheless.

EastEnders understands that a good plot line, like life, or even plonk, takes time to mature. Eventually he had a girlfriend; I had a boyfriend. Sometimes you've got to introduce new characters. His lived in a foreign country, and mine was a Yugoslavian fashion designer that even I couldn't take seriously.

I think we even mentioned the D word, but really we were all talk and no trousers. But word got round that the foreign girl had moved to the New York set. His apartment. Well I couldn't give a monkey's, and a cheeky monkey she was. Just your run-o-the mill Dolly little barmaid.

The gooseberry forever destined for third place in the triangle. Like poor little Lisa, first Matthew's dad and now Phil. The Slav started giving me clothes and shaved his head like Grant. The audience slowly started to warm up to the new characters. If it did work out with these new characters, maybe we would be like Pat and Roy and Frank and Peggy. We could all buy a pub somewhere. And watch *EastEnders*.

But the Slav started asking questions like "Why can't I see you on Wednesday nights?" At first, I felt it was the deepest kind of betrayal to the husband to say the word "*EastEnders*" aloud to the boyfriend. So I said I was watching "my" TV show. But when the foreign girl moved into my husband's apartment, I immediately called the Slav to tell him "my" TV show was "*EASTENDERS*." I yelled it into the phone three times. "Ba-dum-bum-bum."

It was Wednesday. The Slav wouldn't leave it alone. "Why can't I watch it with you? If you like it that much I'm sure I would too." I gave him the usual reply, "You won't like it. You won't get it. And most importantly, I don't trust anybody who doesn't know who Reg Cox is." "Who?" he asked. "Exactly my point," I replied.

It was twenty minutes to showtime. I'd called Lenny five times. No answer. He must have had a terrible accident. Did that foreign girl push him down the stairs? (Or a better plot line...he pushes her down the stairs because he slept with her mother; or even better better: did Frank run him over in the street?) I decide to call hospitals after I set the VCR to tape. Ten minutes to showtime. Tape rolling. Five minutes. Phone rings.

"Honey? I can't make it over for *East*. Could you tape it for me?"

"La-la-la-la-la la-la... anyone can fall in love." The image of the Thames like a dark serpent inking its way across London. Phil on a drunk in Paris. Cath is becoming a bit stroppy, as was I, going spare. This was the ultimate betrayal, on a par with sleeping with the wife's mother. Now I know how Tiff felt. But did she know how I feel?

At least Grant kept it all in the family, but this one of mine has to go larking about with the foreign girl's mum (who incidentally happens to be my age), so you do the math, How old is the foreign girl? Not that there's anything wrong with that. This was my internal soliloquy, all thoughts easily read on the final five-second close-up of any *EastEnders* face. The phone was still in my hand.

"Honey, are you there?" Lenny sounded as scary as Steve Owen.

"Did you ever sleep with MY mother?"

"No..." I heard sniveling, swallowed laughter.

"Don't you dare laugh at my mother because she's old."

"Honey, I think you're mixing fiction with reality."

"Life imitates art. Sooo, you jammy toerag, you proxy prat, you just made me the gooseberry!"

"The goose-what?"

"Look it up in the *How to Speak EastEnders*. Oh, too bad I'll be taking our copy with me to the Slav's." I put the phone down on the bed while I dressed up like a dog's dinner. He kept yelling gibberish from the receiver. He sounded like one of Phil's drunken rambles. I had to turn up the volume on the telly. Then I picked up the phone to hang it up.

"Honey, have you gone spare?" I heard him ask.

"Yes, I guess I have, as in spare tyre, spare fat around the waistline, anything that's left over from the two main parts. And I'm not bleaching your y-fronts anymore. So just NAFF OFF!"

I ran outside in the street, shaking and in high heels and nearly got run over by a cab. That would be my luck, dying in the street before I make it to the Slavic Beppe. When I got there the second episode was on. Phil was still drunk. The Slav was deeply engaged in sewing ribbon flowers on a mustard silk charmeuse corset. I turned up the volume on the telly. He must be made to understand that there can be no multi-tasking during *EastEnders*. Cardinal rule. After a silent 15 minutes of him watching me watch it.... "Ba-dum-dum-bum."

"I don't get it," he said. "As far as I can tell, it's a bunch of unattractive people with boring problems in cheap ill-fitting clothes, all improperly accessorised with cheap jewels. Pat has got to quit wearing those candelabra earrings, and those gaudy prints. And I beg them to shave off that little caterpillar where the Christian girl's eyebrows should be."

"But what about the brilliant dialogue, and the superb acting?"

"How should I know? I speak Slav. I barely speak American English. How could I understand cockney?"

And how could they ever understand you, I fumed. Even Simon didn't sit around sewing poxy flowers on ladies' dainties.

"Just one more question. Take your time. Do you like *Sex and the City*?"

The usually darkly tempered Slav was moved to glee. "Those impeccably dressed beautiful women sporting the latest Fendi bag to their glamorous careers and posh dinner joints. There's a new love affair every episode, so you can't get bored."

Bored. He said Bored. Meaning *EastEnders* BORED him! Too speechless to speak, I threw one Manolo Blahnik pump at the telly, and another at his bald head. I saw them later being hawked on eBay. I rushed back into the street, shoeless. Ha-ha: I still had my keys to

Lenny's place. I knew I'd gone off my trolley, sobbing and moaning on a public street corner. Screaming when I realised I left my bag at his house and had no cab money.

Nonetheless, a weird coloured cab drove up. Ali's Cab Service. Nobody ever really leaves the show. A familiar face spoke to me through the rear-view mirror. "I know where you need to go." Fade out. "Ba-dum-bum-bum-bum...."

For a show of whatever power I still maintained, I did not knock. I opened his door with my key. He was playing his guitar in the front room. He looked different, though I didn't know why. She was probably hiding in the bathroom.

"You look a little peaky," he said.

"I desperately have to pee." I said, sure I would find the spoiled little cow in the loo. That's where all the great girl-rows happen. All I found was the *EastEnders* mug sporting one lone toothbrush and some foreign toothpaste.

"You have no shoes," he said. We laughed. No one else could have known I had a long-time-ago, way-underground hit song with that title. It was even before Reg Cox. "And what was all that nonsense about sleeping with your mother?" Lenny gave me the Frank ("Darling, what the hell are you talking about") Butcher look.

I think we would need Dr Legg to unravel that psychology... Dot at the very least.

I could hear through the clear haze of Dot's cigarettes: "Okay, Leonard, you didn't sleep with anyone's mother. But it does happen, and in her state of irrational jealousy, it is easy to see why she could be hurt if you didn't sleep with her mother as well." Thank you Dot for sorting that one out.

"Where is she, anyway?"

"Gone."

I was dying to know the sordid details but I missed that episode.

"Gone where?"

"Forever for now, unless of course, they decide to write her in again."

"Yeah, like they did with Sam." She only lasted long enough for a short affair with the handsome, dark and barely bearded one, Beppe, who these days is obviously returning to his original child bride.

When I looked again at Lenny's face, I knew what was different. He had grown Beppe facial hair. Wasn't he just looking Jack the lad. Ooo-la-la.

"Did you tape *East*?" he asked. I nodded my head smiling like the cat who just ate the gooseberry.

"Then we're off to yours."

The night was dark, but I could still see the sun shining out of his jacksie as we held hands. Over the moon.

I feel this plot line running smooth, sweet and dependable. Arthur and Pauline. I just gotta keep him outta the Nick.

• • •

Why I Have Loved EastEnders for 25 Years

By Mackenzie Lambert Wood

For those of you who have read my pieces in the *Gazette* over the years, you will know that I have been an Anglophile since birth; so much so that I married a Brit and now live in the UK. It would be no surprise that when a friend of mine told me about a new show in England called *EastEnders*, I was more than excited about it. That is, until I found out that it wouldn't be shown in the Dallas area, where I lived at the time.

It was, however, being shown in Virginia, where my parents lived, and my father was kind enough to start taping it for me when it began airing on WETA. I received the first tapes and from the very first episode, I was hooked. I was addicted, waiting for my fix in the form of tapes arriving in the post every few weeks until KERA in Dallas started running it. I still taped every show and though I have moved across the pond, I still have boxes and boxes of those videotapes with only a couple of years' gap when I moved to an area in the US that wasn't showing *EE* in their PBS line-up.

I just loved the feel of the show from the start. The other big soap in the UK, *Coronation Street*, was brightly lit and colourful (it ran briefly on the cable channel USA Network in the States in the early '80s), and along with the drama there was/is a lot of comedic tones to it. *EE*, by contrast, was stark and gritty and seemed more real. It was a taste of life in a part of England at the time. As Tracey Ullman said on public television in her introduction to the series, it didn't shy away from tough subjects, and for me, someone who had never lived in the UK, it just felt compelling and captivating.

From the earliest episodes, I had my favourite and least favourite characters…. The entire Fowler family, Den and Angie, Ethel and Mary made a real impression on me, while bratty Sharon, bitter Sue, and pseudo-posh Debbie all made me want to reach into the television and give them a smack upside the head. It was a show that brought out real emotions in me, and because, in the beginning, I could watch several (up to 12 half-hour shows per tape) episodes in a row, I could submerge myself in the world of Walford. Even on my worst days, and we all have those now and then, when nothing seems to be going right, I could pop in a tape and be taken to a world where lives were definitely harder and more complicated.

Watching the show in the US, you also have the advantage of not knowing what will happen next, so when the father of Michelle's baby was revealed and when Den handed Angie the divorce papers, it was a total surprise. (As was his first exit from the show, along the canal.) I remember gasping in surprise at some of the twists and turns in the

218

show over the years and enjoying the anticipation of what would happen next. But here in the UK now, you can't walk by a newsstand selling TV guides and soap magazines without being assaulted by headlines and posed photos revealing the next big shocking episode in all of the UK soaps. Even reading the newspaper here or surfing the net, you are bound to stumble on a major spoiler. I do my best to avoid the spoilers as much as possible, and my darling husband will toss the weekly TV guide we get with the weekend newspapers before I can see the cover. But it still is annoying that the press spoils the fun of seeing a storyline unfold on the screen without hearing about it first.

And what storylines! From teenage pregnancy to the East End mobsters—never a dull moment in Walford. Some of the storylines were quite tragic and, at least in the early days, well based in reality. Who can forget Sue and Ali's little son succumbing to cot death, Arthur's breakdown over the stress of joblessness, Mary's struggle to provide for her baby and herself, and of course the ongoing marital antics of Den and Angie? As you watched the drama unfold in your living room over the years, some of the characters started to feel like old friends and some like annoying neighbours that you have to put up with because you like the area.

My life has taken a lot of twists and turns, changes and relocations in the past 25 years. *EastEnders* has always been there, in the background, changing, twisting and turning, too, allowing me an escape when things were bad, and pure entertainment when things were good. I am very happy to now be able to watch the show as it airs here in the UK. It was always a show I loved to watch and is now a part of my evening telly viewing, four nights a week. A lot of the characters have come and gone, but as in real life, people change and move on. But the backbone of the show, the Queen Vic pub and the Square itself, the caff and the Arches are still there, and I can't wait to see what happens next.

• • •

Walford: No Place Like Home

By Michael McCarthy

Albert Square, a packet of green, surrounded by the shops and council flats that make up an East End neighbourhood, is an oasis of seasons come and gone, as well as promises that are yet to be.

Old faces mingle with new, fashions and cars come and go, but the Square endures. There really is no place like home.

Try as they might, like migrating birds taking flight, its denizens feel the pull of home and memories call them back, across London and across the sea. Time is meaningless, only brief reminders of losses, both personal and professional. The residents of Albert Square rise to face yet another day, hoping for the best, preparing themselves for the worst, and all along, taking strength from their neighbourhood.

Hearts are broken, promises fulfilled, at least for the moment, in the ebb and flow of one season consuming another. Children are born, they grow, make mistakes, learn, and then, too soon, they forget.

Pauline frets, Ian plots, Peggy carries on, Pat is a pair of open arms, Barry tries the best he can, the Slaters amaze, Phil broods, Sonia loves, Dot prays, Alfie charms, Laura plods on. Their faces age with the traces life etches on all of us.

It may hurt for a while; hope may seem to abandon them; a winter long blots out the sun—but as surely as love survives, spring returns.

When we hear those familiar chords and see the aerial view of the East End glide across our television screens, we all know it, we can feel it in our bones, yes we are finally, fully, happily home, said Jack the lad, Bob's your uncle, on Albert Square.

. . .

The Unseen EastEnders

By Larry Jaffee

Here's a treatment for an EastEnders *script written by me, circa 1996. I pitched it in person at the studio to then-*EastEnders *producer Jo Ward. The creative team at Elstree decided in its infinite wisdom to pass.*

Synopsis: A Yank, backed by an unspecified major American media conglomerate, makes an offer to buy the *Walford Gazette*. The potential sale has galvanized Albert Square, with most residents firmly against the idea (i.e., yet another British institution turned over to foreign hands).

Most vocal among the opposition is Arthur Fowler, who yearns for the good ole days when Britain was a world leader and still controlled something of an empire. For two local citizens (half-brothers David Wicks and Ian Beale), the issue has presented a means for them to change their lives. David realises that this is the way he can launch a political career (although he has never voted) and capitalise on his TV-friendly good looks. Ian, after failed catering and financing businesses, fancies himself a newspaper publisher like Rupert Murdoch even though he knows nothing about the business, doesn't read the *Gazette* or any other publication for that matter.

David and Ian forge an unlikely alliance—extraordinary considering that David is having an affair with Ian's wife Cindy, and especially implausible since they never trusted each other before. But Ian remembers in a flashback that his late father Pete pleaded with him before he got killed to get along with his half brother.

The first item on David's agenda, if he's elected, will be to spearhead an effort to pass a law in the British Parliament that would ban foreign ownership of any media property. David decides if the *Gazette* is sold to anyone—it should be an Englishman, and who better than Walford businessman Ian Beale. Ian sells his fish & chips shoppe to buy the newspaper, not realising that the *Gazette* costs £1 million—a bit more than the £1,000 that Phil gives him on the spot for the chippie.

In any case, Ian becomes David's campaign manager and prepares a dirty tricks campaign, after taking out a book from the Walford Public Library on Richard Nixon and the Watergate scandal.

Ian offers his uncle Arthur a job as campaign worker and *Gazette* circulation manager if he helps make and distribute "WICKS FOR MP" posters.

Carol Jackson, although up to this point like David and Ian, is apolitical, decides that she must jump into the race to get back at David for abandoning her pregnant when they were teenagers.

Epilogue: Carol wins the election and becomes Walford's representative in Parliament. The Yank gets the *Gazette*, leaving David, Ian and Arthur on the dole.

• • •

A World Without Pat: The End of an Earring

By Larry Jaffee

Jan. 20, 2012—A week later, I am still coming to grips with Pam St Clement permanently hanging up her earrings, or more accurately, the infamous, diverse collection of jewelry that hung from the ear lobes of her character Pat for 25 years on *EastEnders*.

Being in the States watching *EastEnders* episodes on 'public TV' (more than seven-and-a-half years behind what's broadcast in the UK by BBC1), I'm living in an *EastEnders* time warp. For example, the night before last on WLIW, the station here in New York, Pat was the centre of attention in two back-to-back episodes, during which she coerced Janine into confessing that she was responsible for Barry's death.

222

Melodrama at its best, the episode also contained Pat trying to get Janine to ease up in her harassment of unlucky Laura, who ten minutes later ends up leaving little Bobby motherless after an accidental fall down the stairs. Pat was the only person in the Square who showed any compassion to Laura, and naturally she took charge of informing everyone who needed to know of her friend's death. In that episode, Pat realises how evil Janine has become, even way beyond what she thought was possible.

That's why it was so strange to see Janine and Pat—in the scene at Pat's deathbed—proverbially bury the hatchet, even though Janine's plan was to evict the dying woman and her extended family from the house. Obviously the barely conscious Pat had other things on her mind (i.e., the afterlife). Meanwhile, Janine underwent a complete personality change in a split second. Well, just chalk it up to occasional soap slip-ups. Could it have really been her pregnant status that made Janine a human being, at least for a minute?

In the past, Janine laughed at death in her face (i.e., Barry) and she would have relished being at the bottom of the staircase where Laura met her plight. I could hear her say, 'Oops... Laura, you cow ... You're so clumsy!' (Hey, I should be writing for the show, Elstree.) More often than not, *EastEnders'* kitchen-sink realism wrenches the guts of the converted. Why do we care about these fictional characters? But we do.

[In the interest of full disclosure, I occasionally sneak an online peek at what's playing in the UK for a monumental storyline, such as Pat's death, as we Stateside fans wait for the official launch of the iPlayer, for which we're going to have pay monthly about US$8. It was announced in the summer that it would be available in the fall, but still no signs of it.]

Back to Pam, who was interviewed twice by *Walford Gazette* contributor Tim Wilson—once in 1995 (reprinted on page 67 of my book *Albert Square & Me: The Actors of EastEnders*) and again in 1999.

WG contributor Suzanne Lafrance stayed at her New York hotel when the actress was in town 13 December 2000 to help fundraise to keep *EastEnders* on the air at WLIW-TV, out on Long Island. That's where I first met St Clement. Unfortunately, it was the same night that Al Gore decided to concede the presidential election, so contributions weren't as good as they could have been. We can blame George W. Bush for that too, in addition to bankrupting the global economy.

A few months later, I unexpectedly met Pam again on a happier night in Manchester at Granada's studios when we were both booked for a taping of the talk show *Soap Fever*, whose presenter was *EastEnders* alumnus Nadia Sawalha (Annie Palmer). I was planted in the audience, and Nadia introduced me as 'the editor of the world's only *EastEnders* fanzine', prompting me to ask Pam a question. I nervously bellowed, 'Who was Wicksy's dad?!?' Pam must have been asked that same question a thousand times, but responded with a quick quip: 'A lady never tells, Larry'.

EastEnders will sorely miss the moral compass that Pat Beale Wicks Butcher Evans—whom we fans no doubt took for granted—held for a quarter century as Albert Square's streetwise elder stateswoman. At least I have more than seven years to come to cherish her importance.

About Larry Jaffee

Larry Jaffee has published and edited the quarterly *Walford Gazette* (www.wgazette.com) continuously since 1992. It is the world's only regularly published newspaper dedicated to *EastEnders*. Jaffee has edited several magazines, and has been published in *The New York Times, Rolling Stone, Parade, Vibe* and numerous other publications. He is the author of *Albert Square & Me: The Actors of EastEnders*, and may be reached at walfordgazette@gmail.com.

Contributors

Dan Abramson co-founded with Larry Jaffee the *Walford Gazette* in 1992. He was a widely published freelance journalist and contributor to such publications as the *NY Daily News*. Abramson, a historian, comedy writer and supreme Anglophile, died in April 1999 at the age of 45.

A.S. Berman was the first and only managing editor of the *Walford Gazette*, while he was still in high school. He is a former *USA Today* writer and editor, and the author of *30 Years of British Television*.

Melissa Berry is an avid *EastEnders* fan since it first was broadcast in the US—and has been lucky enough to have been invited to the set twice! She has been involved with all three North Carolina *EastEnders* fan clubs.

Suzanne Campbell, daughter of Joan and Bill Campbell and wife of JD Lafrance, is currently living in Philadelphia and working on a [horror] screenplay trilogy. In addition to writing, her passions include Northern Ireland, Liverpool FC, Hard Rock music, Kubrick movies, HST and Guinness.

Sherry Chiger is a professional journalist, currently working as editor at large for Penton Business Media in New York. She spent about two years living in Great Britain with her husband and daughter, but they have since happily moved back to Connecticut.

Andrew Collins is a scriptwriter, journalist and broadcaster, in no particular order. Having learned his TV trade writing for *Family Affairs* and *EastEnders*, he has since written two sitcoms, *Grass*, with Simon Day (BBC3 and BBC2), and *Not Going Out* with Lee Mack (BBC1). He is also the film editor of *Radio Times*, occasional presenter of *The Film Programme* on Radio 4 and regular contributor to *Front Row*. He began his journalistic career at the NME, going on, via Select, to edit *Q* magazine and *Empire*. He currently writes for *Word*, *The Times* and *Radio Times*.

Kent Gibbons is a writer and editor at the US cable-TV-related trade magazine *Multichannel News*. He has been watching *EastEnders* since the early 1990s, first on PBS in Washington, D.C., and now in New York City.

Lenny and Stephanie Kaye met at the Mudd Club in October, 1979, and married in July 1980. Born in New York City, Lenny is a guitarist, writer, and record producer best known for his work with Patti Smith. He is the author of *You Call It Madness: the Sensuous Song of the Croon*, a study of the romantic singers of the early 1930s. Stephanie escaped Spokane, Washington, to migrate to New York City. She spent time on the downtown art scene in a band called Shox Lumania, and worked as a fashion stylist for music videos. In need of something completely different, she then studied Religious Philosophy at Hunter College. The Kayes live in East Stroudsburg, Pennsylvania, with two cats and a turtle; their daughter, Anna, is studying to be a chiropractor. They continue to watch *EastEnders* each Sunday night on WLVT.

Estelle Lazarus was born in the East End of London, where both her parents were also born and raised. She eventually moved to New York, where she still lives, and worked as a publicist in the music and entertainment industry.

Sherry Lehman works as a financial editor in New York. She has been a fan of *EastEnders* since the show was first seen in the US in 1988.

Priscilla Mayfield, founder of the Orange County-centric food discussion site OCFoodNation.com, writes the Taste of Orange County food blog for *Orange Coast* magazine, and has watched *EastEnders* since its US debut.

Michael McCarthy is a playwright living in Hartsdale, New York.

Claire Meyerhoff has been watching *EastEnders* for 22 years and finds that experience quite useful as an on-air fundraiser for North Carolina's UNC-TV.

Pamela Vera is a professor of music at Bergen and Passaic County Community Colleges; and earned a post-masters degree from the Brooklyn Conservatory of Music.

Tim Wilson is a New York-based actor who has worked primarily as a stand-in on film and television productions for more than 30 years. He has been a fan of *EastEnders* for a slightly shorter period of time.

Mackenzie Lambert Wood is living every Anglophile's dream. After kicking around the US—Texas and California—for most of her adult life, she fell in love with a Brit and has happily lived in the UK since 2004.